i-Net+™ Certification For Dummies®

Cheat Sheet

G000152927

TLAs (Two- & Three-Letter Acronyms) to know

ACL	Access Control List
ARP	Address Resolution Protocol
API	Application Program Interface
ASP	Active Server Page
AVI	Audio Video Interleaved
CGI	Common Gateway Interface
DLL	Dynamic Link Library
DoS	Denial of Service
DNS	Domain Name Server
DSL	Digital Subscriber Line
EDI	Electronic Data Interchange
FTP	File Transfer Protocol
GIF	Graphics Interchange Format
GUI	Graphical User Interface
ICQ	I Seek You
ISP	Internet Service Provider
IP	Internet Protocol
MAC	Media Access Control
MP3	MPEG version 3
NAP	Network Access Point
NOS	Network Operating System
POP	Post Office Protocol
PPP	Point-To-Point Protocol
RGB	Red, Green, and Blue
SQL	Structured Query Language
TCP	Transmission Control Protocol
URL	Uniform Resource Locator
VPN	Virtual Private Network
WAV	Waveform audio
XML	Extensible Markup Language

...etter

	...on Protocol
HTML	...ge
HTTP	Hypertext Transfer Protocol
FQDN	Fully Qualified Domain Name
JPEG	Joint Photographers Experts Group
L2TP	Level 2 Tunneling Protocol
LDAP	Lightweight Directory Access Protocol
MIME	Multi-Purpose Internet Mail Extensions
MPEG	Moving Picture Experts Group
PING	Packet Internet Groper
POTS	Plain Old Telephone Service
PPTP	Point-To-Point Tunneling Protocol
PSTN	Publich Switched Telephone Network
SAPI	Server Application Program Interface
SLIP	Serial Line Internet Protocol
SMTP	Simple Mail Transport Protocol
TCP/IP	Transmission Control Protocol/Internet Protocol
TFTP	Trivial File Transport Protocol
TIFF	Tagged Image File Format
VRML	Virtual Reality Modeling Language

Bandwith units to know

Unit	Bandwidth
DS0	64 Kbps
T1	1.54 Mbps
E1	2.048 Mbps
E3	34.368 Mbps
T3	44.736 Mbps
OC1-48	51.84 Mbps to 2.488 Gbps

i-Net+™ Certification For Dummies®

Cheat Sheet

TCP/IP utilities

Utility	Name	Function
ARP	Address Resolution Protocol	Displays and edits the ARP cache
NBTSTAT	NetBIOS over TCP/IP Statistics	Displays the contents of the NetBIOS name cache and repairs the contents of the HOSTS file
NETSTAT	Network Statistics	Displays current TCP/IP connections
PING	Packet Internet Groper	Checks validity of a remote IP address
TRACERT	Trace Route	Traces the route used to reach an IP destination

Common well-known port assignments

Port Number	Assignment
20	FTP data transfer
25	SMTP (Simple Mail Transfer Protocol)
53	DNS (Domain Name System)
80	HTTP (Hypertext Transfer Protocol)
110	POP3 (Post Office Protocol)

Elements in an HTML document

<HTML>

<HEAD> <META> </HEAD>

<BODY>

<TABLE> <TR><TD></TD></TR></TABLE>

<FORM><INPUT><TEXTAREA></FORM>

 </BODY>

</HTML>

Common subnet masks

IP Address Class	Subnet Mask
Class A	255.0.0.0
Class B	255.255.0.0
Class C	255.255.255.0

For Dummies®: Bestselling Book Series for Beginners

TM

References for the Rest of Us! ®

BESTSELLING BOOK SERIES

Are you intimidated and confused by computers? Do you find that traditional manuals are overloaded with technical details you'll never use? Do your friends and family always call you to fix simple problems on their PCs? Then the *...For Dummies*® computer book series from IDG Books Worldwide is for you.

...For Dummies books are written for those frustrated computer users who know they aren't really dumb but find that PC hardware, software, and indeed the unique vocabulary of computing make them feel helpless. *...For Dummies* books use a lighthearted approach, a down-to-earth style, and even cartoons and humorous icons to dispel computer novices' fears and build their confidence. Lighthearted but not lightweight, these books are a perfect survival guide for anyone forced to use a computer.

> *"I like my copy so much I told friends; now they bought copies."*
>
> — Irene C., Orwell, Ohio

> *"Quick, concise, nontechnical, and humorous."*
>
> — Jay A., Elburn, Illinois

> *"Thanks, I needed this book. Now I can sleep at night."*
>
> — Robin F., British Columbia, Canada

Already, millions of satisfied readers agree. They have made *...For Dummies* books the #1 introductory level computer book series and have written asking for more. So, if you're looking for the most fun and easy way to learn about computers, look to *...For Dummies* books to give you a helping hand.

IDG
BOOKS
WORLDWIDE

i-Net+™
Certification
FOR
DUMMIES®

i-Net+™ Certification FOR DUMMIES®

by Ron Gilster

IDG BOOKS WORLDWIDE

IDG Books Worldwide, Inc.
An International Data Group Company

Foster City, CA ◆ Chicago, IL ◆ Indianapolis, IN ◆ New York, NY

i-Net+™ Certification For Dummies®

Published by
IDG Books Worldwide, Inc.
An International Data Group Company
919 E. Hillsdale Blvd.
Suite 400
Foster City, CA 94404
www.idgbooks.com (IDG Books Worldwide Web site)
www.dummies.com (Dummies Press Web site)

Library of Congress Catalog Card No.: 99-69368

ISBN: 0-7645-0654-4

Printed in the United States of America

10 9 8 7 6 5 4 3 2 1

1B/SU/QS/QQ/IN

Distributed in the United States by IDG Books Worldwide, Inc.

Distributed by CDG Books Canada Inc. for Canada; by Transworld Publishers Limited in the United Kingdom; by IDG Norge Books for Norway; by IDG Sweden Books for Sweden; by IDG Books Australia Publishing Corporation Pty. Ltd. for Australia and New Zealand; by TransQuest Publishers Pte Ltd. for Singapore, Malaysia, Thailand, Indonesia, and Hong Kong; by Gotop Information Inc. for Taiwan; by ICG Muse, Inc. for Japan; by Intersoft for South Africa; by Eyrolles for France; by International Thomson Publishing for Germany, Austria and Switzerland; by Distribuidora Cuspide for Argentina; by LR International for Brazil; by Galileo Libros for Chile; by Ediciones ZETA S.C.R. Ltda. for Peru; by WS Computer Publishing Corporation, Inc., for the Philippines; by Contemporanea de Ediciones for Venezuela; by Express Computer Distributors for the Caribbean and West Indies; by Micronesia Media Distributor, Inc. for Micronesia; by Chips Computadoras S.A. de C.V. for Mexico; by Editorial Norma de Panama S.A. for Panama; by American Bookshops for Finland.

For general information on IDG Books Worldwide's books in the U.S., please call our Consumer Customer Service department at 800-762-2974. For reseller information, including discounts and premium sales, please call our Reseller Customer Service department at 800-434-3422.

For information on where to purchase IDG Books Worldwide's books outside the U.S., please contact our International Sales department at 317-596-5530 or fax 317-572-4002.

For consumer information on foreign language translations, please contact our Customer Service department at 1-800-434-3422, fax 317-572-4002, or e-mail rights@idgbooks.com.

For information on licensing foreign or domestic rights, please phone +1-650-653-7098.

For sales inquiries and special prices for bulk quantities, please contact our Sales department at 800-762-2974 or write to the address above.

For information on using IDG Books Worldwide's books in the classroom or for ordering examination copies, please contact our Educational Sales department at 800-434-2086 or fax 317-572-4005.

For press review copies, author interviews, or other publicity information, please contact our Public Relations department at 650-653-7000 or fax 650-653-7500.

For authorization to photocopy items for corporate, personal, or educational use, please contact Copyright Clearance Center, 222 Rosewood Drive, Danvers, MA 01923, or fax 978-750-4470.

About the Author

Ron Gilster (i-Net+, Network+, A+, MBA, and AAGG) has been involved with the Internet and World Wide Web for more than seven years as a trainer, teacher, developer, merchant, and end user. He has more than 33 years of total computing experience, including more than 13 years networking computers. Ron is employed by HighSpeed.Com, a leading LMDS, DSL, and broadband communications company and regional ISP, where he is responsible for the internal and external networking infrastructure of the corporation, including VPN, telephony, intranet, extranet, and Internet operations.

He is the author of *A+ Certification For Dummies*, *Network+ Certification For Dummies,* and *CCNA For Dummies,* plus several books on networking, the Internet, computer and information literacy, and programming.

Ron is also the proud father of Jeana, Rob, Kirstin, and Mimi, and the loving husband to Diane. He and his wife show Irish Wolfhounds and Bichon Havanese dogs, that is, when he's not pounding on the keyboard.

ABOUT IDG BOOKS WORLDWIDE

Welcome to the world of IDG Books Worldwide.

IDG Books Worldwide, Inc., is a subsidiary of International Data Group, the world's largest publisher of computer-related information and the leading global provider of information services on information technology. IDG was founded more than 30 years ago by Patrick J. McGovern and now employs more than 9,000 people worldwide. IDG publishes more than 290 computer publications in over 75 countries. More than 90 million people read one or more IDG publications each month.

Launched in 1990, IDG Books Worldwide is today the #1 publisher of best-selling computer books in the United States. We are proud to have received eight awards from the Computer Press Association in recognition of editorial excellence and three from Computer Currents' First Annual Readers' Choice Awards. Our best-selling ...For Dummies® series has more than 50 million copies in print with translations in 31 languages. IDG Books Worldwide, through a joint venture with IDG's Hi-Tech Beijing, became the first U.S. publisher to publish a computer book in the People's Republic of China. In record time, IDG Books Worldwide has become the first choice for millions of readers around the world who want to learn how to better manage their businesses.

Our mission is simple: Every one of our books is designed to bring extra value and skill-building instructions to the reader. Our books are written by experts who understand and care about our readers. The knowledge base of our editorial staff comes from years of experience in publishing, education, and journalism — experience we use to produce books to carry us into the new millennium. In short, we care about books, so we attract the best people. We devote special attention to details such as audience, interior design, use of icons, and illustrations. And because we use an efficient process of authoring, editing, and desktop publishing our books electronically, we can spend more time ensuring superior content and less time on the technicalities of making books.

You can count on our commitment to deliver high-quality books at competitive prices on topics you want to read about. At IDG Books Worldwide, we continue in the IDG tradition of delivering quality for more than 30 years. You'll find no better book on a subject than one from IDG Books Worldwide.

John J. Kilcullen
John Kilcullen
Chairman and CEO
IDG Books Worldwide, Inc.

**Eighth Annual
Computer Press
Awards ≥1992**

**Ninth Annual
Computer Press
Awards ≥1993**

**Tenth Annual
Computer Press
Awards ≥1994**

**Eleventh Annual
Computer Press
Awards ≥1995**

IDG is the world's leading IT media, research and exposition company. Founded in 1964, IDG had 1997 revenues of $2.05 billion and has more than 9,000 employees worldwide. IDG offers the widest range of media options that reach IT buyers in 75 countries representing 95% of worldwide IT spending. IDG's diverse product and services portfolio spans six key areas including print publishing, online publishing, expositions and conferences, market research, education and training, and global marketing services. More than 90 million people read one or more of IDG's 290 magazines and newspapers, including IDG's leading global brands — Computerworld, PC World, Network World, Macworld and the Channel World family of publications. IDG Books Worldwide is one of the fastest-growing computer book publishers in the world, with more than 700 titles in 36 languages. The "...For Dummies®" series alone has more than 50 million copies in print. IDG offers online users the largest network of technology-specific Web sites around the world through IDG.net (http://www.idg.net), which comprises more than 225 targeted Web sites in 55 countries worldwide. International Data Corporation (IDC) is the world's largest provider of information technology data, analysis and consulting, with research centers in over 41 countries and more than 400 research analysts worldwide. IDG World Expo is a leading producer of more than 168 globally branded conferences and expositions in 35 countries including E3 (Electronic Entertainment Expo), Macworld Expo, ComNet, Windows World Expo, ICE (Internet Commerce Expo), Agenda, DEMO, and Spotlight. IDG's training subsidiary, ExecuTrain, is the world's largest computer training company, with more than 230 locations worldwide and 785 training courses. IDG Marketing Services helps industry-leading IT companies build international brand recognition by developing global integrated marketing programs via IDG's print, online and exposition products worldwide. Further information about the company can be found at www.idg.com.   1/26/00

Dedication

To my loving, patient, and understanding wife, Diane, and to my truly fantastic children, Jeana, Rob, Kirstie, and Mimi, and granddaughter, Jordan.

I would also like to dedicate this book to my absolutely magnificent readers, students, and co-workers. I am grateful that you have shared your hopes, dreams, successes, and failures with me. You keep me inspired. Best of luck!

Author's Acknowledgments

I would like to thank the wonderful folks at IDG Books who helped get this book published, especially Joyce Pepple, John Pont, James Russell, Christine Berman, Carmen Krikorian, and Megan Decraene. And I owe an ever-growing debt of gratitude to Nate Holdread, who continues to save my sanity and shield me from the cold, cruel, technical part of the process.

Special thanks to Laura Tolan for the excellent technical editing job she provided.

I would also like to thank Linda Stark and Kim Darosett for their continued moral and spiritual support.

Publisher's Acknowledgments

We're proud of this book; please register your comments through our IDG Books Worldwide Online Registration Form located at http://my2cents.dummies.com.

Some of the people who helped bring this book to market include the following:

Acquisitions, Editorial, and Media Development

Project Editor: Nate Holdread

Acquisitions Editor: Joyce Pepple

Copy Editors: James Russell, Christine Berman, Tonya Maddox

Technical Editors: Laura Tolan, Andrew W. Wing

Media Development Editor: Marita Ellixson

Associate Permissions Editor: Carmen Krikorian

Media Development Coordinator: Eddie Kominowski

Editorial Manager: Leah P. Cameron

Media Development Manager: Heather Heath Dismore

Editorial Assistant: Beth Parlon

Production

Project Coordinator: Maridee V. Ennis

Layout and Graphics: Amy Adrian, Karl Brandt, Barry Offringa, Tracy K. Oliver, Jill Piscitelli, Brent Savage, Brian Torwelle, Erin Zeltner

Proofreaders: Laura Albert, Corey Bowen, Rachel Garvey, John Greenough, Marianne Santy

Indexer: C² Editorial Services

Special Help

Publication Services, John Pont

General and Administrative

IDG Books Worldwide, Inc.: John Kilcullen, CEO

IDG Books Technology Publishing Group: Richard Swadley, Senior Vice President and Publisher; Walter Bruce III, Vice President and Associate Publisher; Joseph Wikert, Associate Publisher; Mary Bednarek, Branded Product Development Director; Mary Corder, Editorial Director; Barry Pruett, Publishing Manager; Michelle Baxter, Publishing Manager

IDG Books Consumer Publishing Group: Roland Elgey, Senior Vice President and Publisher; Kathleen A. Welton, Vice President and Publisher; Kevin Thornton, Acquisitions Manager; Kristin A. Cocks, Editorial Director

IDG Books Internet Publishing Group: Brenda McLaughlin, Senior Vice President and Publisher; Diane Graves Steele, Vice President and Associate Publisher; Sofia Marchant, Online Marketing Manager

IDG Books Production for Dummies Press: Debbie Stailey, Associate Director of Production; Cindy L. Phipps, Manager of Project Coordination, Production Proofreading, and Indexing; Tony Augsburger, Manager of Prepress, Reprints, and Systems; Laura Carpenter, Production Control Manager; Shelley Lea, Supervisor of Graphics and Design; Debbie J. Gates, Production Systems Specialist; Robert Springer, Supervisor of Proofreading; Kathie Schutte, Production Supervisor

Dummies Packaging and Book Design: Patty Page, Manager, Promotions Marketing

◆

The publisher would like to give special thanks to Patrick J. McGovern, without whom this book would not have been possible.

◆

Contents at a Glance

Cartoons at a Glance

By Rich Tennant

page 351

page 85

page 43

page 9

page 301

page 219

page 337

Fax: 978-546-7747
E-mail: richtennant@the5thwave.com
World Wide Web: www.the5thwave.com

Table of Contents

Introduction

· ·

*I*f you have purchased or are considering purchasing this book, you most likely fit one of the following categories:

✔ You know how very valuable i-Net+ certification is to an Internet technical professional's career and advancement.

✔ You're wondering just what i-Net+ certification is all about.

✔ You think that reading this book may be a fun, entertaining way to learn about the Internet and its components.

✔ You love all *For Dummies* books and wait impatiently for each new one to come out.

✔ You're a big fan of mine and can't wait to read my new book.

Well, if you fit any of the first four scenarios, this is the book for you! However, I'm not certified in the appropriate medical areas to help you if you chose the last category! But, I do appreciate the support.

If you're already aware of the i-Net+ Certification program and are just looking for excellent study aids, you can skip the next few sections of this introduction, in which I do my best to convince you that this is the book you are looking for, because your search is over. However, if you don't have the foggiest idea just what i-Net+ Certification is or how to prepare for it, read on!

Why Use This Book?

Beginning as an obscure research project in the late 1960s, the Internet has since become the largest network in the world — a global nexus combining networks together to form a worldwide network of networks. Unfortunately for anyone trying to get started as an Internet technical professional, the Internet is very complex, involving a wide range of different hardware types and software technologies. The result of this is that even the most knowledgeable Internet professional usually needs at least a little help getting ready for the i-Net+ exam. The sole purpose behind this book is to help you to shorten your preparation time for the i-Net+ exam.

As with all other *For Dummies* certification books, this book is a no-nonsense reference and study guide. This book focuses on the areas likely to be on the exam, with a little background information thrown in here and there to help you understand some of the more complex concepts and technologies. I present the facts, concepts, processes, and applications included on the exams in step-by-step lists, tables, and figures without long explanations. The focus of the book is on preparing you for the i-Net+ exams, and not on overwhelming you with my obviously extensive and impressive knowledge of the Internet and its related technologies (nor with my modesty, I might add).

In developing this book, I have made two groups of assumptions:

- ✔ You have an entry-level knowledge of the Internet and the electronics, computers, software, networking, protocols, and troubleshooting procedures associated with it, and need a review and study guide for the exam.

- ✔ You have some experience with the Internet and its electronics, computers, software, TCP/IP protocols, network operating systems, networking devices, and cabling. You need a refresher on these basics along with a review and study guide for the exams.

If my assumptions in either case suit your needs, then this is the book for you!

Using This Book

This book is organized so you can study a specific area without wading through stuff you may already know. I recommend that you skim the whole book at least once, noting at least the points raised by the icons. For your last minute cram before the exam, each part and chapter of the book is independent and can be studied in any order without confusing you.

Each chapter also includes a pre-test (Quick Assessment quiz) and post-test (Prep Test questions) to help you determine where your knowledge is weak and where you need to continue studying. The following sections tell you what I've included between the covers of this book.

Part I: The Basics

Part I provides you with some general information about taking the i-Net+ exam, an overview of the topic areas you should study, and a primer of the terms and concepts you must know for the exam. This primer includes: an overview of the i-Net+ exam, its objectives and benefits, an explanation of who CompTIA and Sylvan Prometrics are, how to arrange to take the test, and some general tips on what to study and how to get ready for the test.

Part II: The Anatomy of the Internet

Part II provides you with the fundamentals and background information you should know about the general structure, operations, addressing, and problems of the Internet. This info includes a look at the make up and use of a URL, how caching works and its benefits, and what to do when things go wrong.

Part III: On the Client-Side

Part III includes a review of all of the topics you need for the i-Net+ exam relating to the configuration of an Internet-client workstation and building a Web site. Included in Part III is a review of HTML, and the use of forms, tables, and multimedia.

Part IV: The Internetwork

Part IV has everything you need to know about the Internetwork (another term for the Internet), including DNS, remote access, the various kinds of servers on the Internet, how to deal with problems, and security.

Part V: Doing Business on the Internet

As its name implies, this part of the book covers the concepts and technologies used to conduct business over the Internet, including the planning that must go into an Internet business site and the concepts of e-commerce.

Part VI: The Part of Tens

This section provides additional motivation and study guides to help get you ready for the test, with advice about how to be sure that you're ready to take the test on Test Day plus ten great Web sites where you can find study aids.

Part VII: Appendixes

This section gives you even more practice test questions, with ten sample test questions on each domain, as well as information about what's on the CD in the back of this book and how to use the CD.

i-Net+ Certification For Dummies CD-ROM

The CD-ROM included with this book contains a variety of study aids and practice tests to help you prepare for the i-Net+ exam. In addition, the QuickLearn game is on the CD-ROM to provide you with an easy, fun way to study, as well as a few links to the Web sites of companies with training sites and sample copies of their wares.

Studying Chapters

i-Net+ Certification For Dummies is a self-paced method of preparing for the exam. You don't have to guess what to study; every chapter that covers exam objectives guides you with

- Preview questions
- Detailed coverage of topics
- Review questions

This step-by-step structure identifies what you need to study, gives you all the facts, and rechecks what you know. Here's how it works.

First page

Each chapter starts with a preview of what's to come, including

- Exam objectives
- Study subjects

Not sure that you know all about the objectives and the subjects in a chapter? Then turn a page and keep going.

Quick Assessment questions

Beginning on the second page of each chapter, you find a brief self-assessment test that helps you gauge your current knowledge of the topics that chapter covers. Take this test to determine which areas you already understand, as well as to determine the areas that you need to focus on the most.

- If you're in a hurry, just study the sections for the questions you answered incorrectly.

> ✔ If you answered every question correctly, jump to the end of the chapter and try the Prep Test questions to double-check your knowledge.

Study subjects

When you're studying a chapter, carefully read through it just like any book. Each subject is introduced — very briefly — and then you discover what you need to know for the exam.

As you study, special features show you how to apply everything in the chapter to the exam.

Labs

Labs are included throughout the book to walk you step by step through some of the processes you need to know for the exam, such as the installation or configuration of a particular component. Here is an example of a lab included later in the book:

Lab 6-2   Setting TCP/IP Properties on a Windows Client

1. **Double-click the Network icon in the Windows Control Panel to open the Network Configuration dialog box shown in Figure 6-1.**

2. **Highlight the TCP/IP protocol in the components list and click the Properties button to open the TCP/IP Properties window (see Figure 6-4).**

   Use the tabs across the top of the dialog box to access each of the property types.

3. **Click the IP Address tab.**

   In most situations, you choose Obtain An IP Address Automatically to indicate that the workstation client IP address is assigned by the DHCP server. In those situations where a static IP address is assigned, click the indicator for an assigned (static) IP address and enter it in the box provided.

4. **Click the DNS Configuration tab.**

   To indicate that DNS lookup is used on the network, click the adjacent radio button and then enter the host ID, the domain ID, and the IP address of the DNS server. You can enter more than one DNS server, and you can set an order of access.

5. **Click the Gateway tab.**

6. **Enter the IP address of the gateway(s) on the network, as illustrated in Figure 6-5. You can set the access order for gateways; the first one listed is the default gateway.**

7. Click the WINS Configuration tab.

You use the WINS Configuration tab to indicate whether the network supports WINS services. If it does, you need to click the Enable button and enter the IP address of the WINS server. If DHCP is in use, it's likely that you would click the button that indicates that DHCP should be used for WINS service.

Tables

Sometimes you need just the facts. In such cases, tables are a simple way to present everything at a glance. For example:

Table 12-2	Top-Level Domains
Domain	*Organization Type*
.com	Commercial entity
.edu	Education institution
.gov	Branches of government
.org	Non-commercial and non-profit organizations
.mil	Branches of the military
.net	Internet service providers

Prep Tests

The Prep Tests at the end of each chapter gauge your understanding of the entire chapter's content. The Prep Test questions are structured in the same manner as those you may see on your exam, so be sure to try your hand at these sample questions. If you have difficulties with any questions on the prep test, review the corresponding section within the chapter.

Icons Used in This Book

Time Shaver icons point out tips that can help you manage and save time while studying or taking the exam.

Instant Answer icons highlight information to help you recognize correct and incorrect exam answers.

 Remember icons point out general information and subjects that you should know and understand for the test. While the information may not appear directly on the exam, it provides you with information you need to identify the correct response.

 Tip icons flag information that can come in extra-handy during the testing process. Take note of these tidbits!

Feedback

I'd like to hear from you. If an area of the test isn't covered as well as it should be, or if I've provided more coverage than you think is warranted about a particular topic, please let me know. Your feedback is solicited and welcome. You can e-mail me at `rgilster@bmi.net`.

Part I
The Basics

The 5th Wave   By Rich Tennant

"He aced the i-Net+ exam, and he's a great technician, but he still lacks people skills."

In this part . . .

You've decided you want to become i-Net+ certified and let the world know how much you know about the Internet, the World Wide Web, and networking. So where do you start? In this part of the book, I give you the particulars about the test, such as who CompTIA and Sylvan Prometric are, how to schedule the test, where to go, what to do, and so on.

The i-Net+ exam does not include questions on everything there is to know about setting up, configuring, developing, installing, administering, and maintaining or connecting to an Internet site, but it does cover some of it in varying degrees. You won't find questions on computing and technical basics; you should know the bits and bytes and the basics of how data moves over wires and around computers. The i-Net+ exam either assumes you know this stuff or that it isn't relevant to the work of an Internet Technical Professional. However, you had better know the ins and outs of installing a TCP/IP client and connecting it to the Internet.

The i-Net+ exam includes just about everything you should know to be effective as an entry-level Internet Technician (CompTIA prefers Internet Technical Professional). Of course, this assumes you have been exposed — either in experience or study — to the opportunity to work with or learn about each of the technologies that together form the Internet and the Web.

The i-Net+ exam is strictly pass-fail. If you get a 70 percent, you pass, and if you don't, well, you don't — it's that simple. Don't over study. Let me be your guide on what you should and shouldn't worry about for the test. And, oh yes — best of luck!

Chapter 1

The i-Net+ Examination

CompTIA, the A+ and Network+ certification people, has a new certification program. This program designed for the entry-level Internet technician who has an excellent general knowledge of the Internet, the World Wide Web, and the design, installation, and support of Internet user Web pages, e-mail, browsers, and the like — is called the i-Net+ certification.

A typical exam candidate should have some practical knowledge of Internet-related technologies from training, school, or personal experience, but there are no other requirements.

Your chances of passing the exam and getting certified are better if you have experience with the hardware and software used to install an Internet client, knowledge of the server-side hardware and software, and the activities performed to administer and support both, as well as Internet users. However, this experience is not required, only recommended.

Like Network+ certification, the official title of the certification granted by the i-Net+ exam is officially just the i-Net+ Certification. What this means to you is that after you pass the test — and you will — you are i-Net+ Certified. CompTIA unofficially calls it "the Internet professional's" certification. By passing the i-Net+ exam, CompTIA certifies to the world that you are an Internet professional who possesses the knowledge required to perform a full range of Internet and World Wide Web design, development, and technical support activities. The i-Net+ certification was developed by a team of subject matter experts from around the world and is a globally recognized certification.

There are no other certifications like the i-Net+; it is the first of its kind, being both brand and platform neutral. Products from Microsoft, Novell, Cisco, and other manufacturers may be referenced on the i-Net+ test, but this is done only to represent what the Internet technician works with in the real world and to make the test a true measure of the Internet technician's overall knowledge of internetworking, the Internet, and the World Wide Web.

Who Is CompTIA?

Computing Technology Industry Association (CompTIA) is a membership trade organization formed in 1982 to promote standards of excellence in computer technology. The organization's goals are to develop ethical, professional, and business standards and to provide educational opportunities to the industry. CompTIA members include more than 7,500 computer resellers, computer repair shops, VARs (value-added resellers), distributors, manufacturers, and training companies in the United States and Canada. CompTIA members range from large multinational corporations to local computer repair shops and individual entrepreneurs.

A Little History

A group of CompTIA companies has been working on the idea of an industry-wide Internet technician's certification since 1998. A team of subject matter experts (SME), including yours truly, was organized to develop the i-Net+ job task analysis, a list of duties, responsibilities, and the skills that are needed to carry them out. The goal of the SME committee has been to identify, categorize, and distribute skills standards for Internet technicians and professionals working in three types of organizations: Internet service providers (ISPs), VARs and resellers, and private business and government agencies. The job task analysis formed the basis for the exam objectives and the beta test which was offered in November, 1999. The report on the i-Net+ job task analyis can be purchased from CompTIA, should you be interested.

The i-Net+ SME panel includes companies and organizations such as the Association of Internet Professionals, Comark, Global Training Solutions, HyCurve, Inc., IBM, Microsoft, Novell, ProsoftTraining.com, Sysoft, and Wave Technologies International. This is truly a global committee with not only companies from around the world, but also several multi-national companies as well. Their participation on the SME committee speaks volumes about the acceptance of the i-Net+ certification.

Why Get i-Net+ Certified?

That's a very good question. And just where i-Net+ fits into the mix of certifications and resume alphabet soup is another good question. One thing for certain is that certification of any kind is fast becoming the minimum requirement for nearly all IT and Internet-related jobs. CompTIA sees i-Net+ as a complementary certification to its A+ certification with the entry-level skills needed to qualify for a position as an Internet technician.

i-Net+ certification tells the world that its holder possesses demonstrated knowledge of general Internet and internetworking technology. Employers and consumers can use this, and other certifications, to indicate a baseline of capability and quality in a technician or a service organization. Given a choice, it is believed that a customer will choose an i-Net+ certified Internet provider over one that is not certified.

Is i-Net+ better than MCP+I, CCDA, or any of the other Internet-related certifications? No, but then it is not worse either, just different. i-Net+ says something different about its holder than the other certifications, but that's the point. In fact, it may take some time before people are even aware of i-Net+. But make no mistake, like it's A+ and Network+ cousins, i-Net+ is certain to become a recognized and respected certification, and soon a common minimum requirement for many Internet jobs.

What Are the Benefits of i-Net+ Certification?

That's another good question. Why would you want to cram for a test and then sweat bullets taking it, just to get a piece of paper that says, "This person really knows their Internet stuff?" The i-Net+ certification, like all industry certifications, provides benefits to everyone in or using Internet technology: you, employers, employees, job seekers, and especially consumers. Here are just a few of these benefits:

- ✔ **Proof of professional achievement:** The i-Net+ credential validates to your employer and your customers that you have reached a level of competence established by the computer industry, using criteria that are accepted and valued by the industry.

- ✔ **Increases your marketability:** i-Net+ certification makes you a more desirable employee who can often attract a higher starting wage because the cost to train you is lower than that of a non-certified employee. Many ISPs and other employers will most likely make i-Net+ certification a minimum requirement for employment.

✔ **Provides opportunity for advancement:** The knowledge you possess as an i-Net+ certified employee enables you to be a more efficient worker, which means that you are more productive. In most companies, at least in mine anyway, the most productive people get ahead.

✔ **Fulfill training requirements:** i-Net+ certification meets the prerequisite classes and training requirements for other certifications and advanced training courses. Much of the preparation for the i-Net+ exam is relevant to other industry certifications, such as the Network+ and MCSE+I certifications.

✔ **Apply for jobs with confidence:** i-Net+ certication provides you with the reasonable assurance that you meet a job's minimum requirements. You can apply for an Internet technician's position with the confidence that you are a certified entry-level technician. Employers can immediately assume a basic skill set from applicants holding i-Net+ certification. You have a much better chance of getting the job, but the end result is really up to you.

✔ **Raises customer confidence:** As more and more technicians display the i-Net+ certification logo on their business cards, and as companies begin advertising that their technicians are i-Net+ certified, the public will begin to accept it as a sign of Internet excellence and believe that an i-Net+ certified technician is more qualified to work on networked systems than an uncertified technician.

✔ **The envy of all of your friends and the respect of your peers:** Passing the i-Net+ exam verifies that you truly do know your stuff, just like you knew you did, and of course this is a very good thing. Earning the i-Net+ certification is a matter of personal pride and self-esteem. You have new self-worth, you can get the big job, and it may even get you a date — hey, it could happen!

What the i-Net+ Exam Covers

The i-Net+ exam is the result of an industry-wide analysis performed by companies from around the world of the necessary skills and knowledge that a networking technician needs to obtain an entry-level position as an Internet technician. The initial version of the i-Net+ test, published in January 2000, reflects the culmination of over two years of skill set and test development by the i-Net+ SME (Subject Matter Experts) task force.

The i-Net+ exam consists of 70 questions that covers six specific knowledge areas of Internet-related technologies, as listed in Table 1-1. As is indicated by the percentage each area represents of the whole test, some areas are emphasized more than others and accordingly the number of questions varies with this emphasis.

Table 1-1 lists and describes the six major knowledge areas (which are called domains by CompTIA) of the i-Net+ exam, the topics within each major area, and the percentage (and number of questions) of the total test each area represents.

Table 1-1	i-Net+ Exam Knowledge Areas		
Area	*Number of Questions*	*Percentage of Test*	*Content*
1.0 Internet Basics	7	10%	URL functions and components, including the different types of URLs and how they are used; the issues affecting the functionality of an Internet site; caching and how it works; the different types of search indexes; and how to perform Internet searches
2.0 Internet Clients	14	20%	The infrastructure of an Internet client; the use of Web browsers, plug-ins, helper applications, and other clients; configuring a computer as an Internet client; what MIME types are and how they're used; the problems associated with legacy clients; the issues and problems associated with updating and patching client software; and the pros and cons of using cookies
3.0 Development	14	20%	Programming terminology as relates to the development of Internet applications; server-side versus client-side programming languages; integrating a database with a Web site; popular multimedia extentions and plug-in applications; the benefits and use of popular multimedia file formats

(continued)

Table 1-1 *(continued)*

Area	Number of Questions	Percentage of Test	Content
4.0 Networking	18	25%	Network access points; the purpose and use of various Internet servers; domain names and the use of DNS; the components and operations of TCP/IP; setting up and using remote access protocols; the protocols and services used in e-mail, the World Wide Web, and file transfer; when and how to use TCP/IP diagnostic tools; hardware and software connectivity devices; and the specifications and use of Internet link types (bandwidth technologies)
5.0 Internet Security	10	15%	Applying Internet security concepts, including ACL, encryption, and authentication; what a VPN is and what it does; detecting and preventing suspicious network activities; file permissions and access control; antivirus software and its use; and the differences between an intranet, an extranet, and the Internet
6. 0 Business Concepts	7	10%	The issues of copyrighting and licensing; launching a multinational Web site; the tools used to attract and hold an audience; and e-commerce terminology and concepts

The format of the i-Net+ exam is strictly multiple-choice questions that have only one correct answer. There are no choose-all-that-apply questions, no true-false, no pick-the-object-from-the-diagram, and no required-objective/optional-objective scenario questions common to MCSE exams.

This book has been organized to match the sequence and content of the i-Net+ objectives to help you plan your studies. You may also want to use Table 1-1 as a cram checklist right before you take the test.

You really need to know the functions of the TCP/IP suite of protocols. You should have knowledge of Web browser software, e-mail, HTML, and general networking operations in Windows and NetWare environments as well. Use the test percentages shown in Table 1-1 as a gauge of how you should spend your time preparing for the test. Concentrate on the areas in which you don't have knowledge or experience. By all means, review everything you can, more than once, and take as many sample tests as possible.

The following sections provide you with a little more detail on each of the exam domains listed in Table 1-1. Please understand that I have not expanded the acronyms and mnemonics in the table for the sake of space. Each of these abbreviations and techno-names is defined and explained in later chapters.

Internet basics

Ten percent of the total test is comprised of questions that measure your basic knowledge of the Internet. These questions measure your ability and understanding of the following topics:

- ✔ **URLs:** Including the structure and components of a URL, the different types of URLs, and the server type with which each URL type is associated.

- ✔ **The issues affecting an Internet site's functionality in terms of its performance, security, and reliability:** Including bandwidth requirements, network connection points, ISPs, slow servers, graphics resolution, and connection types.

- ✔ **Caching and its impacts:** Including server caching, client caching, and proxy servers.

- ✔ **Different types of search indexes:** Including specific search methods, types of search engines, and the use of meta tags.

Internet clients

Approximately 20 percent of the i-Net+ exam concerns the setup, configuration, and operations of an Internet client. The questions from this area measure your knowledge and understanding of these topics:

- ✔ **The infrastructure of an Internet client:** Including the TCP/IP protocol stack, IP addresses, network connections, Web browser software, e-mail, and the hardware platform of the client.

- ✔ **The use of a Web browser and a variety of plug-in applications:** Including when you would use a particular helper application and the basic commands used with each client application.

✔ **Issues involved with configuring a client computer:** Including TCP/IP configuration, along with the IP address settings for WINS, DNS, default gateways, subnet masks, the use of DHCP and static IP addresses, and host file configuration.

✔ **Different MIME types and their components:** Including the reason for MIME and how it is used.

✔ **Problems relating to the use of legacy clients:** Including TCP/IP sockets and their relationship to the operating system.

✔ **The impact of software patches and updates on client components:** Including security, virus protection, encryption, Web browsers, and e-mail.

✔ **Advantages and disadvantages of using cookies:** Including the format of a cookie and the service life of a cookie.

Development

The exam devotes 20 percent of its questions to the processes and programming languages used to develop Internet and Web sites. The questions from this domain ask about your ability to perform or define the following:

✔ **Programming-related activities and terms:** Including API, CGI, SQL, SAPI, DLL, and client/server scripting languages.

✔ **Client-side and server-side programming languages:** Including Java, JavaScript, Perl, C++, Visual Basic, VBScript, XML, VRML, and ASP.

✔ **When to integrate a database into a Web site:** Including the technologies used to do so.

✔ **The tools for creating HTML pages:** Including the structure of an HTML document, and the tags used to create tables, forms, and ordered and unordered lists.

✔ **Popular multimedia extensions and plug-ins:** Including QTVR, Flash, Shockwave, and RealPlayer.

✔ **When various multimedia file formats should be used:** Including GIF (87 and 89), JPEG, PNG, TIFF, AVI, BINHex, streaming media, and non-streaming media.

Networking and infrastructure

The biggest single domain of the i-Net+ exam concerns networking and the infrastructure of the Internet. This domain accounts for 25 percent of the entire test, and concentrates on your abilities, knowledge, and understanding of the following topics:

✔ **The core components of the Internet and their interrelationships:** Including network backbones and network access points.

✔ **Internet connectivity problems:** Including those common to e-mail, slow servers, and Web sites.

✔ **The use of Internet domain names and the DNS:** Including DNS levels, top-level domains, and country-level domains.

✔ **The operating essentials of TCP/IP:** Including IP address classes, subnet masking, and public versus private IP addresses.

✔ **The purpose and use of remote access protocols:** Including SLIP, PPP, PPTP, and point-to-point/multipoint.

✔ **The protocols and services that are used in e-mail, the Web, and file transfers:** Including POP3, SMTP, HTTP, FTP, TCP/IP, and LDAP.

✔ **The use of diagnostic protocols to identify and resolve Internet problems:** Including PING, WinIPCfg, ARP, TRACERT, and NETSTAT.

✔ **The different hardware and software connectivity devices and their uses:** Including NIC, DSL, router, bridge, gateway, and firewall.

✔ **The various types of Internet bandwidth and link types used:** Including T1/E1, T3/E3, OC1, OC3, frame relay, X.25, ATM, and DSL.

✔ **The purpose of various server types found in a local or wide area network:** Including proxy, mail, cache, web, certificate, directory (LDAP), e-commerce, Telnet, and FTP.

Internet security

Only 15 percent of the i-Net+ exam is specifically on Internet security. This may be somewhat misleading because the client and server areas include questions regarding security issues, which do not count against this percentage. The questions from this area require you to demonstrate your knowledge of the following topics:

✔ **Internet security concepts:** Including access control lists, encryption, authentication, the use of digital certificates, and public, private, symmetrical, and asymmetrical keys.

✔ **Virtual Private Networks (VPNs):** Including the basic structure of a VPN, encrypted communications, and connecting remote users to a VPN.

✔ **The identification and control of suspicious network activities:** Including multiple logon failures, denial-of-service attacks, spam, SYN floods, and spoofing.

✔ **How access is controlled to various Internet servers:** Such as e-mail servers and Web servers, including user name and passwords, file level controls, digital certificates and signatures.

✔ **Antivirus software:** Including its use with and effect on browsers and servers.

✔ **Security issues:** Especially those relating to an intranet, an extranet, and the Internet.

Business concepts

In terms of its number of questions, this area has the least emphasis, but it still represents ten percent of the total exam. In this exam domain, you will be asked questions that test your knowledge of these topics:

✔ **Copyrighting, trademarking, and licensing:** Including the use of the copyright and trademark symbols, and how to copyright material.

✔ **Working in a global environment:** Including the issues of multi-language support, and the use of slang and colloquialisms on Web pages.

✔ **Push and pull technologies:** Including how they can be used to attract and hold an audience.

✔ **The use of an intranet, an extranet, and the Internet from a business viewpoint:** Focusing on the situations when each is best used.

✔ **E-commerce terms and concepts:** Including EDI, business-to-business, merchant accounts, e-commerce servers, credit card processing, online catalogs, and Internet marketing.

Scoping Out the Exam and the Questions

If you are new to online, interactive testing, have no fear; you'll be very pleased with the experience — provided you are prepared. If you're not prepared for the test, it is far too easy to blame the test for your failure. Even if you don't pass the exam, I'm positive you'll learn from the experience.

Number of questions

The i-Net+ exam has 70 questions for which you will be given 120 minutes. The time allotment does not include time you are given to use the tutorial provided to orient you to the test and the various question types you will encounter. Two hours is plenty of time for the test and a review of questions you marked for review during the exam.

You are allowed to mark questions as you proceed through the test. I recommend that you use the test engine's built-in mark-and-review features and use any remaining time you have at the end of the test for review. In fact, many people have time to completely review the entire test in the time available. One tip on reviewing your answers: Trust your first instinct.

The questions from all of the six domains are randomly mixed throughout the test. You won't get all of the Networking or Development domain questions together in one dose. However, it is also not unusual for questions relating to close topics to follow one another.

Multiple-choice questions

The questions on the i-Net+ exam are in the multiple-choice format. Each question has only a single answer and none require two or more answers. Be sure you read the question carefully because a question may be asking which in a list does NOT meet the criteria stated in the question.

Some of the questions included in this book ask you to provide more than one answer. This is done more to maximize the practice test subjects than to get you ready for that type of question. You will not see any "Choose all that apply" or "Choose 3 answers" questions on the exam.

Some reading required

One thing you don't have to worry about is long questions. Other than one or two situational questions, which can have up to three sentences, nearly all the questions are short and to the point, with only one or two sentences.

There is no attempt to trick you or mislead you with unnecessary information. The i-Net+ exam is designed to give you the best possible chance of passing, provided you know your stuff.

Working a Study Plan

Knowing your stuff is the key to passing the i-Net+ exam. So, how should you get ready? Use the questions in this book or on a test simulator to determine the parts of the test that you need to study. This doesn't mean you shouldn't study all the topics on the test, but you need to focus on those areas where you need to improve your knowledge.

Quick Assessment quizzes at the beginning of each chapter and the Prep Tests at the end of each chapter cover the topics in each chapter. There are a number of commercially available test simulators you can use. I've included URLs for some of the better ones later in this chapter and in Chapter 18. (Some are even free!)

Go through this book and mark the pages that have lists, tables, and diagrams — it is a fact of certification testing that there is a body of information that must be memorized. Which protocols are in the TCP/IP suite, the default subnet mask of a Class C IP address, or the commands used to edit a HOSTS file entry are the type of answers you cannot figure out from the data in the question. You have to know this stuff. Begin committing this information to memory as soon as you can.

Allocate time right before the test as cram time. Do a good general review of your notes, lists, tables, and diagrams at least twice. Finish by reviewing the lists that must be memorized. Give yourself enough time that you can remain relaxed during this time. Take as many deep breaths as necessary, but keep calm.

When you get into the testing room, use the plastic or paper you are given to quickly write down all of the lists you've memorized and then quickly go through the test and answer all of the questions requiring memorized information. If you haven't taken a Sylvan Prometric test before, use the tutorial to acquaint yourself with its operation. Remember that the tutorial time is not a part of the time allotted to you for the actual test, but don't dilly-dally, your short-term memory may be expiring.

How much studying is enough?

Gilster's Law of Test Preparation says: You never can tell, and it all depends. How much studying you need to do depends on you, your experience, your education, and so on. Seasoned veterans of the networking wars may need only to catch up on the very latest stuff, and someone just starting out in network technology may have a more difficult time getting ready for the exam.

Because you are paying to take this test, I would certainly err to the side of too much studying, if that is possible. If you are intent on passing, your goal should be to pass the first time — unless you can afford to take the test just to find out what you should study. All I can say to that is that this book is much less expensive than the test, and tells you what to study. But, it is your money! (Any excess funds you just have to spend, send it to me in care of IDG Books Worldwide, Inc.)

Keep yourself focused on the topics identified as being on the test and avoid studying any new technologies that have come out since about three months before the test was released in January, 2000. Anything newer than that won't be on the test — guaranteed.

Practice tests and test simulators can be good measurements of whether you are ready or not. If you can consistently pass the practice exams (with the answers hidden), chances are that you are ready. Many of the practice tests are actually much more difficult than the actual test anyway.

Where to start

The best place to start is right in your hands! Use the quizzes, tests, lists, and tables in this book to prepare for the memorized portions of the test and then read through its topics to shore up your understanding of concepts and principles.

You may want to use other resources as well. Sometimes a little different explanation is the one that works for you. The CompTIA Web site (`www.comptia.org`) has information about the exam, its objectives, and lists of other possible sources for practice exams.

Planning for success

The benefits of i-Net+ certification are well worth the time you invest in passing the test. Whatever method you use to prepare for the test, create a plan and then stick to it. Give yourself ample time to prepare for the test. Go for understanding rather than just memorization. If you truly understand the concepts behind the facts, the facts come easier, and might even begin to make some sense.

Here are a few tips to consider as you prepare for the test:

- ✔ **Focus on the exam objectives.** CompTIA is very good at staying within the boundaries established by the exam objectives.

- ✔ **Use the Quick Assessments, Prep Tests, and sample exam questions in this book and on its CD as well as any other practice tests to which you have access.** You can't take too many practice tests.

- ✔ **Beware of wrong or misleading answers on practice tests.** I have taken every possible step to ensure the accuracy of the sample test questions in this book and on the CD-ROM, but I can't vouch for the accuracy of the sample tests from other sources. It is a shame — especially if you are learning most of this stuff from scratch — to have practice tests give bad answers, but it happens. This is one reason you should use more than one set of practice questions.

- ✔ **Take occasional short breaks, if possible, of a day or two, from studying.** You can overdo it and burn out. This test is very important, but it is not a life and death thing. Keep your perspective . . . and your sanity.

If you pass the test, I was glad to be of help. If you don't pass and you've used this book and its resources to their full potential, you need to study longer and better and possibly supplement this book with additional practice tests. Of course you *will* pass the test, I have confidence in you!

Taking the Exam

The test is online and interactive, and very well designed to provide you with every possible opportunity to pass. Each question is presented one at a time on the screen in an easy-to-read format with help always available to help you proceed. Unfortunately there is no subject-matter help available on the test. You are allowed to mark, using a check box, questions you would like to review later. In fact, you are allowed to review the entire test if you wish. The test even goes so far as to mark any questions for which you didn't provide an answer. Contrary to what you may have heard or believe about certification tests, the i-Net+ exam wants you to pass if you have the right knowledge, and attempts to remove the test itself as a barrier to that goal.

To become i-Net+ certified, you must get at least a 70% on the i-Net+ Certification examination. This means you must get 49 of the 70 questions on the exam correct — it also means that you can miss, incorrectly interpret, misconstrue, or choke on 21 questions and still pass.

You have 2 hours to complete the test, allowing you plenty of time to work through the entire test as well as for reviewing your answers. However, you must also understand that when time is up, the test is over! Bam, zoom, no last minute quesses — over, done, fini! So watch the time carefully!

One other thing about taking the test. The physical setup of the testing facility varies from site to site. The test centers are in training companies, community colleges, universities, and the like. Regardless of how the testing center is organized, you will be assigned to a specific computer workstation to take the test. You are not allowed to take breaks, talk to anyone, or get up and move around. Many test centers have open microphones and video cameras in the room to monitor the test takers. This is intended to prevent somebody from cheating or disturbing other test takers. As strict as this all sounds, your best bet is to forget about it and plan on sitting at your workstation for the duration, quietly taking your exam.

Where to Go to Take the Exam

The i-Net+ Certification examination is conducted by Sylvan Prometric testing centers located in over 700 locations worldwide. To schedule an appointment to take this test, call them at 877-803-6867 (toll-free). Call at least two days before your desired test date and the friendly and knowledgeable testing counselor helps you set a date, time, and location that is convenient for you. Sylvan Prometric helps you to find a testing center near your home or the vacation spot in which you wish to celebrate after the test. You must give them your credit card information or mail them a check or money order (not a great option if you are in a hurry).

The test is not given at specific times or dates. You pick the date, time, and place. Some testing sites are not available every day of the week, or even every month of the year, and some offer testing during only certain hours of the day. So the earlier you contact Sylvan Prometric, the better. I would recommend calling as soon as you think you are entering the final stages of your exam preparation.

How Much Does It Cost?

The cost of the i-Net+ exam is $125 for CompTIA members and $175 for nonmembers. Sylvan Prometric accepts all generally accepted credit cards. You can make other payment arrangements with them, but before you can take the test, you must be paid in full.

Web Sites to Help You

Here are some URLs that have either free information, sample tests, or products to help you prepare for the i-Net+ exam:

CompTIA: www.comptia.org

Global Training Solutions: www.gtspartner.com

Super Software, Inc.: www.rotw.com

Wave Technologies: www.wavetech.com/trainingsolutions

A Little Luck Never Hurts

I know I speak for the entire *For Dummies* team when I wish you the very best luck on the i-Net+ exam. And let us be the first to congratulate you on earning your i-Net+ certification!

Chapter 2

Speaking the Language of the i-Net+ Exam

● ●

In This Chapter

▶ Looking at the i-Net+ exam

▶ Understanding what's on the test

▶ Reviewing terms and concepts used on the i-Net+ exam

▶ Crafting a study plan

● ●

*T*he i-Net+ exam is intended to certify the knowledge of Internet professionals with around six months of experience. However, it is also an excellent way to demonstrate that you are a well-rounded computing professional as well.

As I see it, there will be four groups of people taking the i-Net+ exam:

✔ A+ and Network+ certified service technicians. (You don't need either of these certifications to take the i-Net+ test, although it is a natural next step, adds to your resume, and certainly can't hurt.)

✔ Experienced Internet technicians looking to add more letters to their resume.

✔ Experienced Internet technicians certifying their knowledge to meet an employer's minimum requirements.

✔ Internet technicians fresh out of training programs, schools, or colleges who are looking to get job credentials.

If you have seven years of Internet experience and can set up a TCP/IP client and design an HTML document blindfolded and without cursing, then maybe — just maybe — you have a good chance of passing the i-Net+ exam without studying. You should remember that this test covers the Internet from soup to nuts, including all the stuff you never quite got around to learning or using. Keep in mind that the technology cycles on the Internet are measured in days and weeks rather than months and years.

On the other hand, if you are coming straight out of school and want to establish your job credentials, i-Net+ can give you a hand up out of the feeding frenzy for entry-level jobs in networking.

The intent of the i-Net+ exam is to certify a general knowledge of the Internet and the TCP/IP client at an entry-level. How much you need to study is directly related to the length and breadth of your experience. Regardless of your experience, you should at least review what's on the test and study the areas in which your experience or knowledge is less than perfect.

Speaking i-Net+: A Primer

There is a whole new language, loosely based on English, used on the Internet. Although this new Internet language was not necessarily intended to be a spoken language, in places where Internet people hang out, which is just about anywhere these days, you can hear this strange language and its odd sounding TLAs (three-letter abbreviations), FLAs (four-letter abbreviations), nouns, and verbs. There aren't too many adjectives, but those that are used pack a lot of definition into a single word.

The i-Net+ exam draws heavily on the language of the Internet and — just in case you haven't figured it out yet — i-Net+ is an attempt at naming the test something like Internet+ without actually staking claim to that name. If you can speak, write, and understand the language of the Internet fluently, then you are on your way to i-Net+ success! I know you didn't expect to get a language lesson as a part of your preparations for the i-Net+ exam, but I think that may be one of the better ways to get ready for the test. Much of the exam is built around your understanding of what a certain term represents or how it is applied.

So, here are some short definitions to the common terminology you will see on the i-Net+ exam. If you study these terms before delving into the rest of the book, you can maximize your study time.

Basic Internet terms

Here are the major terms and concepts you need to know for the Internet basics domain:

Address

There are actually two types of addresses you need to know about for the exam: the IP (Internet Protocol) address and the MAC (Media Access Control) address. An IP address is the logical address of a host, server, peripheral, or connectivity device on a network using TCP/IP protocols. An example of an IP address is 192.53.105.2. A MAC address is the physical address permanently assigned to a network interface card (NIC) or a network adapter. For more information on how IP and MAC addresses are used, see the description of ARP in the "Real important networking terms" section later in this chapter.

Bandwidth

Technically, bandwidth is the highest signal rate a connection can support. Bandwidth is often used to describe the transfer speed of a network (including its connectivity devices, such as hubs, bridges, routers, and cabling). Bandwidth for a digital circuit is always expressed as bits per second (bps) and normally as either thousands of bits per second (Kbps) or millions of bits per second (Mbps). Where bandwidth is concerned, bigger is better.

Cache and caching

A cache is RAM (random-access memory) set aside to keep data readily available. Caching is storing data in cache. On the i-Net+ exam, *cache* and *caching* are used to describe how Web documents and objects are stored on cache servers so that frequently requested data is available to a network without the need to fetch it from its original server. Some Web browsers store recently downloaded pages on the hard disk of the client computer to create a *local cache* or *client cache*.

Clients and servers

The Internet is a very large client/server network. Clients and servers are just about what you would expect them to be. Because the terms originated in real life instead of in the computing world for a change, it is easy to understand that a client is the one that is asking for something and the server is the one providing it. An HTTP client (see "Terms relating to the Internet client" later in this chapter) requests that a document be downloaded from a Web server (see "Real important networking terms").

The short version is that a client is a workstation capable of connecting to a network and interacting with a server. A server is a network-connected computer that receives and processes client requests.

ISP

ISP stands for Internet service provider. ISPs come in all sizes and offer differing levels of services, ranging from dialup access to the Internet and e-mail to a full-range of development services, such as Web page design and hosting as well as different bandwidth and link types such as ISDN, DSL, and others (see the "Real important networking terms" section later in this chapter).

Network access point (NAP)

At the highest levels of the Internet infrastructure are very high speed inter-connection points called *network access points* (NAPs). There are 12 major NAPs, plus a growing number of lower-level NAPs, in the U.S., and several others around the world. The interconnections between these links create the spine of the Internet's backbone.

Port

A *port* is used in computing to describe the physical connection that allows data to enter and leave a computer to a network or peripheral device. On most computers, there are serial and parallel ports to which cable connectors are attached.

The term port is also used among Internet professionals as a shorthand term for port number, which is a TCP/IP-based number assigned to an application program running in the computer. The port indicates the application to which incoming data is to be assigned. TCP/IP has a number of standard port numbers known as *well-known ports.* For example, port 80 is the well-known port number for HTTP or Web traffic.

Protocol

A protocol is a set of rules and standards that prescribe how two computers, operating systems, or applications communicate with each other. A protocol may define the media type, the packet format, the timing issues, and error handling involved with sending data between two points. The primary protocols on the Internet are in the TCP/IP protocol suite.

Search index

Actually, there are many different ways to search for information on the Internet, including search indexes, directories, catalogs, and more. *Search index* is a generic term that describes the software tools used to find specific content on the Internet. Also known as a *search engine,* a search index catalogs data about Web sites into databases (indexes) that can be searched with user-defined criteria to find Web sites of interest.

Socket

The combination of a computer's IP address and a port number make up a socket. Also known as a UNIX socket, representing its origins, a socket connects incoming data directly to the computer and application that will process it. Web page data would have a socket in the form of 192.234.10.1:80.

Stateful

I'm including this term only because it shows up as one of the multiple choices on one or more i-Net+ exam questions. Stateful computers and programs track the state of their interactions by storing values in special fields. The Internet Protocol (IP) is a stateless (and connectionless) world.

Computers and your creditors are stateful (which rhymes with hateful) things. So, this term cannot possibly be a correct answer for any question relating to the Internet.

Terms relating to the Internet client

As simple as it may seem from outward appearances, the Internet client has a variety of different components and processes associated with it. Here are the major terms and concepts you need to know for the i-Net+ exam.

Browser

A Web browser is a software application that runs on a local computer to establish it as a World Wide Web and Internet client. The browser performs the requested actions of the user, including requesting and downloading Web documents, and transferring documents via FTP, Gopher, and other protocols. The browser interprets the Web document's HTML commands and displays the document and any linked objects for the user. The browser also processes any hypertext links embedded in the document. Most browsers also save recently visited sites in temporary Internet files, history folders, or in a disk cache.

Cookie

A cookie is a bit of information saved on a client computer's hard disk by the client's browser at the request of a Web server. Cookies are used to record user preferences, speed up banner ad rotations, and store some e-commerce information that the Web server can later request to assist the user on its site. The average cookie ranges in size from 50 to 150 bytes. Cookies carry expiration dates and if one is not included, the cookie disappears at the end of the current browser session.

DHCP

DHCP stands for Dynamic Host Configuration Protocol. This protocol is used on networks to dynamically assign host IP addresses to workstations as they log on to the network. DHCP is what is designated when you choose to let the server supply the IP address in your TCP/IP settings. The opposite of a dynamic IP address is a static, or permanently assigned, IP address.

DNS

DNS stands for Domain Name System, which is the mechanism used on the Internet to look up domain names such as www.dummies.com and change them into IP addresses. The DNS distributes its databases of domain names around the world so that names common to each region are located in that region for faster lookup. One single, central database would be very impractical and cause a major bottleneck on the Internet.

E-mail

In the Internet world, where just about everything begins with an "e", e-mail is an abbreviation for electronic mail. E-mail consists of personal messages transmitted over the Internet and delivered to a private electronic mailbox on a local mail server. If you are reading this book to prepare for the i-Net+ exam and don't know what e-mail is, then I recommend you put this off while you learn more about the Internet in general.

FTP

FTP stands for File Transfer Protocol, and is the TCP/IP protocol used to transfer files between two computers, typically an FTP client and an FTP server. FTP is commonly used as a way to transfer files too large to be attached as e-mail attachments.

Gateway

You will see the term *gateway* used a couple of ways on the i-Net+ exam. One way is as a default gateway, or the IP address of the device used to connect a network to the Internet. The other way is hardware or software used to connect two dissimilar networks, which typically mean they are running different network operating systems (NOSs). Be sure which definition of gateway a question is referencing before picking your answer.

MIME

MIME stands for Multi-Purpose Internet Mail Extensions. MIME is an extension of the original SMTP (Simple Mail Transport Protocol) e-mail protocol that enables users to exchange data files in different formats over the Internet, including audio, video, graphics, programs, and more, in addition to the ASCII text files handled in SMTP by default.

NOS

NOS stands for network operating system. The NOS, along with other local area network (LAN) activities, provides services to the local client computer, including access to the Internet and other supporting services, such as the cache server, proxy server, and default gateway.

TCP/IP

TCP/IP stands for Transmission Control Protocol/Internet Protocol, which is the suite of protocols and utilities used as the protocol foundation for the Internet. TCP/IP protocols handle all phases of transferring data from one point to another over the Internet. TCP/IP is also commonly used as the primary protocol for intranets, whether they connect to the Internet or not.

Telnet

Telnet is a TCP/IP protocol that is used to gain access and log on to a remote server (appropriately called a Telnet server). Telnet is used to conduct a character-based interaction on a remote computer in terminal emulation mode.

Speaking about development

The i-Net+ exam has more on the details of developing Internet and Web applications than you might expect. If you are not experienced with writing server-side or client-side scripts and programs, you should review the terms in this section.

API

API stands for applications program interface. An API is created to support application functions in a specific task or activity. For example, the Mail API (MAPI) contains DLL files that contain routines that can be used by a mail-enabled program to perform standard e-mail related actions. Other common APIs are ISAPI (Internet Server API), TAPI (Telephony API), and ODAPI (Open Data API).

AVI

AVI stands for Audio Video Interleaved, although it is rarely, if ever, referred to as anything other than AVI. An AVI file is a Windows multimedia format that interleaves 8-bit audio and digital video frames to store animated images that playback at 15 frames per second in 160 x 120 x 8 resolution. AVI is a common Web file format for multimedia.

BinHex

The name *BinHex* is a shortened form of binary-to-hexadecimal. BinHex is actually a utility that is used to encode Macintosh mail files into a 7-bit ASCII format for transmission over the Internet as e-mail attachments.

CGI

CGI stands for Common Gateway Interface. CGI is a hardware and platform (operating system) independent standard. A CGI script, which is commonly written in Perl, is a script of instructions that executes on the Internet or Web server to process data supplied by client software. The functions now performed by CGI scripts, which are stored in a folder typically named bin-bin, will likely be done by Java and ActiveX in the future.

Client-side programming languages

There are a variety of client-side programming languages that create applications that run on the client computer rather than the server. Examples of client-side programming tools are JavaScript, VBScript, some Java routines, and VRML.

DLL

DLL stands for dynamic link library. DLL files are created to provide a common library of preprogrammed routines and objects that usually relate to a common activity or task. An API is usually made up of a number of DLL files.

GIF

GIF stands for Graphics Interchange Format. GIF files are the most common form of graphic images on the Internet and the Web. There are two standards in use for GIF images: GIF87, which is the oldest GIF standard, and GIF89, which includes the ability to make a part of the GIF image transparent and the ability to create an animated GIF image.

HTML

HTML stands for Hypertext Markup Language. HTML is the standard coding language used to develop Web pages. Web browser software interprets the HTML tags and attributes of the document to display it as the developer intended. Two very important terms you must know for the exam are

- ✔ **Tag:** HTML instructions are encased in < and > symbols and instruct HTTP, search indexes, and browsers how to transfer, categorize, and display Web documents. Examples of HTML tags are <P> (paragraph) and <OL> (ordered list). You may also run into the term *tag set,* which means the opening and closing tags of certain tags. An example of a tag set is <HTML> ...</HTML>, which includes and requires both tags to complete the set.

- ✔ **Attribute:** An HTML attribute is a specific value within an HTML tag instruction. Attributes are used to define colors, sizes, file locations, and other data the tag needs to complete its purpose. Within the <FONT> tag, you can usually find FONTSIZE= and COLOR= attributes.

JPEG

JPEG is the abbreviation for Joint Photographic Experts Group. JPEG is the de facto standard on the Internet for highly compressed photographs and other high resolution documents. With GIF, JPEG is one of only two image file formats generally supported by all software on the Internet and the Web.

Server-side programming languages

CGI and some Java programs are server-side programming languages. This means the programs created with these programming languages must (in the case of CGI) or may need to (in the case of Java) run on an Internet server. Server-side programming uses data supplied by the client to complete a task and either record it in a database, respond to the user, or both.

SQL

SQL (often pronounced "sequel") stands for Structured Query Language, although it is generally not often referred to as anything other than SQL. This is a query language used, among other tools, to retrieve data from a database and insert it in a Web page.

Streaming media

There are two types of multimedia, audio, and video that are sent over the Internet: streaming format and non-streaming format. The streaming type is fast becoming a standard for delivering audio/video/multimedia files over the Internet. Streaming media sends enough of its content ahead that it can be buffered, and then begins playing the downloading file from the buffer while staying ahead of the actual playback. Non-streaming media files must be completely downloaded before playback can begin.

TIFF

TIFF, a.k.a. TIF, stands for Tagged Image File Format. TIFF is a widely-used bitmapped graphics format for monochrome, gray scale, 8-bit, and 24-bit color. To display a TIFF graphic your browser typically must use a plug-in or helper application.

Real important networking terms

In this section, I define the terms and concepts that appear not only in questions about networking and infrastructure, but also in nearly all of the other domains in one way or another. Be sure you are familiar with these terms.

ARP

ARP stands for Address Resolution Protocol, which is the TCP/IP protocol used to convert physical (MAC) addresses to their IP address equivalent. ARP uses a file called the ARP cache to hold the mappings of network nodes' addresses. The ARP cache is built by ARP sending out broadcast messages with the IP address it's looking for and the node responding with its MAC address.

Bandwidth/Link types

Carrier lines are often described in terms of their bandwidth, which is also synonymous with the link type or common name of the carrier line. On the i-Net+ exam, you will find references to T-carrier, E-carrier, and Optical carrier lines:

✔ **T1:** A T1 line transmits signals at the rate of 1.54 Mbps and can transmit 1MB of data in about 10 seconds. This is fast enough for nearly all the data and still graphic formats found on the Internet. It is not fast enough for full-motion video, which needs around 10 Mbps. A T1 line consists of 24 channels that can be fractionalized into smaller lines in multiples of the 24 64 Kbps channels that make up the T1 line. Common increments are 128 Kbps, 256 Kbps, 384 Kbps, 512 Kbps, and 768 Kbps.

✔ **T3:** A T3 line is the equivalent of 28 T1 lines and can transmit signals at 44.736 Mbps.

✔ **E1/E3:** These carriers, which are used in South America and Europe, are similar to the T1 and T3 lines used in the US. The E1 is about one-fourth larger than the T1 (2.048 Mbps versus 1.54 Mbps) and the E3 is about one-fourth smaller than the T3 (34 Mbps versus 44.736 Mbps), but they are often referred to as equivalents.

✔ **OC lines:** The Synchronous Optical Network (SONET) — a U.S. standard for transmitting signals over fiber-optic cables — defines a set of carrier lines and signal rates. The most commonly used OC (Optical Carrier) lines are the OC-1, which transmits at 51.84 Mbps, and the OC-3, which transmits at three times the base rate (hence the three) or 155.52 Mbps. Other commonly used OC signal rates are OC-12 (622.08 Mbps) and OC-48 (2.488 Gbps). Optical carrier lines are used for the Internet backbone or tier-1 links to the NAPs.

Bridge

A bridge is a protocol-independent Data Link (Layer 2 of the OSI Reference model) that is used to connect two or more networks or network segments. A bridge uses the information inside of a network packet to forward the message to the appropriate network segment.

Digital certificate

A digital certificate is like an electronic passport and credit card all in one and is used to establish who you are and that you are trustworthy when doing financial or legal transactions on the Web. A digital certificate, which is issued by a certification authority such as Verisign, has your name, a serial number assigned to the certificate, its expiration dates, a copy of your public key, and the digital signature of the certificate authority that issued the certificate. The information in the digital certificate is used by the merchant or the transaction processing authority to verify your transaction.

Domain

In technical terms, a domain is a group of network servers and hosts that appear to remote users to be a single network. In terms of the Internet, a domain is a network's name that can be referenced by Internet users and also used to look up the network's (meaning its gateway's) IP address using the DNS (Domain Name System). Internet domains are organized into a hierarchy with the top-level domains standardized into categorical groupings:

com (commercial), edu (educational), gov (governmental), int (international), mil (U.S. military), net (network service provider), and org (non-profit). There are also top-level domains for most countries around the world. Examples of country-level domains are au (Australia), br (Brazil), es (Spain), uk (United Kingdom), and us (United States). See Chapter 12 for more information on domains.

DSL

DSL stands for Digital Subscriber Line. This term shows up in quite a few questions on the i-Net+ exam, but beyond what its acronym stands for, what you really need to know is that it is a bandwidth option (also called a link type) that enables you to download at higher speeds than you upload. In most cases, DSL lines upload data at speeds ranging from 128 Kbps to 6.1 Mbps, with typical service offering from 512 Kbps to 1.5 Mbps download speeds and 128K upload speeds. There are several types of DSL services, but don't sweat them for the exam.

Firewall

A firewall prevents unauthorized network traffic — for instance, broadcast messages — from entering a network. The firewall, which is commonly a combination of hardware and software, sits at a network's Internet gateway and screens incoming (and outgoing) messages to determine if they have the authority or permission to continue to their destination. A firewall is a network's first level of security.

Frame relay

Frame relay is a type of packet-switching WAN system that transmits signals over a Permanent Virtual Circuit (PVC) that is established between two points.

HTTP

HTTP stands for Hypertext Transfer Protocol, which is the TCP/IP protocol used to transfer HTML documents on the World Wide Web. HTTP provides the rules under which any document can establish hyperlinks to any other document or location on the Internet.

LDAP

LDAP stands for Lightweight Directory Access Protocol, which is used to locate domains or an object located on a domain on the Internet. If you know the directory of an item on a network, then you basically know where it is. Likewise, on the Internet or any other TCP/IP network, the DNS can be searched to find the location (IP address) of a domain name. LDAP comes into play if you don't know the domain name; it enables you to search for the domain, or an individual, or a file, on the network.

NETSTAT

NETSTAT is a utility program that is used to display protocol statistics and current active TCP/IP network connections, having a variety of options that can be used to display a full range of statistics and configuration information for a network, workstation, or server. Expect a question on the exam about what the NETSTAT utility does.

PING

PING actually stands for Packet Internet Groper, but you don't really need to remember that. What you do need to know is that PING is used to determine if an IP address or domain name is valid by sending a series of packets out and waiting for their responses from the targeted IP address or domain.

Point-to-Point Protocols

There are actually five point-to-point protocols mentioned on the i-Net+ exam: the actual point-to-point protocol (PPP), the Serial Line Internet Protocol (SLIP), the point-to-point tunneling protocol (PPTP), Layer 2 Tunnel Protocol (L2TP), and the point-to-point/multilink protocol.

- **PPP:** This is the protocol most commonly used with dialup connections, and is usually considered to be a part of the TCP/IP protocol suite. PPP is a full-duplex protocol that works on a wide variety of physical media, including PSTN, copper twisted-pair wire, fiber-optic cabling, or even wireless transmission. PPP encapsulates packets using a variation of High-speed Data Link Control (HDLC).

- **SLIP:** This was the first protocol for transmitting IP packets over a dialup connection. About all SLIP does is define an encapsulation method, and lacks significant abilities such as error-checking and encryption. SLIP, which has been largely replaced by PPP, is going the way of the dinosaurs.

- **PPTP:** This WAN protocol allows users to build virtual private networks (tunnels) through the Internet. PPTP (and L2TP) are used to create virtual private networks (VPNs).

- **L2TP:** This is a new tunneling protocol standard that extends the capability of PPTP. L2TP is used to create private virtual circuits over the Internet.

- **PPP/Multilink:** This protocol combines two PPP links into a new virtual link with greater bandwidth of the two separate links, and is commonly used to distribute the bandwidth load of two links evenly over their combined capacity.

POP3

POP3 (Post Office Protocol 3), which is known simply as POP mail to its friends, is an e-mail standard that collects user e-mail in a mailbox and then transfers the e-mail to the user's computer when the user logs on to the mail server.

Be careful on the i-Net+ exam that you know which POP is being discussed in a question. The connection point for dialup Internet customers is also called a POP (Point of Presence).

POTS/PSTN

Despite the fact that these two terms are technically different, they are often used interchangeably. POTS stands for the Plain Old Telephone System, which is the standard analog telephone service typically found in most homes, offices, or schools. On the other hand, PSTN is the Public Switched Telephone Network, which doesn't at face value sound anything at all plain or old. In the PSTN, the phone company becomes a service provider that uses circuit-switching to create a network with unrestricted access. Oh, that's what I thought you said: the POTS.

Router

A router is a type of connectivity hardware or software that determines the best route a packet should take to its destination. The router is connected to at least two networks: the internal (intranet) and the external (Internet). Its decision on which network a packet should be forwarded to is based on where the destination address resides, or doesn't reside in many cases. If a destination address lies outside the internal network, the router sends the packet to the next upstream address it has (usually another router) that also makes a routing decision on the packet. A router is typically used as the default gateway for a network.

SMTP

Where POP3 delivers e-mail to the end-user, SMTP (Simple Mail Transport Protocol) is the TCP/IP protocol used to transmit e-mail over the Internet. SMTP has limited mailbox capabilities, so it is not uncommon for SMTP to be used to send e-mail and POP3 to be used to receive it.

X.25

X.25 is the international standard that defines how e-mail and graphics are coded and transmitted between different types of computers. In a nutshell, X.25 defines how you connect with a common carrier to use a packet-switched network for which you are billed for your time on the network.

The secret language of Internet security

If the Internet has a language all its own, then Internet security is a major sub-dialect all its own. The good news is that if you understand the terminology used in Internet and World Wide Web security, you should have no fear of this portion of the exam.

ACL

ACL stands for access control list. An ACL is maintained by virtually every operating system and network operating system, and lists the available services on a system and the users or nodes that have been granted access (and the kind of access) to those services. Once a user is authenticated on a system, the ACL controls what the user can and cannot access.

Antivirus software

Although not always thought of as a security issue, viruses pose a serious threat to the integrity of a system. This is why antivirus software is considered a security measure. Antivirus software is used to detect and remove computer viruses.

When installing new versions of application programs, it is a good idea to disable antivirus software, which monitors memory and the hard disk for changes.

Authentication

Authentication is the process that verifies that a user, node, or workstation has the authority or permission to gain access to a system. The most common form of authentication is through the use of a user account name and a password. If the account name and password are valid, then the user is authenticated and granted permission to access the system, subject to other restrictions.

Denial-of-service attack

A denial-of-service (DoS) attack is a hostile action taken against an Internet server that causes the server to begin denying services normally provided to users because it is overloaded with bogus requests for service. However, a DoS situation isn't always the result of some mean-and-nasty action. A site may shut down — that is, begin denying services — due to sudden popularity.

Encryption

Encryption is the process that converts data into a form that cannot be deciphered by an unauthorized person. The encrypted data, called a cipher, must be converted back into an understandable form using a process called decryption.

Types of networks

For the i-Net+ exam, you should know the differences between the three basic types of TCP/IP networks. They are

> ✔ **Intranet:** This is any internal private network that uses TCP/IP as its base protocol. On an intranet, information is viewed by users with browsers. Most intranets are connected to the Internet, but they do not need to be.

✔ **Extranet:** This is actually an intranet that has been extended to include trusted external users or networks. In most cases, an extranet allows certain outside users, such as customers, suppliers, or other businesses, to gain access to part or all of an internal network's resources.

✔ **Internet:** About the only thing an intranet and an extranet have in common with the Internet is that they all use TCP/IP and share data through HTTP transfers. The Internet is the dynamic, global network of networks.

Spoofing

On the Internet, spoofing has a few different meanings, but the definition you need to know for the i-Net+ exam is faking an Internet or e-mail address for the sole purpose of gaining unauthorized access to a server or host computer. The context of the verb "to spoof" is the same as one would use in "oh, you're spoofing me!"

VPN

A Virtual Private Network (VPN) is the connection made between two computers using a tunneling protocol, usually the PPTP (Point-to-Point Tunneling Protocol), over which data can be transmitted privately. A VPN encrypts data and then encapsulates the encrypted data in a PPTP packet so that it is transmitted over the Internet without the danger of interception and misuse. VPNs are gaining popularity with wide-area-network intranets and extranets.

Getting down to business

About ten percent of the test concerns the concepts of doing business on the Internet. Here are some of the terms and concepts you should review for the i-Net+ exam.

Copyright

A copyright protects the ownership of intellectual property and provides the owner of a writing, piece of art, idea, or other intellectual property with the exclusive right to print, distribute, and copy the work. The property cannot be reused for any purpose without the express written permission of the owner, the Seattle Seahawks, and the National Football League (actually, only the property copyright owner must give permission, I got carried away).

A copyright is provided automatically to the creator or author of any original work, and the copyright takes effect the instant the work is created. So, if you publish an original piece of art to the Web, it is yours, you can claim your copyright with a disclaimer and the © symbol. You aren't required to register your copyright, although that does make it more visible and defensible.

E-commerce

E-commerce involves the buying and selling of stuff on the Internet and the Web. Just about any kind of merchandise or service that is sold over the Web in an auction, e-store, or e-mall, creates e-commerce.

EDI

When two businesses exchange data — such as orders, shipments, quotes, and catalogs — via the Internet or by directly connecting to each other over communications lines, they are engaging in Electronic Data Interchange (EDI). This is not a new concept and it is not unique to the Internet or the Web.

Push/pull technology

Push technology delivers data directly to a user's browser or computer, and is pushed to the host computer from a server. This contrasts to what can be called pull technology, in which the user uses a search engine or browser to find and download information. A commonly used form of push technology is the PointCast (www.pointcast.com) portal.

A couple of great sites to study Internet terms and concepts

Here are the URLs for a few sites that are great for looking up Internet and networking terms and concepts:

- ✓ **The TechWeb Encyclopedia:** www.techweb.com/encyclopedia/
- ✓ **Whatis.com:** www.whatis.com

Part II
The Anatomy of
the Internet

In this part . . .

The Internet isn't actually a thing, but rather a whole bunch of things that work together to create a global network of networks. Just about everyone has a different image of what the Internet is and does. Some see it as the World Wide Web with a browser face that allows them to find documents on the Web and then surf from site to site. Some see it as a searchable reference library that contains millions and millions of information sources. Others see it as a meeting place, a conversation pit, a game room, a store, a car dealer, and countless other things. However, there is one thing everyone agrees on: Without the correct tools and the knowledge to use them, the Internet can be an intimidating place.

This part takes a look at the tools, functions, and components that make up the Internet, focusing on those you will find on the i-Net+ exam. I explain the URL, the different types of servers used on the Internet and Web, the issues that affect the functionality of an Internet site, including security, caching, and accessibility, the kinds of things that can go wrong, and what you can use to identify and correct these situations.

Chapter 3

Moving about the Internet: URLs and Internet Sites

● ●

Exam Objectives

▶ Defining the various types of URLs and their uses
▶ Understanding the issues that affect an Internet site's performance

● ●

*Y*ou must understand the primary vehicle used for moving about the Internet: the URL (Uniform Resource Locator). If you think of the Internet as a city (a very large city) with traffic circles, streets, intersections, and large apartment houses, then you can probably see the functionality of the URL.

Like the house number, street name, and apartment number in the address of a single domicile in a high-rise building, the URL identifies a domain, a server in the domain, a directory on the server, and a particular file in the directory. It even identifies the name of the public transportation you should use to get to it, in the form of the protocol.

As I discuss in this chapter, there are several types of URLs, called schemes, but, in general, they are all variations on a basic functionality theme: a URL locates the resources you want and then brings them to you. Pretty slick stuff, this.

On the i-Net+ exam, you'll be asked questions regarding the use of a URL and how the different URL schemes are used to access different types of servers.

I also include in this chapter some general guidelines to address the issues you face when launching an Internet site, including bandwidth, access, and site performance. Although not specifically related to the discussion on URLs, this part of the chapter does point out potential problems that visitors (using your URL) may have in reaching, accessing, downloading, or viewing your site content. You need to be aware of these issues for the exam.

Quick Assessment

Defining the various URLs and their uses

1 The acronym URL stands for _____.

2 The first element in a URL is the _____.

3 The _____ scheme is used to send e-mail to a particular address.

4 The _____ protocol is used to transfer files across the Internet.

5 The address portion of the URL contains the _____ and Web server.

6 The abbreviation FQDN stands for _____.

7 A(n) _____ is used to designate the specific TCP/IP service or driver to be used to process a request.

8 The _____ part of a URL is used with a search engine or Internet directory.

9 An ISP located one level from an NAP is a(n) _____ ISP.

Understanding the issues that affect an Internet site's performance

10 The _____ creates Internet-ready and platform-independent documents.

Answers

1 *Uniform Resource Locator.* See "The Wonderful World of URL."

2 *TCP/IP protocol or URL scheme.* Review "Following protocol."

3 *Mailto.* Take a look at "Developing the scheme of things."

4 *FTP.* Check out "Following protocol."

5 *Domain name.* Look over "Looking up the domain address."

6 *Fully qualified domain name.* See "Looking up the domain address."

7 *Port.* Review "Specifying a port."

8 *Search.* Look over "Striving for better search ports."

9 *Tier 1.* Check out "Making the right connection."

10 *Portable document format.* Take a look at "Working with files."

The Wonderful World of URL

Whether you say "earl" or "you are ell," a URL (Uniform Resource Locator) is the key to moving about the Internet and World Wide Web. A URL, which is also known as a Universal Resource Locator, is to the Internet what the telephone number is to the POTS (plain old telephone system). In the same way that the phone number identifies the area code, the exchange within the area code, and the number within the exchange, the URL identifies a protocol, the domain server and host computer, and a specific document on that server. The URL can also include other information to help identify locations or transport files over the Internet.

The anatomy of a URL

As shown in Figure 3-1, a URL has several parts: the scheme, the slash, the host computer's name, a port number, and a document name, or perhaps some search data. The URL and its parts enable your browser to ask just the right questions when it's looking to perform the actions or to retrieve the documents you've requested of it.

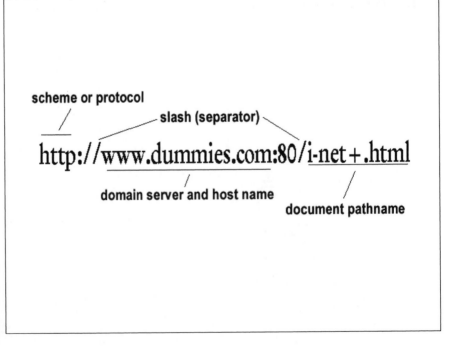

Figure 3-1: The parts of a URL.

Take the time to learn the parts of a URL, including the purpose and role of each part. This is the key to the different types of URLs. Expect to see questions on the test about the protocol and port parts of a URL.

Essentially, a URL is an address, and like other types of addresses, it helps you find a particular location. When you write an address on an envelope, you must include all the elements needed to get Aunt Sally's birthday card to her house. It must include each of the general addressing elements, including zip or postal code, state or province, and city, as well as the specific addressing elements, such as street, house number, and person. Occasionally, you can get away with only a bare minimum of addressing elements on a letter, and because the postal service helps you, it may still get to its destination.

However, a URL must have all of its elements present to work. Your browser may fill in some of the elements by default for you, but it doesn't yet have anything like a postal or zip code to generally identify the destination's location. When you type in just the domain information, such as `www.dummies.com`, your browser automatically adds the `http://` part to the front and perhaps even the `:80` part to the back, completing the essential parts of the URL needed by the Internet to find the location. The following sections describe each of these parts in more detail.

Following protocol

The first element in a URL is the particular TCP/IP protocol or scheme (see the next section) used to transfer the file over the Internet. Each file type stored on an Internet server or host has a particular protocol that's best suited to transferring its format or content to your computer.

The URL protocols that you should know for the i-Net+ exam are

- ✔ **HTTP:** The most commonly used protocol and the default scheme for virtually all browsers is HTTP (Hypertext Transfer Protocol). This TCP/IP protocol transfers HTML (Hypertext Markup Language) documents over the Internet.

- ✔ **FTP:** Another frequently used TCP/IP protocol, FTP (File Transfer Protocol) downloads and uploads complete and intact files between remote host computers and your local computer. Nearly all browsers have built-in support for FTP transfers.

- ✔ **Telnet:** The Telnet protocol, one of the TCP/IP protocol suite, initiates a logon session on a remote host computer, usually a UNIX system or a network server.

- ✔ **Gopher:** The gopher protocol, another TCP/IP protocol, accesses sites running a gopher server to peruse its index and download documents.

Developing the scheme of things

A URL *scheme* is a specialized URL that uses specific syntax and format to access a particular type of document or information on the Internet. The URL schemes you may see on the i-Net+ exam are

✔ **Data:** This URL scheme transfers small groups of information, usually less than 1,000 characters, over the Internet and the Web.

✔ **IMAP:** This scheme accesses those servers, mailboxes, messages, and search programs on host computers accessible through the IMAP (Internet Message Access Protocol).

✔ **File:** This URL scheme retrieves files or displays a directory listing from a remote host in your browser.

✔ **Mailto:** This scheme specifies an e-mail address to which information, such as the current browser window, is to be sent.

✔ **News:** Browsers support several schemes to access NNTP (Network News Transfer Protocol) newsgroup postings. Other schemes your browser may use to display newsgroup messages are snews, newspost, newsreply, snewspost, and snewsreply.

✔ **POP:** This scheme logs onto a POP3 (Post Office Protocol) server using a logon name and password to access a mailbox and its messages.

✔ **WAIS:** This scheme retrieves resources using the WAIS (Wide Area Information System) search protocol.

Looking up the domain address

The portion of the URL that contains the domain name and server of an Internet location is the bare minimum you must enter for your browser to attempt to find the location. For example, entering www.dummies.com in the URL, address, or location bar of your browser, opens up the full URL — http://www.dummies.com/default.html.

The address portion of the URL includes the domain name (dummies.com) and the Web server that services access requests for that domain (www). These two elements combined also form what's called the Fully Qualified Domain Name (FQDN).

Reviewing your options

You can include some options in a URL that help the browser and Internet to set up specifically the connection you want to use when downloading the information you need. The most frequently used URL options are a port number and what is called a *search port*.

Specifying a port

Port is one of those terms in computing that has more than one meaning. A port can refer to the plug on the back of the computer onto which a cable is plugged, as in "put the cable on the serial port." When you translate software from one operating system so that it's compatible with another operating system, you port the software. *Port* may even refer to your choice of wine when surfing the Net. Or a port can be used to designate the specific TCP/IP or other protocol or driver that should be used to process the request. It's this type of port that you need to remember in conjunction with a URL.

As you navigate through some sites, you may have seen ports used as a part of the URL address in your browser. It may have looked something like the following example:

```
http://www.dummies.com:80
```

The :80 indicates that the default HTTP port is being used to track the connection to a remote site.

TCP/IP ports are categorized into three types:

- ✔ **Well-known ports:** The most commonly used TCP/IP ports, which are in the range of 0 through 1023.

- ✔ **Registered ports:** Ports in the range of 1024 through 49151, used by user-developed programs for logical connections between proprietary programs.

- ✔ **Dynamic (private) ports:** Ports in the range of 49152 through 65535, which are unregistered and can be used freely for private connections.

On the i-Net+ exam, you'll be asked to identify the port assignment of several common TCP/IP protocols. If you know the ports listed in Table 3-1, you'll definitely be ready for any port questions on the test. Table 3-1 lists most of the commonly used TCP/IP port assignments.

Table 3-1   TCP/IP Well-Known Port Assignments Used with URLs

Port Number	Assignment
20	FTP data transfer
23	Telnet
70	Gopher
80	HTTP (Hypertext Transfer Protocol)
110	POP3 (Post Office Protocol)

Striving for better search ports

A URL with a search port is somewhat unusual and is in most cases the by-product of working with a search engine or directory. For example, if I search on the AltaVista search engine for "Dummies," the URL that AltaVista generates to itself contains the following search port:

```
pg=q&kl=XX&stype=stext&q=dummies&search.x=26&search.y=9
```

The search port contains search instructions that the search engine programming understands. As I said, this is not something you'd necessarily enter yourself, but the search port is one of the optional ports of a URL.

Optimizing Internet Site Performance

Although you certainly need to pay lots of attention to the artistic and word-smith skills applied to the development of a Web site, you also must address several other issues when launching the site on the Internet. It's one thing to create a thing of beauty and a beacon of clarity, but it's quite another to create a site that is easily accessed, quickly downloaded, and displays on a browser as designed.

On the i-Net+ exam, you must be aware of how certain issues impact the functionality of a site in terms of its operation, access, and consistency. In the following sections, I describe each of the functionality issues you should know for the test.

It's big, but it's slow

You should address several functionality issues when launching a Web site on the Internet. Functionality issues include bandwidth usage and requirements, file sizes and download times, and the Internet connection points for your site.

Handling bandwidth issues

One of the key issues involved with designing an effective Web page is its bandwidth impact. How big a Web page is, in terms of its total amount of bits (including graphics, text, meta tags, and so on) directly affects its effectiveness. Even the very best Web documents can turn into real turkeys, if they are slow to download because of their size. The bandwidth issues of a Web page concern how much of the available bits-per-second tranmission rate the page takes up. The more it uses, the slower it goes. In this case, less is truly more.

If your idea of a great looking Web page is wall-to-wall graphics, animations, several crazy fonts, and a very busy background wallpaper, all accompanied with some very snazzy synthesized elevator music, you're not alone. Many developers have taken golf's greens-fee approach, which justifies bad golf scores as getting your money's worth, and adapted it for Web publishing. This "more is better" approach produces Web pages that consume huge amounts of bandwidth. Unfortunately, if downloading your Web page takes a long time, your visitor loses interest and moves on, missing your message altogether — assuming you have one.

There are even organizations springing up to educate people on the tricks they can use to minimize bandwidth requirements and still retain their sense of artistic expression. One such organization is the Bandwidth Conservation Society (`www.infohiway.com/faster/`), which has tips on sharper, yet smaller graphic files, style sheets, logos, embeddable fonts, and more — all things you can use to reduce the bandwidth requirements of a Web page.

Making the right connection

A hobbyist ISP, not that there's anything wrong with them for general and local usage, may be too far removed from a backbone connection point to provide efficient and sure access to your site. You may notice that some ISPs brag about being a *Tier 1* or *Tier 2* ISP. This means that they're connected directly to a Network Access Point (NAP) or are just one hop removed from the backbone. Being closer to a NAP is a good thing! Chapter 12 discusses NAPs in more detail.

Your ISP can really affect the performance of your site. If you're connected to an ISP that's not located near a top-level Internet connection point, accessing your site may prove difficult for some visitors. Some systems limit the distance (measured by the number of hops or routers) that the download request message must travel over to reach the destination.

An ISP can buy access services from another ISP, who in turn buys access services from a third ISP, and so forth. The higher your site is in the access hierarchy, the greater the chance of your visitors finding and downloading your site.

The agony of the slow server

The most efficient bandwidth and highest possible access point location can be for naught, if your site is supported on an undersized or overloaded server. Your visitors don't know or care how big your server is; they only care that they get bored waiting for the download and move on. Large files can be one of the problems, but a server supporting a potentially popular site that can't handle the traffic is Web page death just as sure as no bandwidth or a page requiring 15 hops.

Finding faster roads

Many of the larger or national ISPs can also support a range of connection types, including dial up, DSL (digital subscriber lines), ISDN (integrated services digital network), and other dedicated connections, to allow you to connect to the Internet backbone. Should you wish to host your own Web server, faster connection types with higher bandwidth can facilitate your needs. See Chapter 13 for more details about the various connection types.

Can you have too much security?

In order for an Internet site to be effective, it must have an audience, and the audience must be able to access the site. Too little or too much security on a site can affect the size of your audience.

Letting the audience in

Launching a site from a LAN workstation located behind a firewall is probably not in the recipe for a highly visible and successful Web site. Of course, if you remove the firewall or adjust it to allow everyone in, you can undermine the security of the local network. However, placing the site on the Web server at your ISP retains the security of your LAN and places your site directly on a service intended to support visitors.

Hiding behind the ISP

Most ISPs are aware of the security steps that must be used to protect your data, as well as the data of all their subscribers. As a result, your site and its data are generally quite safe on an ISP server.

An ISP should employ a wide range of security policies, and procedures, including

- A formal, written, and enforced security policy
- Measures that prevent network traffic from using unauthorized routes into the ISP's network
- The use of VLANs (Virtual Local Area Networks) or nonbroadcast networks to segment internal and external server customers
- The prompt application of security patches to your server software or firmware
- Measures that protect network servers and subscriber data in the event of denial of service attacks
- A monitoring system to detect network attacks, and a reporting procedure that subscribers can use to report suspicious activities or security events

See Chapter 15 for more information on Internet security.

Reliable is better than fast

An Internet site must perform reliably and consistently to gain an audience. Why publish a site if you don't want people to visit it (and more than once)? The consistent performance of a site's elements plays a large part in how it builds an audience.

Is that a mountain or a mole?

If you must have graphics (and who doesn't?), you absolutely must pay attention to the quality, clarity, and resolution of your graphics. Just because you know that a picture of Mount Everest illustrates your recent hiking expedition even though it's a little blurry, grainy, and underdeveloped, doesn't mean anyone else can. I won't lecture you on the word value of a picture, but unless you use good, clear images with good resolution, don't bother.

Working with files

There's nothing worse than downloading a very large file from a site, only to find that the file is corrupted and cannot be opened. Or that the file format is not supported by your software, and there was no indication of its version, platform, or size.

Files placed on a site should be clearly labeled as to their format, software, size, and date. They should also be opened and tested regularly to ensure their continued usability.

You may want to consider using the portable document format (PDF) created with Adobe Acrobat to create an Internet-ready and platform-independent document.

Prep Test

1 A URL includes which of the following parts? (Choose all that apply.)

A ❑ Scheme

B ❑ Port

C ❑ Domain name

D ❑ IP address

2 A commonly used URL protocol is _____.

A ○ PING

B ○ HTTP

C ○ HTML

D ○ Archie

3 A specialized URL format that uses a specific syntax to access a particular type of document or service is called a(n) _____.

A ○ Protocol

B ○ Search port

C ○ Domain name

D ○ Scheme

4 The address portion of a URL includes which of the following? (Choose two.)

A ❑ Web server

B ❑ Browser type

C ❑ Protocol

D ❑ Domain name

5 Optional parts of a URL include which of the following? (Choose two.)

A ❑ Domain name

B ❑ Protocol

C ❑ Port

D ❑ Search port

6 The well known port assignment for HTTP is _____.

   A ○ 20

   B ○ 23

   C ○ 80

   D ○ 110

7 An ISP connected directly to an NAP is considered to be _____.

   A ○ High-level

   B ○ Business-oriented

   C ○ Tier 1

   D ○ Tier 4

8 Which of the following may be symptoms of a Web site with slow page downloads? (Choose all that apply.)

   A ❑ Slow server

   B ❑ Low bandwidth

   C ❑ Large file size

   D ❑ Tier 1 or 2 ISP

9 Security policies and procedures that an ISP should employ include which of the following? (Choose all that apply.)

   A ❑ Formal written security policies

   B ❑ VLANs

   C ❑ Limited access to its Web server

   D ❑ A procedure for subscribers to report suspicious activity

10 A document format that produces Internet-ready and platform-independent documents is the_____ file format.

   A ○ DOC

   B ○ RTF

   C ○ PDF

   D ○ QSP

Answers

1 *A, B, and C.* The URL is used in lieu of the IP address and includes a scheme or protocol, a domain and server name, and a document reference. *See "The anatomy of a URL."*

2 *B.* The HTTP (Hypertext Transfer Protocol) is probably the most commonly used protocol, especially with Web documents and browsers. *Review "Following protocol."*

3 *D.* URL schemes define the syntax and content of the specialized URLs used to access particular services (such as Telnet, POP3, and others) or document types (news, file, and so on). *Take a look at "Developing the scheme of things."*

4 *A and D.* The *address* is the portion of the URL that includes the FQDN (Fully Qualified Domain Name), which is made up of the domain name and server (for example, www.dummies.com). *Check out "Looking up the domain address."*

5 *C and D.* The domain name and protocol are required parts of the URL, although the protocol can be supplied automatically by the browser at times. The port and the search port of the URL are optional and used only in certain cases. *See "Reviewing your options."*

6 *C.* Port 80 is the standardized TCP/IP well-known port for HTTP Web-document transfers. *Review "Specifying a port."*

7 *C.* A Tier 1 ISP is connected directly to a network access point (NAP), which is in turn directly connected to the Internet backbone infrastructure. *Take a look at "Making the right connection."*

8 *A, B, and C.* Any one of these conditions, or any combination of them, can create a functionality problem for a site. *Check out "It's big, but it's slow."*

9 *A, B, and D.* Limiting access to a Web server kind of defeats its purpose, but an ISP should have other security policies, procedures, and processes in place to protect its software and data, as well as and especially that of its subscribers. *Look over "Hiding behind the ISP."*

10 *C.* Adobe Acrobat creates PDF (portable document format) files that can help prevent corrupted file or incompatible file format problems across the Web. *See "Working with files."*

Chapter 4

Caching: Speeding Up the Internet

· ·

Exam Objectives

▶ Describing the concepts of caching

▶ Explaining the implications of caching

· ·

*1*n general terms, a *cache* is simply a temporary storage place where you hold something in reserve for later use. If you're like me, you've created personal caches of very valuable stuff that you plan to use again real soon. For example, I have a bedroom closet cache of undersized clothes I'll wear again, someday; a basement cache of exercise equipment I'll use again, someday; and a garage cache of tools I'll use again, someday.

My caches tend to serve as long-term storage, but each is, in its own right, a cache. As my examples illustrate, several different types of caches exist, including supply caches, weapons caches, and Web caches. Of course, for the i-Net+ exam, you need to know about Web caches, as well as server-side caching, proxy and cache servers, and how you manage and maintain caches.

Quick Assessment

1 A(n) _____ cache is a storage area, usually on a computer's hard disk, where copies of files are stored temporarily.

2 The type of caching mechanism that's located closest to the Internet is a(n) _____.

3 Virtually every cache server is also a(n) _____ server.

4 A(n) _____ cache works on the same principle as a Web cache, with the exception that cache entries are only from the local network.

5 A large part of what a caching system does is maintaining the _____ of the cache.

6 One way a cache is maintained is by passing _____ requests to a document or object's server.

7 Some entries in the cache have _____ expiration data in their headers.

8 The most popular approach to maintaining a cache is the _____ method.

9 The _____ caching method issues requests to remote servers when the caching server is not in use.

10 To increase the space used for disk caching in Netscape Navigator, you access the _____ window.

Answers

1 *File.* See "Caching In on the Web."

2 *Cache server.* Review "Caching In on its name."

3 *Proxy.* Take a look at "In the far corner, wearing the fire-red trunks . . ."

4 *Local.* Check out "Other forms of cache gladly accepted."

5 *Freshness.* See "Keeping the cache fresh."

6 *Get if modified.* Review "Modify it, and it will come."

7 *HTTP.* Look over "When it's past its freshness date, throw it out."

8 *Heuristics.* Check out "The very complicated approach to freshness."

9 *Active.* Take a look at "Active caching."

10 *Preferences.* See "Choosing cache options."

Caching In on the Web

Caching solves some very specific problems of the Internet and the Web. Without caching, the Internet would literally be the World Wide Wait. There isn't nearly enough bandwidth to service all of the document requests that are issued at any given moment. Caching absorbs a great many of these requests and avoids the delay that would be experienced without it.

By storing Internet documents on servers and clients in anticipation of future requests for one of the documents, you eliminate unnecessary traffic — both out- and inbound — on the Internet. The more caching is used around the Internet, the more likely that requests will get through and the documents being sought will actually get to the requestor for display.

A *file cache* is a storage area, usually on your hard disk, where copies of files are stored temporarily in anticipation of future requests for one of the files. A *Web cache* is a file cache that stores copies of Web pages and documents under the assumption that the pages or documents will be requested again soon.

One benefit of caching involves something called *Quality of Service (QoS)*. This telecommunications term generally means that the service you expect to get is the service you actually do get. In relation to the Internet, QoS refers to the reliability and speed of the response to your requests for Web page downloads. If your requests don't time out, and your browser quickly displays the page you want, you have pretty good QoS levels.

Caches, near and far

Different types of file caches exist on a system. What differentiates them is how far (or close) they're located to either the requesting workstation or the Internet itself. I describe the different types of file caches in the following sections.

Caching in on its name

The type of file cache located closest to the Internet is the *cache server,* which is a server located between the network workstations and the Internet gateway. The cache server is normally located behind the network firewall (see Chapter 15) and it caches (saves) Web pages, FTP files, and other files requested by network users from the Internet.

Have you ever downloaded a Web page and then e-mailed the URL to a coworker on the same LAN so that person could also visit the site? Well, in all likelihood, your network cache server enabled your coworker to see the Web page without downloading it again so soon after you downloaded it. By providing the page to the network without a second download, the cache server not only eliminates unnecessary Internet traffic, but also speeds up the delivery of the page to the requesting workstation.

In the far corner, wearing the fire-red trunks . . .

Virtually every cache server is also a proxy server. In fact, many people view the function of a proxy server to be primarily that of a cache server. A proxy server acts as a surrogate for the users of a network to the Internet. To the outside world, your Internet address is that of the proxy server. All replies sent to you and the other workstations on your internal network are actually sent to your network's proxy server; it gets its name from acting as the network's proxy for Internet activities. Because it serves as the portal to your network from the Internet, most proxy servers are also firewalls as well.

Not all firewalls are also proxy servers, and not all proxy servers are cache servers. However, nearly all cache servers are proxy servers and all proxy servers are firewalls. Got it?

Casting out the Web cache

If you understand this caching stuff, it should come as no surprise that you have a cache for your Web browser. No matter whether you call it the history, or temporary Internet files, or some such name, a Web browser cache contains the Web files that you've recently downloaded and stored on your hard disk.

Only a small percentage of all Web and Internet documents are actually being downloaded at any time. As Pareto would reason, about 20 percent of the files create about 80 percent of the Internet traffic. Literally billions of Web pages exist on the Net, but a handful (okay, a big handful) are actually requested by users, with a chosen few hundred sites getting the lion's share of the activity.

If you've visited a site once, odds are that you'll visit it again, and especially in the very near future. It would be a waste of valuable Internet resources to download every unchanged object of a previously visited site. So, a Web cache stores each and every document, object, and hypertext link of a Web document, on the chance that you may request it again.

For example, if you were to visit my favorite online bookstore, `amazon.com`, its logos and graphics would be stored in the cache of the Web browser and provided from this content bank the next time you request an Amazon page. However, the Web page objects stored in the Web cache have a shelf-life and eventually expire. The length of time that a Web object is useable is called its *freshness*.

Other forms of cache gladly accepted

A network may also include a *local cache server* that caches frequently accessed network files to reduce data transfer time and activity on the input/output (I/O) channels. A local cache works on the same principle as the Web cache, with the exception that all the activity being buffered by the file cache is totally local in nature.

Keeping the cache fresh

Of course, none of the objects and documents stored in your cache ever change, your disk space is never-ending, and your cache is perpetual. As you visit new sites, your system adds them to your ever-expanding cache. Should you ever need to download a previously visited site, bingo — there it is, right there in your cache. You only need to venture out onto the Internet for new sites. Your cache forms a safe cocoon of your favorite sites around you.

Sound too good to be true? Good, because it is. True to the dynamic nature of the Internet, sites change, move, and disappear every day, and disk space is not endless. A large part of what a caching system does is maintaining the freshness of its cached entries.

A system can use four approaches to manage a cache, as I describe in the following sections.

Modify it, and it will come

One of the four ways a cache keeps its contents fresh is by passing a `get if modified` request to the server on which the desired object or document is stored. In most situations, HTTP uses the `get` command to request an object from a remote server. However, the caching system can issue a `get if modified` request, which asks that the object be sent only if it has changed since the last time the same object was requested. The cache and the server compare dates to see which is older: the version in the cache or the one on the server. If the cache is older, the object or document is downloaded and displayed, and the cache is updated with the fresher copy.

When it's past its freshness date, throw it out

Just like cottage cheese with a two-month old expiration date, some entries in the cache have HTTP expiration data in their headers. When a page is requested, its freshness date is evaluated, and if it should no longer be used, it's thrown out and a fresh copy is requested, displayed, and stored in the cache.

The very complicated approach to freshness

The most popular approach to maintaining cache freshness is the *heuristics* method. This approach is popular because it keeps the cache slimmed down and is based solely on the life expectancy of each object or document.

Here is how the heuristics approach to caching works: When an object or document is downloaded from a server, the cache makes special note of the date the object was last modified. The cache then calculates how long it's been since the object or document was last modified. A fixed percentage is then used to calculate the expected remaining usable life of the object. If the object is deemed to be still alive, the cache continues to use it. However, if the object is determined to be no longer useful, it's thrown out and a fresh copy is requested.

For example, if a Web page that's downloaded for the first time was last modified 10 days ago, the cache, using a fixed 10 percent to calculate remaining freshness, would use the page for one more day. Beyond the one-day freshness period, the page would be replaced with a fresh copy when requested.

Active caching

Caching software systems use a fourth approach to maintaining a fresh cache, called *active caching*. In general terms, the cache server actively seeks to keep only the freshest copies of objects in the cache. The three primary methods used in active caching are

- ✔ The cache server can issue `get if modified` requests to remote servers for the objects in its cache whenever it's idle.
- ✔ The cache server can just refresh portions of the cache on specific time intervals.
- ✔ The cache server can determine which objects in the cache are the most popular and refresh them more frequently.

Setting Up a Browser's Cache

To reduce the load on the Internet even further, most browsers maintain a cache of Web documents and objects. Not every network includes a cache server or a proxy server, so often the Web browser's cache may be the only caching scheme in use.

There is a direct relationship between the size of your cache and the amount of time a document takes to download. Increasing your cache size speeds up the document download. Restricting the size of the cache increases download time. The moral of this story is: For faster downloads, increase the cache's disk space.

Choosing cache options

The size of a local Web cache is typically maintained through a Web browser. Lab 4-1 details the process used to change the Web cache options using Netscape Communicator. You can set the amount of space in kilobytes that you want to use for memory cache and for the disk cache, as well as set the disk directory or folder in which the cache is to be stored. If you are using Internet Explorer or another browser, you'll find the process is very similar to this.

Lab 4-1 Setting Web Browser Cache Options

1. Choose Edit➪Preferences from the Menu bar.

Figure 4-1 shows the Preferences dialog box that is displayed by these menu choices.

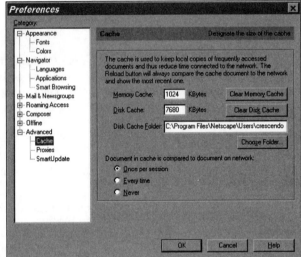

Figure 4-1:
Cache
settings in
Netscape
Commun-
icator.

2. Choose the Cache option.

On the option tree shown in the left-hand side of the window, collapse the advanced list and then click on the cache option to display the cache options window.

3. In the bottom-center area of the window (refer to Figure 4-1), option buttons enable you to specify when a cached document is to be evaluated for freshness.

The choices in this case are only once in each session, every time the object is requested, or never check and use the copy in the cache. This last option is most commonly used when working in an offline mode.

As shown in Figure 4-2, Internet Explorer adds an automatic setting to its cache choices, which uses a combination of get-if-modified and heuristic approaches to refresh its cache.

Putting cache on the disk

On your computer's hard disk, the cache store goes by a couple of different names. For example, Netscape calls it the Disk Cache, and Internet Explorer designates it as the Temporary Internet Files. The browser's cache stores

Web pages, objects, and data just as they are viewed. While this may take just a little more disk space, it speeds up the display process for pages that you frequently visit.

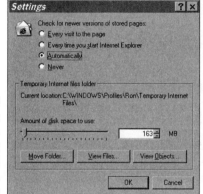

Figure 4-2:
Cache settings in Internet Explorer.

In either of these two major browsers, you can assign the space to be used for the cache (refer to Figures 4-1 and 4-2). Increasing the amount of disk space assigned to the cache generally speeds up the process of fetching and displaying previously visited documents. Remember that increasing cache size also reduces the amount of disk space available for other stuff.

Removing cache from the disk

Should you ever want to remove part of the disk cache maintained by your browser, you can. Both of the major browsers provide a mechanism to remove any or all of the objects and documents stored in the cache. In Internet Explorer, you empty the cache by clicking the Delete Files button in the Internet Options dialog box, as shown in Figure 4-3.

Refer to Figure 4-1 and notice that Netscape Communicator includes a button to Clear Disk Cache.

Both browsers also include other cache removal options unique to their particular methods. Internet Explorer also includes a cached history of the links you have visited, which you can also clear. Netscape goes one better and enables you to clear the current memory cache.

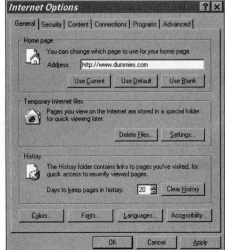

Figure 4-3:
The Internet
Options
dialog box in
Internet
Explorer.

A Really Cool Site About Caching

If you want to know every possible thing there is to know about caching,
including things you would never think that you'd want to know, visit
www.caching.com.

Admit it! You knew such a site had to exist!

Prep Test

1 A Web cache _____.

   A ○ Is a file cache

   B ○ Stores copies of uploaded Web pages

   C ○ Is always fixed in size

   D ○ Is stored on a remote server

2 Which statement best describes the action of a Web cache?

   A ○ A Web cache keeps a copy of only the last Web document downloaded in case the browser display needs to be refreshed.

   B ○ A Web cache eliminates unnecessary Internet traffic and speeds up document delivery to the requesting workstation.

   C ○ A Web cache benefits only internal network users.

   D ○ None of the above.

3 Virtually all cache servers are _____.

   A ○ Located outside a network's firewall

   B ○ Located parallel to a network's firewall

   C ○ Also proxy servers

   D ○ Also firewalls

4 The type of caching tool usually located closest to the Internet is a _____.

   A ○ Proxy server

   B ○ Firewall

   C ○ Web browser

   D ○ Cache server

5 A cache server located on a LAN that's used to reduce data transfer time and the amount of I/O activity on only the local network is called a _____.

   A ○ Proxy server

   B ○ Local cache

   C ○ Cache server

   D ○ LAN server

6 Beyond caching downloaded Internet documents and objects, much of the activity of a caching server is spent doing what?

A ○ Maintaining the freshness of the cache
B ○ Resizing the disk files
C ○ Mirroring the cache
D ○ Downloading anticipated requests

7 A caching method *not* used to maintain the currency of the cache is _____.

A ○ `get if modified` requests
B ○ `send if modified` requests
C ○ HTTP header expiration data
D ○ Heuristics

8 The caching approach that uses the last modified date of a file to determine how much usable life the document has is called _____.

A ○ Expiration data method
B ○ `get if modified` method
C ○ Heuristics method
D ○ Active caching

9 Internet Explorer stores its cache in what it calls _____.

A ○ Disk cache
B ○ Memory cache
C ○ History
D ○ Temporary Internet Files

10 In a Web browser caching scheme, disk space used for caching is assigned in _____.

A ○ Kilobytes
B ○ Megabytes
C ○ Gigabytes
D ○ Sectors

Answers

1 *A.* A Web cache is a file cache that stores copies of Web documents and objects under the assumption that each will be requested again very soon. *See "Caching In on the Web."*

2 *B.* By eliminating unnecessary Internet traffic, the overall bandwidth requirement is reduced, and the fact that the document is supplied from the local network speeds up its delivery. *Review "Caching In on the Web."*

3 *C.* Virtually every cache server is also a proxy server. However, not all proxy servers are cache servers, but most are. In addition to serving as the Internet surrogate for a network, a proxy server usually hosts the cache server as well. *Take a look at "In the far corner, wearing the fire-red trunks . . ."*

4 *D.* A cache server is located between a network's workstations and its Internet gateway. It intercepts requests intended for the Internet to see if it can better fulfill the request rather than sending it on out to the Internet. *Check out "Caching In on its name."*

5 *B.* Local cache servers provide the same benefits to a LAN that Web cache servers provide to Internet-connected workstations. *Look over "Other forms of cache gladly accepted."*

6 *A.* Many of the activities of a cache server involve keeping the cache entries fresh. Depending on the approach used, the cache is maintained as a result of document requests or as a result of proactive action the cache server initiates. See "Keeping the cache fresh."

7 *B.* All the other answers are different approaches used to maintain the freshness of the cache. `get if modified` requests that a remote server only refresh a document if it has changed since last requested. The expiration data in the HTTP header is used to expire a cache entry. I explain heuristics in the answer to the next question. *Review "Keeping the cache fresh."*

8 *C.* This approach to maintaining the currency of the cache involves a calculated remaining life based on a percentage of the time since it was last modified. *Look over "The very complicated approach to freshness."*

9 *D.* The Temporary Internet Files include all documents, graphics, and other objects downloaded with a Web page. They are maintained separately, which enables only the required, or expired, part of a page to be refreshed. *Check out "Putting cache on the disk."*

10 *A.* Using too much disk space for the disk cache can put a bind on the amount of disk space available for normal disk storage. A disk cache should not be put inside of a compressed disk drive. *Take a look at "Choosing cache options."*

Chapter 5

When Things Go Wrong

● ●

Exam Objectives

▶ Solving common dialup problems

▶ Correcting connectivity problems

▶ Resolving IP address problems

● ●

*W*hen you're connecting to and interacting with the Internet, trouble may lurk in any piece of hardware or software involved in the process. If a file fails to download, or you can't connect to your ISP, the list of suspects may include your computer, possibly a modem, most likely a switch and a router, probably a gateway, and with all odds a server or two, cabling, addressing, databases, flat files, and much more. Where a problem can happen is anyone's guess, but with experience and some troubleshooting help, you'll figure out that a certain kind of problem typically happens in about the same place every time.

Often, you can overcome an Internet-related problem simply by trying again. On the second attempt, the error that prevented your file from downloading or disrupted your connection to the ISP seems to disappear. However, any problem that persists with a second try obviously needs your expert attention.

On the i-Net+ exam, you can expect to see several questions that present a dialup, download, or access problem and then ask you to place the blame, or at least find the fault. As an Internet professional, you should be able to promptly and knowledgably respond to user errors. You need to be a walking encyclopedia of the cause and effect of Internet, Web, file, LAN, WAN, and modem errors. For the i-Net+ exam, however, you need to know only the troubleshooting basics that I cover in this chapter.

Quick Assessment

Solving common dialup problems

1 The protocol most commonly used for dialup connections is _____.

2 _____ is the process of verifying that an account name and password are valid.

3 Some passwords are _____ and must be entered exactly as originally entered.

4 A dialup connection may be disconnected because _____ is active.

5 Most e-mail systems limit the size of _____.

Correcting connectivity problems

6 If you can download the ISP's homepage, but no sites beyond the ISP, the problem is likely to be with the _____.

7 Another reason why you cannot access sites beyond the ISP may involve the _____.

Resolving IP address problems

8 If your server is rejecting a valid e-mail address, the error may be a _____ lookup problem.

9 The two primary mail server types are _____ and _____.

10 The error code that indicates a URL was not found is _____.

Answers

1 *PPP (Point-to-Point Protocol).* See "The modem answers, but nothing happens."

2 *Authentication.* Review "I enter the password, and nothing happens."

3 *Case-sensitive.* Take a look at "I enter the password, and nothing happens."

4 *Call-waiting.* Check out "Killing call-waiting."

5 *Attachments.* Look over "I'm connected, but I still have problems!"

6 *ISP.* See "I'm connected, but I still have problems!"

7 *Proxy server.* Review "I'm connected, but I still have problems!"

8 *DNS.* Look over "Problems of the e-mail kind."

9 *POP3, SMTP.* Check out "Problems of the e-mail kind."

10 *404.* Take a look at "What's the 411 on the 404?"

I Call Your Number, but Nobody's There: Fighting the Dialup Blues

When connecting to the Internet, you can have problems in three general areas (four, if you count the user): the dialup modem, protocol setup and connectivity issues, and URLs and IP addresses. This section focuses on the first area, problems with dialup connections and modems. I cover the other two areas later in this chapter (see the "Pardon Me, Are You My Server?" and "What's the 411 on the 404?" sections later in this chapter).

Making the connection

In any problem related to modem and dialup networking issues, if the modem doesn't work, you should always check that it is connected to the computer, and that the modem is powered on. In fact, your computer will probably let you know that one of these is likely the problem anyway. So, I'll skip right over that part.

On the i-Net+ exam, you need to have a good understanding of the kinds of problems that can happen when connecting to an ISP through a dialup modem. You'll encounter questions on the test that ask you to identify the likely problem in a given situation from a list of choices. As long as you're aware of the kinds of problems that can occur and the typical cause of each, you're in good shape for the test.

I don't get no dial tone

If the dialup networking dialing routine reports an error that no modem is detected or that no dial tone is present, be sure that the modem and the computer are connected to each other and that the modem is connected via the cable with the RJ-11 plugs to a phone jack.

If the modem has worked in the very recent past (like in the past hour or two) chances are that the modem is being detected as busy and you may need to reset your system.

The modem answers, but nothing happens

Before you make yourself crazy, make sure that you have the dialup networking settings, modem settings, and TCP/IP settings configured properly with the values supplied by your ISP or the network administrator. If any of these are wrong, you've found the problem and it is you, or children in your home, or perhaps just a gremlin.

Another possibility is that you may be using the wrong protocol. The PPP (Point-to-Point Protocol) is the protocol most commonly used for dialup connections. However, it's possible that the server you're connecting to uses SLIP (Serial Line Internet Protocol) instead.

Another possibility, although generally a remote possibility, is that the ISP servers may be down. Most ISPs protect their servers, their main money-makers, with failover technologies to keep them functioning, but nothing is absolutely failsafe.

PPP is the most commonly used dialup protocol.

I enter the password, and nothing happens

So, the modems answer and go through their tonal mating ritual, the login dialog box is displayed, you enter your account name and password, and then . . . nothing.

This happens for one of two major reasons: You're using the wrong account information, or you entered the right information wrong. The first is that either your account name or the password is not what is on file at the ISP or server. *Authentication servers,* the servers that verify that the combination of account name and password entered is valid as a combination, only allow users with a good account and password set to have access to the system.

The remedy for this problem is try, try again. Then give up because the system will most likely lock you out after three tries anyway. Also remember that passwords and account names are case-sensitive on many Internet servers (especially those that are UNIX-based).

The second common reason for failing to authenicate is that what you have entered for your account name and password are simply wrong. If you've forgotten your password or account name, chastise yourself and then call your friendly ISP's technical support staff. They usually provide these to you. If they don't require some stringent form of identification, such as your mother's second-cousin-by-marriage uncle's mother's name, or your last white blood cell count, you may want to worry about who may be using your account along with you.

Killing call-waiting

If you connect alright, but get disconnected frequently, it could be that you have call-waiting on the phone line you're using to connect. Call-waiting signals can be interpreted by the modem as disconnect signals, which it does obediently. In most cases, dial *70 to deactivate the call-waiting feature on your telephone. After you finish your PPP session, you can enter *71 to reactivate it.

I'm connected, but I still have problems!

If you succesfully enter your account name and password and then get authenticated, but you still have problems, you need to consider some possibilities beyond those that I describe in the preceding sections. Here are some of the more common connection-related problems you may see on the exam:

- ✔ **You can't access your e-mail:** Some e-mail programs ask for your account name (username) and password again. Be sure you entered it correctly this time as well. If that's not the problem, you may be suffering the dreaded e-mail blockage, which is an irregularity caused by an unusually large e-mail file or attachment. Most e-mail systems limit message and attachment sizes, with 1MB to 5MB being common. If someone were to send you a 10MB file, your mail server or mail client could get clogged by the file. However, a good e-mail server or client will simply reject the file as undeliverable. Contact your ISP technical support to verify and clear this error.

- ✔ **You can't download a really great Web site:** It could be that this great Web site is too busy to service your request. Try downloading other Web sites, if you can. In all likelihood the problem is with the first site, in which case you should wait and try it later.

- ✔ **You can't download anything beyond the ISP's server:** If the ISP's homepage displays, but no other sites will, the ISP's Internet connection is probably down. If you can access your e-mail, but cannot access any Web sites, including your ISP's, it's time to call technical support to check out your TCP/IP settings. Your ISP may have a proxy server in use.

- ✔ **You can't download anything beyond the ISP's server, Part II:** Another reason that you may not be able to download any sites beyond your ISP's server is that the ISP may have a proxy server installed and it may be on the fritz. Try temporarily removing the browser settings that turn on the use of a proxy server. The option to use or not use a proxy server is usually located in the Connection and local network portion of your browser's preferences or options. If you can download remote sites with the proxy settings turned off, call the ISP and let them know that they have a proxy problem.

- ✔ **You can't download some sites, but you can download others:** The problem here isn't you or your ISP. Chances are that there's a traffic problem or another problem somewhere on the Internet that's affecting you. The best remedy for this is to simply try again later.

- ✔ **You get a DNS error when trying to connect to a site:** First check the URL you're seeking. If it's alright, check out the DNS server settings in the TCP/IP settings of your operating system. On a Windows computer, these are displayed through the Network icon on the Control Panel. If you're unsure what they should be, call the ISP's technical support.

Problems of the e-mail kind

You have access to your e-mail and all appears okay, but when you send a message out, it's immediately returned as undeliverable. The first thing to check is which server (actually a MAILER-DAEMON) rejected it: your server or the mail server of the remote domain. If it's your server, the error is likely a DNS problem and you should contact your ISP or network administrator. However, if the problem is at the other end, verify the address and try resending the message a couple more times.

If the message isn't rejected, but doesn't make it to its destination, the message could very well be the victim of network lag or a temporary condition. Just wait a bit and then resend it.

Whatever the problem, always read the entire message received from the MAILER-DAEMON. You may find that what appeared to be a rejected message was actually delivered after a network-controlled delay. You may even be advised on how long to wait before resending the message.

Table 5-1 includes some possible e-mail errors and their causes. TCP/IP contains a number of utilities that you can use to solve most e-mail problems (and HTTP problems, for that matter) such as FINGER and PING.

Table 5-1	E-mail Errors and Their Causes
Error	*Cause(s)*
Undeliverable mail	Incorrect username or host domain name
Local configuration error	An error in the recipient's mail account
Bad host name	Typing error or DNS lookup problems
Looping message detected	Disagreement between two mail systems as to where the recipient's mailbox is located
System timeout during mail transfer	Network traffic, a server overload, or some network error

Pardon Me, Are You My Server?

A problem that can affect just about every type of service you may want to access is having the correct server specified in the appropriate settings. You may want to access mail servers, DNS servers, gateways, cache, news, and more, and you must provide an IP address for each server if you want the services associated with it to function. In fact, just about every Winsock application, such as Internet Explorer, Netscape Communicator, Pegasus, Eudora, and others, must have a server's IP address specified in order to do its thing.

Mail servers

Your e-mail client is not likely to work very well if it's not connected to an e-mail server. Most e-mail client setup procedures have settings that take the domain names for its mail servers, usually a POP3 or IMAP server (to receive mail) and a SMTP server (to send mail). They can be the same server, in which case you enter the same domain name for both settings.

News servers

USENET news is generally supported by most popular e-mail clients. However, you need to specify a news server in order for it to download the newsgroups you've indicated you want to receive.

Gateways and other servers

Be absolutely sure that you get the IP address or domain name of every server your connection and ISP requires. You must enter them exactly as specified or you won't get the results you expect. If you're having trouble and you're on a Windows system, you can use the WINIPCFG utility to check your TCP/IP settings before calling your ISP.

What's the 411 on the 404?

The HTTP (Hypertext Transfer Protocol) is the protocol that moves HTML (Hypertext Markup Language) documents around the Internet. Built into this standard protocol are a variety of error codes and messages that are displayed when certain situations arise. If you surf the Web much, then undoubtedly you've seen some of these codes, probably some more than others.

For the i-Net+ exam, you should be familiar with the more common error codes. Be sure you know the error codes listed in Table 5-2, which includes the more commonly seen HTTP error codes and those found on the i-Net+ exam.

Table 5-2	Common HTTP Error Codes	
Error Code	**Meaning**	**Possible Cause**
200	Okay	While not actually an error code, this code means that you successfully downloaded a document.
302	Redirection to new URL	The URL you entered has been forwarded to a new site.
304	Use local copy	The server is directing the browser to retrieve a document from its cache.
400	Bad request	There's probably a typing error somewhere in the URL, or the case-sensitive parts of the URL are incorrect.
401	Unauthorized	You are not on the access list for the URL you've entered.
403	Forbidden	Much like error 401, only a little harsher.
404	Not Found	This is usually caused by typing errors or a URL that no longer exists.
500	Server error	An error occurred on the server trying to service your request.
503	Service unavailable	Normally caused by a failure in either an ISP's server or gateway, and occasionally even your own computer.

Prep Test

1 Which of these problems is not likely the reason for a modem connection problem?

A ○ Modem not connected to phone line

B ○ Caller-ID feature enabled on phone line

C ○ Incorrect modem settings

D ○ No dialtone detected

2 Which protocol is most commonly used for dialup connections?

A ○ SLIP

B ○ CSLIP

C ○ PPP

D ○ PPTP

3 The process of verifying the user's account name and password is called _____.

A ○ Verification

B ○ Verify and connect

C ○ Login

D ○ Authentication

4 You use the _____ command to disable call-waiting on most telephone systems.

A ○ #70

B ○ *70

C ○ #71

D ○ *71

5 An e-mail message arrives in your mailbox that references an attachment, but no attachment is present. What could likely be the problem?

A ○ Your e-mail client is not configured for attachments.

B ○ The sender neglected to attach the attachment.

C ○ The attachment was larger than your e-mail server allows.

D ○ The attachment was lost in transit.

6 After connecting to your ISP, you're not able to download several very popular remote Web sites, but you are able to display the ISP's homepage. What is a possible cause?

A ○ The ISP's Internet connection is down.

B ○ Your account is no longer authorized for Internet access.

C ○ The Web sites have all ceased operation.

D ○ None of the above.

7 If you're unable to access remote URLs, but can display the ISP's homepage, what could be the problem?

A ○ The ISP's proxy server is faulty.

B ○ You need to turn on the ISP's proxy server in your browser.

C ○ Your gateway server settings should be changed to the proxy server.

D ○ All of the above.

8 E-mail error messages are typically generated by the _____.

A ○ E-mail client

B ○ Mailer-daemon

C ○ E-mail server

D ○ HTTP daemon

9 You can use the _____ Windows utility to display the TCP/IP settings.

A ○ TRACERT

B ○ PING

C ○ NETSTAT

D ○ WINIPCFG

10 The HTTP error code _____ indicates that a document cannot be found.

A ○ 302

B ○ 400

C ○ 404

D ○ 8181

Answers

1 *B.* Caller-ID is not a telephone feature that interferes with a modem connection or its operation. However, call-waiting will. The other answers listed are all fatal errors that will stop a modem connection in its tracks. *See "Making the connection."*

2 *C.* Point-to-Point Protocol is the primary dialup protocol. Repeat the previous sentence about 20 times to permanently etch it on your brain for the exam. *Review "The modem answers, but nothing happens."*

3 *D.* Authentication matches the username or account name to the password and to the services to which the user has access. Authentication takes place as a part of the logon process in most dialup services. *Look over "I enter the password, and nothing happens."*

4 *B.* The command *71 is used to reactivate it after you are no longer using the phone line for a modem. The reason you want to turn it off is that incoming calls disconnect the modem connection. *Check out "Killing call-waiting."*

5 *C.* Most e-mail servers allow message attachments up to 5MB in size. A message that references an attachment indicates the sender attached it (the source of the reference), but the attachment was removed or not received, probably due to its size. *Take a look at "I'm connected, but I still have problems!"*

6 *A.* On the i-Net+ exam, you'll encounter several questions like this one. Carefully consider all the answer choices before giving in to the temptation to choose the none or all of the above escape route. *See "Pardon Me, Are You My Server?"*

7 *A.* The proxy server is, among other things, a caching server that caches Web pages that have been recently visited by users. If the proxy is malfunctioning, it could impact your ability to access sites beyond it on the Internet. *Review "I'm connected, but I still have problems!"*

8 *B.* Yes, this daemon is the source of much e-mail bad news. You should always read the messages sent by the mailer-daemon to be sure of what actually happened. Often, what looks like an error is just an advising note. *Take a look at "Problems of the e-mail kind."*

9 *D.* For the exam, be sure that you know how and why each of these utilities is used. There is definitely a question on the exam about WINICFG, so lock this away. *Check out "Gateways and other servers."*

10 *C.* This is another of those answers you need to memorize. The 404 — Not Found error message is generated when a document URL is bad, but can also be displayed when the Internet is clogged and traffic times out. *Look over "What's the 411 on the 404?"*

Part III
On the Client-Side

In this part . . .

This part contains information for about 40 percent of the questions on the i-Net+ exam. You must know about the software, such as browsers and protocol clients, how to search for a specific subject, how and why cookies (the Internet kind) are used, as well as the programming languages used to create a Web page. But that's not all! You must also be ready for questions that test your knowledge of the infrastructure required to support an Internet client and the issues that must be considered when configuring a client, including any legacy components.

Be sure you know which programming languages are used on the client-side and those that belong on the server-side. You should also be aware of the tools and protocols involved with including data from a database in a Web page. This includes a good working knowledge of HTML and the tags used to create the standard HTML page's structure, including tables, forms, and lists.

One other very important area you should study for the i-Net+ exam is multimedia and the browser extensions and plug-ins that are used to support the more popular multimedia formats.

Chapter 6

Configuring the Internet Client

● ●

Exam Objectives

▶ Describing the infrastructure needed to support an Internet client

▶ Explaining the issues of configuring a PC client

▶ Identifying problems related to legacy software clients

● ●

*U*nderlying all the fun and games of surfing the Net, you must have a solid Internet-client foundation. Like the little pig's house made of straw, a poorly constructed Internet client quickly falls apart when faced with the rigors of the Internet and Web.

One of the more important parts of an Internet technician's expertise is the ability to construct an efficient, effective Internet client on a networked PC. Most Internet users lack the skills needed for configuring a PC to access the Internet. It falls to you, the highly-skilled, keen-eyed, sharp-witted, and tireless Internet professional, to put together a system that navigates the complex waters of the Internet and Web successfully.

The i-Net+ exam places great emphasis on testing your ability to install and configure an Internet client, as well as troubleshoot any problems that may arise. This chapter and Chapter 7 cover just what you should know to be successful on the i-Net+ exam in this area.

Along with reviewing my suggestions as to what you should know, I suggest that you configure a workstation for TCP/IP, network access, and dialup access. Also, install and use several Web browsers. Understanding the nuances of configuring an Internet client is a matter of practice. Actually doing the task is an excellent way to prepare for the test. My advice is: Just configure it!

Quick Assessment

1 In a client/server network, the device or software that asks for a service is the _____.

2 A(n) _____ establishes the sequence or hierarchy in which communications protocols are applied.

3 You add the TCP/IP protocol to a Windows computer through the _____.

4 _____ assigns each workstation an IP address to use temporarily for its TCP/IP activities.

5 The _____ database is a series of connected files, each representing a group of local host names and their IP addresses.

6 Windows computers use _____ to resolve NetBIOS names to their IP addresses.

7 The _____ is the IP address of the router that provides the connection to the Internet.

8 A _____ is hard disk storage where temporary copies of downloaded objects are stored.

9 _____ clients are left behind when you upgrade portions of a client configuration.

10 The HTTP error message _____ indicates that a site no longer exists or that an URL was entered incorrectly.

Answers

1 *Client.* See "There are clients, and then there are clients."

2 *Protocol stack.* Review "Stacking up the client."

3 *Control Panel (the Network Icon).* Check out "Creating the client."

4 *DHCP.* Take a look at "Understanding the dynamics of the client."

5 *DNS.* See "The Internet's city directory."

6 *WINS.* Look over "Making WINS work."

7 *Default gateway.* Review "Is this the path to the IP gateway?"

8 *Cache.* Take a look at "Caching in on a good thing."

9 *Legacy.* Check out "Dealing with Legacy Clients."

10 *404 — Not Found.* See "Troubleshooting a moving target."

Setting Up the Client

One of the more important concepts you must know for the i-Net+ exam is that of client/server. You must be able to immediately and intuitively separate and differentiate the client from the server when you encounter either or both terms.

There are clients, and then there are clients

The *client* is the device or software that is asking for a service, such as data from a database, or a document from a remote computer. The *server* either fulfills or rejects a request. When you go to a restaurant, you are the client, the one asking for the food, and the restaurant folks are the servers, fulfilling your request. In fact, the person that comes to take your order usually identifies himself or herself as the server, saying, "Hi, I'm StacyJoeBiffRasheed and I'll be your server." Can't get much simpler than that! So, if SJBR is the server, then you are the . . . ? That's right, client! See how easy this is?

Well, not so fast. There are a few wrinkles to this, as you knew there'd be. The roles of client and server relate to which one makes the request and which one processes or services the request. Depending on the transaction, two computers can take the role of either the client or the server, depending on which is asking and which is answering. A computer on the Internet can be a client one minute, asking to download a Web document from a remote computer server, and then become a server the next minute, providing a document via FTP to a remote computer (client).

Oh, and it gets better! Some people call a computer attached to a local area network (LAN) a client. In this usage, the computer is a client to the network server. However, when the i-Net+ exam speaks of *configuring the client,* it's referring to the various software clients running on the network node. A client is a single piece of software, or a family of related software, running on a personal computer. The client provides the mechanisms for your PC to request and transport documents or files across the Internet and Web from a remote server.

So, when I speak of *configuring the client,* I'm referring to creating the required environment for a PC to function as a client. Yes, the PC will normally be only one type of client (running only a certain software client) at a time, but the whole of it — the hardware, software, protocols, and application software — is what makes the PC an Internet client.

Taking stock of the client hardware

So far, I have referred to the client hardware as a personal computer (PC). However, you can use many different types of hardware as the basis for an Internet client. For the i-Net+ exam, you should be familiar with these hardware types:

- ✔ **Desktop computers:** You can certainly configure your normal, run-of-the-mill PC as an Internet client, providing it has an Intel 486 processor (or better), at least 16MB of RAM, about 500MB of available disk space (for client software and the browser's temporary and history files), and either a modem or a LAN connection.

- ✔ **Portable computers:** A portable computer (laptop or notebook PC) needs to have essentially the same hardware configuration as a desktop computer in order to work effectively as an Internet client. The key is the capabilities of the built-in or PC-Card modem or LAN connection.

- ✔ **PDAs (Personal Digital Assistants):** A wide variety of handheld and palmtop devices can connect you to the Internet. Devices such as the PalmPilot, Psion, Newton, Nokia 9000, and others extend the capabilities of what were once not much more than electronic appointment books to include the ability to connect to the Internet for e-mail and some browsing.

- ✔ **E-mail clients:** One special type of handheld computer is the e-mail client device, a computer specifically designed for, and limited to, the retrieval of e-mail from an Internet e-mail provider. These devices are an inexpensive alternative for people who don't want to surf the Internet, but would like to wade in the e-mail pool.

- ✔ **WebTV:** A service available from Microsoft, WebTV is a combination of hardware (a set-top box and a wireless keyboard) and subscriber services that turn a television into an Internet client.

- ✔ **Internet phone:** By adding specialized wave-table sound processing hardware to a PC, such as the voice cards available from VocalTec, Dialogic, Quarterdeck, and others, you can turn your computer into an Internet client that can use the Internet as a telephone system.

Operating the client

There's no truth to the rumor that in order to do the Internet, you must use Windows. You can use virtually all the commonly used operating systems on an Internet client. Yes, even good old DOS!

Here's a brief overview of the Internet capabilities of the more popular operating systems:

- **DOS (Disk Operating System, a.k.a. MS-DOS, PC-DOS, or DR-DOS):** There are browsers, FTP clients, and add-on applications available for those of you steadfastly refusing to succumb to the Windows or Linux revolution. Browsers, such as ARACHNE (from the Czech Republic) and SPIN (from the Netherlands), also include HTML editing and other features.

- **Linux and UNIX:** Regardless of which flavor of Linux or UNIX you're using, finding the clients you need to configure an Internet client won't be difficult. Keep in mind that the Internet started in the UNIX world, and as a result, myriad utilities, clients, and applications are available for this platform.

- **OS/2:** Although not quite as extensive as the Windows and Linux/UNIX lists, a number of clients are available for OS/2 systems, including browsers, FTP, multimedia, and more.

- **Windows 9x:** Unless you've been away on a Peace Corps mission to find a lost civilization (only to find they're connected to the Internet and are active e-mail users) or you live in Linux Land, you're familiar with Microsoft Windows. Love it or hate it, Windows is the most widely used operating system in use today. It comes bundled with most of the client software you need to configure your PC as an Internet client, including Internet Explorer, a universal client. See Chapter 7 for more information on the various types of client software.

A very good Web site to find resources for the most commonly used operating systems is Browser Watch (`www.browserwatch.com`).

Creating the client

It's not unusual for a Windows 9x computer to have TCP/IP already installed, but Lab 6-1 steps you through the process used to set up the TCP/IP client on a Windows 9x computer.

Lab 6-1	Setting Up a TCP/IP Client

1. **First, check to see whether TCP/IP is already installed (if you can connect to the Internet from this computer, you can be sure it is): Click the Start button and then choose Settings⇨Control Panel.**

2. **On the Control Panel, double-click the Network icon to display the Network Configuration dialog box, which lists the protocols available.**

   Figure 6-1 shows the Network Configuration dialog box.

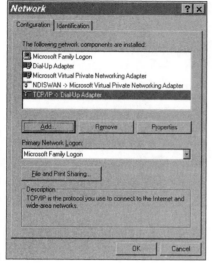

Figure 6-1:
The
Windows 98
Network
Configura-
tion dialog
box.

3. **If TCP/IP isn't listed in any form, click Add.**

   This opens the Select Network Component Type dialog box, as shown in Figure 6-2.

Figure 6-2:
The Select
Network
Component
Type
dialog box.

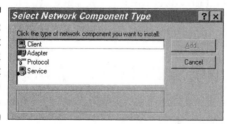

4. **Double-click the Protocol option.**

   Windows takes stock of the system and builds a driver information data-base before displaying the Select Network Protocol dialog box, as shown in Figure 6-3.

5. **Because you're on a Windows computer, choose Microsoft in the Manufacturers list and then double-click TCP/IP in the Network Protocols box.**

   The Microsoft TCP/IP protocol is added to the system, and you're returned to the Network Protocol dialog box shown in Figure 6-1. *Note:* You may be asked for your Windows CD (or disks, if you installed from floppies).

   The settings you select for configuring the TCP/IP client depend on how you connect to the Internet. Lab 6-2, later in this chapter, completes the configuration of the TCP/IP client.

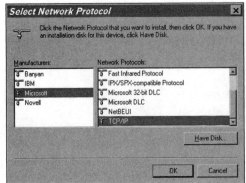

Decisions and Choices: Completing the Internet Client

You must make numerous decisions and choices when completing the configuration of an Internet client. Many of the choices are pre-made by network administrators, but many depend on the preferences of the end-user. In this section, I don't cover every single choice you face — many are just fine with their default values. However, I do cover the ones you need to know about for the i-Net+ exam.

Understanding the dynamics of the client

Each client PC on a TCP/IP network must be assigned an IP address so that it has a source address to send and receive Internet messages. An IP address is assigned to clients in one of two ways: manually by the network administrator or automatically by the server. Manually assigned IP addresses are called *static* addresses. Automatically assigned IP addresses are *dynamic* addresses.

When a static IP address is assigned to a workstation, it's a set-it-and-forget-it situation. Unless some compelling reason exists to change the computer's IP address, the computer retains the static address it was assigned by the administrator.

On the other hand, dynamically assigned IP addresses are assigned to a workstation when the workstation is logged onto the network. The control protocol that controls the dynamic assignment of IP addresses to workstations on a network is the Dynamic Host Control Protocol (DHCP).

DHCP assigns each workstation an IP address to use temporarily, usually a few days, for its TCP/IP activities. The process used to assign each workstation a DHCP IP address goes like this:

1. When the DHCP client (the workstation) boots up, it broadcasts an IP request message using the only identification it has — its MAC (Media Address Control) address and computer name — to the DHCP server.

2. The DHCP server receives the request and, if a valid configuration is available, responds with a message containing the DHCP IP address and the corresponding subnet mask, default gateway, and other data.

3. If an IP address is not available, the request is denied. The client is persistent and pesters the server for the next 5 minutes. If that doesn't work, the client idles for 5 minutes, and then starts the entire process over again.

The advantage that a dynamic IP address assignment has over statically assigned IP addresses is very dramatic in larger networks, especially those on which workstations move frequently. In a dynamic scheme, when the workstations log on after they move, they will be assigned a DHCP address regardless of where they are on the network. In a smaller network, static IP addresses are easily managed.

Dynamic IP addresses are assigned to network workstations using DHCP, and may be different from session to session. Static IP addresses are assigned to network workstations by the network administrator and are the permanent IP address of the workstation.

Reviewing the TCP/IP client configuration settings

For the i-Net+ exam, you need to know the purpose of the primary client configuration settings and the type of value each contains. The TCP/IP configuration settings you need to know for the test are WINS (Windows Internet Name Service), DNS (Domain Name System), subnet mask, and hosts file.

Checking the local directory

NetBIOS over TCP/IP (typically shortened to NBT) is a network service that's used to convert computer (NetBIOS) names to IP addresses, a process called *name resolution*. A computer's NetBIOS name is usually the handle given to the computer when its operating system was installed. It's the name by which the computer is known on the network. A computer is assigned a unique name that can be from one to 15 characters. For example, my computer has the imaginative name of RGILSTER, but yours may be VOODOO, BIGJOHN, FASTLADY, or something a lot more fun.

NetBIOS names enable network users to communicate and share resources over the network. For example, if the user on BIGJOHN has created a network share for a certain folder (RECIPES) on its hard disk, FASTLADY is able to access the contents of the folder by mapping to **\\BIGJOHN\RECIPES**.

Looking up the NetBIOS name (intermission)

If you'd like to see the NetBIOS name of your Windows computer, right-click Network Neighborhood, choose Properties, and then click the Identification tab in the dialog box that's displayed. The computer's NetBIOS name is in the field labeled Computer Name. The NetBIOS settings for a network are stored on the server in an area called the *NetBIOS name cache*.

If you're on a Windows NT system, you can display the name of the computer by typing the following command at a command prompt:

```
nbstat -n
```

Finding hosts on the Internet

TCP/IP has a four-octet, 32-bit address structure that allows for literally millions of network addresses, but they're not at all easy to remember. This is where DNS comes in; it provides a hierarchical means of translating domain names to IP addresses, or vice versa.

For example, what if a user in California wants to access the RECIPE folder on a computer in Indiana with the Internet (domain) name of bigjohn.com? The user in California can access the remote domain using either its domain name (www.bigjohn.com) or its IP address (206.175.162.18). Most users don't remember IP addresses (at least I don't), so they use the domain name.

Domain names are registered in the DNS (Domain Name System) database distributed around the Internet. DNS is used to look up a domain name and convert it into its IP address. The DNS database literally contains all the domain names and associated IP addresses for the entire Internet, a collection of information that requires frequent updating. However, the file is considered to be a static database because its updates are manually entered periodically by the ARIN (American Registry of Internet Numbers) agency.

The effect of DNS name resolution is as follows: If you enter the domain name www.bigjohn.com, DNS lookup changes the entry to 206.175.162.18. In this example, the domain name www.bigjohn.com is converted into its IP address. (Just for the record, you really don't need to know the this IP address for the i-Net+ exam.)

One more thing before I move on: A domain can also be looked up in reverse. Some Web pages record who is visiting their sites. To do this, the IP address really doesn't tell much. What is needed is the domain name. So the IP address can be used in a DNS search to locate the host computer's real name for logon purposes. This is called *reverse DNS*.

The Internet's city directory

The DNS database is actually a series of connected files, each representing a group of local host names and their IP addresses. Each local host database is related to one or more higher-level parent, or *root,* servers in the DNS hierarchy. To translate a domain name, such `www.dummies.com`, into its IP address, the databases up a particular path, from www to dummies.com to .com, are each searched until a match is found.

At the top of the DNS structure are the root domains. The six root domains used in the United States are

- ✔ **.COM:** This domain contains commercial and for-profit companies on the Internet. It's the largest domain in terms of the number of entries.

- ✔ **.EDU:** Educational institutions, public and private, are in this domain.

- ✔ **.GOV:** This domain contains the branches of the United States federal, state, county, and city governments.

- ✔ **.MIL:** The United States military services and their branches are in this domain.

- ✔ **.NET:** Organizations that provide direct Internet related services, such as networksolutions.net, and arin.net, as well as many ISPs, such as internetnw.net and others, are in this domain.

- ✔ **.ORG:** Nonprofit, noncommercial, charitable, or publicly owned organizations, such as redcross.org and mariners.org (the baseball team) are in this domain.

What's in a name?

When FASTLADY, a host at `www.cookingschool.com`, needs to access the recipes at `www.bigjohn.com`, a number of small requests are generated. The first request goes to `bigjohn.com`, an address that `www.bigjohn.com` already has. The primary DNS server at `bigjohn.com` tries to solve the request locally from its own database, but failing that, the request is passed up the hierarchy to the regional .com server, which looks in its databases. If the .com server cannot find an entry for `www.bigjohn.com`, it passes the request to the national .com server, which then searches down its hierarchy until the IP address shows up. If the URL cannot be resolved (for example, you may have entered it incompletely or misspelled it), then an error message is sent to your browser saying the domain name cannot be found. Try entering your name as `www.your_name_here.com` to see this error. That is, of course, assuming you haven't generated your own commercial site using your name.

Don't worry about recanting exactly how a DNS name lookup proceeds — the exam isn't going to ask. But you do need a reasonable understanding of how the process works.

Are you the host?

You can use local files and services in place of the DNS database. These local files provide an abridged and more relevant database of names-to-IP-address and names-to-MAC-address conversions. Generically, these files are called hosts files because they contain a list of network hosts (computers on the network) and their corresponding IP and MAC addresses.

The hosts file associated with NetBIOS name lookup is the LMHOSTS (LAN Manager HOSTS) file, a holdover from LAN Manager, an early network system. LMHOSTS is a manually managed static file that's been replaced by the WINS service. However, many administrators still use LMHOSTS as a backup name resolution method.

HOSTS files are maintained with a variety of transactions. Each transaction type performs a specific task. You should remember that the transaction used to manage the computer names in a HOSTS file is the CNAME command.

Making WINS work

The Windows Internet Name Service (WINS) is a dynamic service used to resolve NetBIOS computer names to their IP addresses on Windows-based networks. Whenever a network-client computer boots up, it registers its name, IP address, the account name of its user, and whatever network services it's using with the WINS server. The word *Windows* in the name of this service tells you that this is a Microsoft product, and that other network operating systems (UNIX, NetWare, and so on) will probably not support its use.

Here's how WINS works: When a computer is moved to a new location, say in a different city, it will undoubtedly now have a different IP address, along with a new subnet mask. (See Chapter 2 for a brief discussion on subnet masks.) As long as it's a part of the same overall network domain structure, WINS will find it and update the computer's resolution data automatically.

The steps used to perform name resolution on a WINS system are

1. The local NetBIOS name cache is searched, and if the name is found, the process ends.

2. If the local NetBIOS cache doesn't contain the name, the client makes a request of the WINS server for the IP address associated with the computer name. If found, the WINS server returns the IP address to the client, and the process stops.

3. If the address isn't found, and a secondary WINS server is in use, the request is forwarded to that server.

4. If the name cannot be resolved by a WINS server, the computer name for the needed IP address is broadcast to the network in the hope that it responds with its IP address.

Is this the path to the IP gateway?

A *gateway* is a mechanism used to connect two dissimilar networks that operate independently of one another, such as a LAN and the Internet WAN. The gateway is also the demarcation point of routing over the Internet.

The primary protocol of a network may or not be TCP/IP. Even if it is, each network operating system functions slightly different from good old regular TCP/IP. Regardless, the LAN and the Internet are separate networks that operate independent of each other. However, on occasion they do need to interconnect.

The local network uses a static IP address for its gateway to and from the Internet. That this address is a static address is very important because other Internet hosts wishing to access a local network host (to deliver e-mail, for example) will most likely use Internet DNS services to find it. So, the gateway must not be a moving target and maintain a static, permanent identity.

To the clients on a LAN, the *default gateway* is the IP address of the router connected to another physical or logical network. Another way to look at it is that the default gateway is the IP address of the device (usually a router) that provides the real connection to the Internet.

All together now . . .

If FASTLADY really wants to access BIGJOHN to see its recipes, FASTLADY needs the IP (Internet Protocol) address for BIGJOHN, wherever it may be. Converting the host name BIGJOHN into its IP address is the process called *name resolution*. On a Windows 9*x* or NT computer, computer name resolution goes like this:

1. The NetBIOS name cache is checked first. If the name is found, the IP address is returned and the process ends.

2. If WINS is in use, the WINS server on the local network is requested to resolve the computer's name to its IP address.

3. If WINS cannot resolve the host name, a broadcast message is sent over the network asking the computer with the name in question to respond with its IP address.

4. If there is still no identification, the Windows client decides the computer name must actually be the name of a remote host on the Internet, in which case it checks the HOSTS file (a listing of remote host computers and their IP addresses) and DNS servers which cross-reference domain names and their IP addresses on the Internet.

5. If all else fails, it's assumed that the name is nonexistent or was misspelled or badly constructed. The moral of the story is: Be sure you spell URLs correctly — a lot of work goes into identifying user error.

Configuring the TCP/IP client

There's absolutely nothing like some hands-on practice to really be sure you're ready for the i-Net+ exam, at least in the area of setting up a TCP/IP client. Lab 6-2 completes the process started in Lab 6-1 to configure a Windows TCP/IP client.

Lab 6-2	Setting TCP/IP Properties on a Windows Client

1. **Double-click the Network icon in the Windows Control Panel to open the Network Configuration dialog box shown in Figure 6-1.**

2. **Highlight the TCP/IP protocol in the components list and click the Properties button to open the TCP/IP Properties dialog box (see Figure 6-4).**

   Use the tabs across the top of the dialog box to access each of the property types.

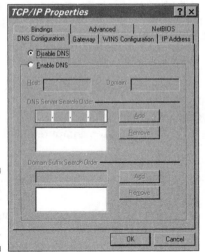

Figure 6-4:
TCP/IP
Properties
dialog box.

3. **Click the IP Address tab.**

   In most situations, you choose Obtain An IP Address Automatically to indicate that the workstation client IP address is assigned by the DHCP server. In those situations where a static IP address is assigned, click the indicator for an assigned (static) IP address and enter it in the box provided.

4. **Click the DNS Configuration tab.**

   To indicate that DNS lookup is used on the network, click the adjacent radio button and then enter the host ID, the domain ID, and the IP address of the DNS server. You can enter more than one DNS server, and you can set an order of access.

5. **Click the Gateway tab.**

6. **Enter the IP address of the gateway(s) on the network, as illustrated in Figure 6-5. You can set the access order for gateways; the first one listed is the default gateway.**

7. **Click the WINS Configuration tab.**

   You use the WINS Configuration tab to indicate whether the network supports WINS services. (See Figure 6-6.) If it does, you need to click the Enable button and enter the IP address of the WINS server. If DHCP is in use, it's likely that you would click the button that indicates that DHCP should be used for WINS service.

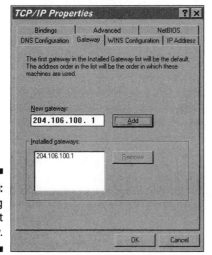

Figure 6-5:
Configuring the default gateway.

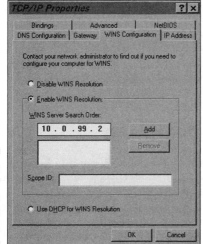

Figure 6-6:
Enable or disable WINS resolution.

Configuring the browser

If you have recently installed a browser with a version number higher than 4, you know that browser installation and configuration requires very little in the way of outside assistance. Browsers have basically gotten to the same maturation point as automobiles. Long gone are the days when you and I could actually open the hood of a car and be able to identify anything beyond the dipstick (and then only because it is labeled). Browsers are now quite capable of installing and configuring themselves, as well as taking over and controlling your entire computer. What with active desktops, smart updates, and all, there's little left for the user to configure.

Regardless of the capability of the browser, however, you need to know some browser configuration details for the i-Net+ exam, such as hardware requirements, configuring for a proxy server, and setting up caching and history.

Do you measure up?

Here are the minimum computer hardware requirements for installing a browser on your system:

- **Processor:** At least a 486DX processor running at 66 Megahertz or higher.

- **Operating System:** Windows 9*x* or Windows NT, Macintosh, OS/2, Amiga, and a few less popular operating systems are supported by some browsers. However, not all browsers support all environments.

- **Memory:** Typically, you need from 16MB to 32MB of RAM at minimum for most of the newer browser releases.

- **Hard-drive space:** Depending on the level of installation you choose (minimal, typical or full installation), you need as little as 45MB of free disk space to as much as 115MB.

- **Obvious other stuff:** Some stuff you may want to have to be able to effectively use your browser are a mouse and either a modem or a LAN connection to the Internet.

Caching in on a good thing

Nearly all Web browsers support what is called *client-side caching,* or the use of a client-based cache. A *cache* is hard disk storage where temporary copies of downloaded objects are stored. A browser uses a cache to store, or cache, any downloaded objects such as documents, graphics, and sound files, on the hard disk. Any later requests for these objects are serviced from the cache area, eliminating some unnecessary network traffic.

A client-side cache, while a good thing, is not the best thing. In contrast, a *cache server* on a network provides a shared cache to be used by all the network clients, thus preventing even more redundant Internet traffic that may be fetching a page that another user on the network had just downloaded.

Local caching

Most browsers allow for local caching or temporary Internet files, as it's also called. You can configure the browser to look for newer versions of a cached object every time you request it, only at the start of a new browser session, or never. You can also set how much disk space is to be allotted to saving downloaded objects. For those users that visit the same sites frequently, allowing for client-side caching can help improve network performance. Plus, fetching a page from cache is always faster than waiting for it to download from the Web.

Server-side caching and proxy servers

Nearly all Web browsers also support using a proxy server, or a server-based cache. There are a variety of reasons for using a networked cache server or proxy server, but the best has to be the reduction of traffic exiting the default gateway router to the Internet.

Configuring the browser to use a proxy server is typically done in the LAN settings area of the browser controls. On a Windows system, the configuration of the client for Internet access is controlled through the Control Panel's Internet Options icon. In addition to setting many personal choice options about the performance of the client and its browsers, you can set whether the client is to use a LAN-based proxy server.

If you choose, you can use both a local cache and a proxy server. Doing so can eliminate even more traffic by eliminating some calls across the network to the proxy server or beyond.

 Proxy servers are also excellent for creating firewall protection on an internal network. Chapter 13 goes into agonizing detail on proxy servers, and the other servers common to a network, and their roles.

Putting on the subnet mask

 One of the items required for configuring a client is the subnet mask that is applied by the network to separate the IP address of the network from the IP address of the client computer (host). The subnet mask itself looks very much like an IP address, but it is actually a preset pattern of binary numbers (ones and zeroes) that the destination address of a network message is filtered through to extract the network ID of the destination computer. A common subnet mask is 255.255.255.255.

Dealing with Legacy Clients

I don't know about you, but despite the constant nagging from the publisher of my browser, I rarely take the time to upgrade my browser and the other clients I use to navigate and download from the Internet and the Web. The result, much to my frequent dismay, is that I end up with legacy clients. Don't panic, having legacy clients is not nearly as bad as gingivitis or hemorrhoids, regardless of what browser and client software publishers or the i-Net+ exam wants you to believe. However, having older clients, helper applications, and viewers can make your experiences with the Internet and the Web less efficient and effective, causing your system to lock up, disconnect, or improperly display downloaded objects.

Legacy clients are left behind when you upgrade portions of a client configuration. Frequently, these are tools that have been around for a while and have worked adequately with newer versions of other client software. For example, when you upgrade your browser to its fresh-off-the-presses version, other software, such as helper applications, viewers, and readers may not have been tested with this browser version. The result is that you get to be the lucky one who discovers that they're as compatible as oil and water. Many systems still sport DOS and early Windows client software, such as Winsock clients, that aren't always compatible with the new stuff. This can cause hard-to-find performance problems, lockups, and uneven displays.

What you should study for the i-Net+ exam in the area of performance issues is:

- ✔ **Troubleshooting browser problems:** Most browser publishers, including the big two, have help or technical support pages to list troubleshooting guides for their products. I think the biggest troubleshooting problem occurs when you have to figure out the meaning of the error messages themselves.

- ✔ **Ensuring currency and compatibility:** Before downloading or installing new Internet or Web clients or editing software, you should check the revision levels of the software and the other Web clients with which it's compatible. Often this information is available from the publisher or vendor.

- ✔ **Incompatibility problems:** Not all clients, helper applications, and viewers are compatible with all other Internet and Web access tools, although this seems to be getting much better as the field of popular browsers continues to slim down. If you're a Web page publisher, you should test the page to avoid compatibility problems, and if they're unavoidable, warn the reader.

Troubleshooting a moving target

Troubleshooting browser and client problems can be like shooting a moving target. In most cases, a download problem can be resolved simply by refreshing the page or accessing the same URL a few times. Often, temporary network problems have taken care of themselves by the time you reload the page.

Don't assume the problem is with the network. Try repeating the problem by accessing different sites that you have previously been able to download successfully. If the same error keeps happening on different sites, tag you're it! The problem is likely with your hardware or connection. Before getting too crazy, be sure your hardware or connection isn't the problem.

Here are some troubleshooting tips for common problems:

- **Unknown file type, no viewer configured for file type, or unable to launch external viewer:** There are standard file types that most browsers will recognize, such as GIF, JPEG, and AU, but on occasion you may encounter a file type for which you don't have a helper application or viewer.

- **Server DNS entry error:** There are a number of causes for this type of error, including the TCP/IP stack not being present, network slowness or congestion, or you can't get to the Internet through a LAN firewall. Another possibility is that the URL you're after simply doesn't exist.

- **404 Not Found:** Everyone's favorite HTTP error message. Either the site has ceased to exist or you spelled it wrong. Always try at least one more time.

- **404 Access Denied:** Tsk, tsk, you're trying to access a site for which you don't have access rights. You can either give up hacking the site, or contact its owner to change the permissions.

- **System call 'connect' failed: connection refused:** This error message is more times than not caused by network slowness. Other reasons are that the remote server is down or out of service. You should try using the TCP/IP PING or TRACERT utilities to test the site's existence and operation.

- **FTP — Error 57:** This error message is a sure sign that the network or the FTP server is extremely busy or overloaded with requests. Just cool your jets and try again later.

Some appearance problems you may also need to troubleshoot involve such issues as font size, colors, frames, and other HTML-related features of a Web page. Reviewing the setup and configuration of the browser itself normally clears this type of error. Most browsers include the ability to override a downloaded page's fonts, colors, and other features, which can cause display problems on some pages.

To help you prepare for the i-Net+ exam, you should visit the help pages of as many browsers as you can. This will help you get an idea of the kinds of troubleshooting help available, along with the kinds of problems that have already been identified. The URLs of the Big Two are

```
http://help.netscape.com/
http://support.microsoft.com/search/
```

Are you compatible?

I'm sure you've seen Web pages that have a nice graphic at the bottom of the page along with the caption that says the page is best viewed with a browser you don't have using a monitor setting you don't have. Whether this indicates extreme laziness on the part of the Web page developer or somebody who owns stock in one of the publishing companies is immaterial.

Web sites with known browser incompatibilities should carry a warning so that users with the wrong browser will know the reason a particular page looks really bad on their computer. This always reminds me of the early days of color television, when I was often told not to adjust my set, the problem was in the broadcast.

Not every Web page is 100 percent compatible with every browser in use on the Web, but the most popular pages seemingly have little problems with any browser used. This is not the result of luck; rather, the site developers tested the site with multiple browsers and adjusted for compatibility.

Here's a really great site that lists the compatibility features of the more popular browsers on each operating system:

```
http://www.ariadne-webdesign.co.uk/ariadne/Resources
```

Prep Test

1 In a client/server network environment, the component that processes service requests is the _____.

A ○ Client

B ○ Server

C ○ Application

D ○ Processor

2 Which of the following are hardware types on which an Internet client can be configured? (Choose all that apply.)

A ❑ Desktop computer

B ❑ Notebook computer

C ❑ WebTV

D ❑ PDA

3 A protocol stack is best described as _____.

A ○ The OSI Reference Model

B ○ TCP/IP

C ○ A sequence or hierarchy of how protocols are used on a network

D ○ The various protocols available on a client

4 The type of IP address that can be permanently assigned to a workstation is a _____ address.

A ○ Dynamic

B ○ Recurring

C ○ Non-recurring

D ○ Static

5 A domain can be accessed by _____ and _____. (Choose two.)

A ❑ Domain name

B ❑ Keyword

C ❑ Meta tag

D ❑ IP address

6 The highest order domains in the DNS hierarchy, such as .COM, .ORG, and .MIL, are called _____.

A ○ Trunks

B ○ Trees

C ○ Roots

D ○ Families

7 The service used on some Windows computers to resolve NetBIOS names into their IP addresses is _____.

A ○ LMHOSTS

B ○ WINS

C ○ HOSTS

D ○ DNS

8 The default gateway is represented by which of the following?

A ○ The IP address of the device that connects to the Internet

B ○ The external firewall

C ○ The Web proxy server

D ○ The IP address of the primary Web server

9 The hard disk storage that is used to store temporary copies of objects downloaded from the Internet is called the _____.

A ○ \TEMP directory

B ○ Cache

C ○ Buffer

D ○ Bookmarks

10 Which of the following HTTP error messages would be displayed if the TCP/IP protocol stack is not present?

A ○ Unknown File Type

B ○ 404 — Access Denied

C ○ FTP — Error 57

D ○ Server DNS Entry Error

Answers

1 *B.* The server provides service and the client receives the service. *See "There are clients, and then there are clients."*

2 *A, B, C, and D.* This is not intended to be a trick question; I just couldn't think of any kind of computer or communications device on which some form of an Internet client could not be built. *Review "Client hardware."*

3 *C.* The sequence and the hierarchy of when and how communications protocols are applied on a network client are established in its protocol stack. TCP/IP is a pre-structured protocol stack. *Look over "Stacking up the client."*

4 *D.* Dynamic addresses are assigned to a network client when it logs on to the network by the DHCP server. Static addresses are assigned permanently when the client is configured by the network administrator. *Check out "Understanding the dynamics of the client."*

5 *A and D.* A domain can be accessed via DNS by its domain name or directly by its IP address. *Look over "Finding hosts on the Internet."*

6 *C.* The root domains are on the highest level in the DNS hierarchy. The root domains list the sites within each domain. *See "The Internet's city directory."*

7 *B.* Not every Windows client or network uses WINS (Windows Internet Name Service) to resolve NetBIOS names into IP addresses. Some use HOSTS files and others use the DNS, but you need to know about WINS for the exam. *Review "Making WINS work."*

8 *A.* A gateway interconnects two dissimilar networks, such as a LAN and the Internet WAN. The default gateway is the IP address of the device that serves as the gateway to the Internet on a network. *Check out "Is this the path to the IP gateway?"*

9 *B.* Your cache of Internet treasures eliminates unnecessary trips to the Internet for Web documents that you have recently visited. *Take a look at "Caching in on a good thing."*

10 *D.* Not the most descriptive message in the library, but it indicates that the domain entered cannot be resolved. Not having the protocol stack would severely hamper name resolution. *See "Troubleshooting a moving target."*

Chapter 7

Working with Internet Clients

●●

Exam Objectives

▶ Using Web browsers

▶ Applying FTP, Telnet, e-mail, MIME, and other Internet clients

▶ Employing different Internet and Web search indexes

▶ Describing the pros and cons of cookies

▶ Discussing the benefits and pitfalls of upgrading client software

●●

*I*n the overall scheme of the client/server world of the Internet, it is the workstation clients that enable you to create, deploy, access, display, and interact with the information on the Internet and the World Wide Web (WWW, or just plain ol' Web). A *client* is typically a stand-alone program that employs an underlying communications protocol. Internet clients, most of which are TCP/IP (which stands for Transport Control Protocol/Internet Protocol) protocols, establish the rules used to connect to remote systems to locate, display, and transfer documents and information such as Web pages and e-mail messages over the Internet.

In preparing for the i-Net+ exam, you need to know and understand the various clients used to interact with the Internet and the Web, especially those used to access and display Web documents. You need to know the processes and protocols involved in displaying the document and why they may not work on occasion.

While you do need to memorize some of this material, for the most part if you have a good working understanding of these tools you should do just fine. Keep in mind that this test assumes you are an entry-level technician, and won't throw too many curves at you.

Quick Assessment

Using Web browsers

1 In the client/server world of the Internet, a Web browser is a(n) _____.

2 A(n) _____ interprets HTML commands and hypertext links in a Web document.

3 A URL has three primary components: _____, _____, and _____.

Applying FTP, Telnet, E-mail, MIME, and other Internet clients

4 The software tools used to display specially formatted files or embedded features of a Web page are called _____, _____, or _____.

5 _____ is an extension of the SMTP that enables documents and files to be transferred via e-mail.

6 To transfer a file from one computer to another computer over the Internet, the _____ is typically used.

Employing different Internet and Web search indexes

7 The letters ICQ stand for _____.

8 The three most common types of search engines are _____, _____, and _____.

Describing the pros and cons of cookies

9 A cookie is normally set by a(n) _____ script.

10 Good places to look for warnings, cautions, and error reports for most software upgrades and compatibilities are _____ and _____.

Discussing the benefits and pitfalls of upgrading client software

Answers

1 *Client.* See "Why *do* they call it browsing?"

2 *Browser.* Review "Browsing for fun and profit."

3 *Transfer protocol, FQDN, document reference.* Take a look at "I think I'm going to URL."

4 *Viewers, readers, helper applications (add-ons* and *plug-ins* are good answers, too). Check out "Taking in the view."

5 *MIME.* See "What's MIME is yours."

6 *FTP (File Transfer Protocol).* Look at "Moving up and down the Internet."

7 *I seek you.* Review "ICQ and you seek me."

8 *Static catalog index, keyword index, full text index.* Check out "The Never-Ending Search for . . ."

9 *CGI.* See "The inner workings of a cookie."

10 *Vendor sites, newsgroups.* Review "Getting help before you need it."

What You Get Is What You See

In the brief history of the computer, nothing has made as big of an impact as quickly as the Web. The Web, which is just one of the Internet technologies, has been the primary catalyst behind the explosive growth of the Internet and its associated networks to this point. Although newer emerging technologies may help reinvent the Internet in the future, the Web is what most people think of as the embodiment of the Internet. Web browsers and other file access clients make the Internet accessible to anyone with a computer and a way to connect to a network. When someone says they "found it on the Internet," they most likely mean they found it on the Web using a browser.

You don't need to know the history of browsers, but a little background information can only help you strengthen your philosophical side for the exam and enable you to impress your friends at parties.

In the beginning (which was about six years ago), there was text, and Web browsers enabled users to browse through text files — hence the name browser. Then as now, hypertext makes it possible to move from one Web document to another in much the same way as you would browse your way around in a magazine. With the addition of the graphical user interface (GUI), the browser now enables you to examine documents containing not only text and hypertext, but also colors, textures, and graphics.

Hypertext is the mechanism that underlies the function and structure of the World Wide Web. Hypertext links are words or images that have been linked to targets in the same document, or the URL addresses of documents on the same server on a remote server.

Why do they call it browsing?

I'll bet you all the marbles in my head (a considerably large bet) that you should know what a Web browser is for the i-Net+ exam. Oh sure, you think you know, but just to be on the safe side, here is my all inclusive definition. A *Web browser* . . .

- ✔ Is a piece of application software known as a client
- ✔ Enables users to view documents created with HTML (Hypertext Markup Language)
- ✔ Uses HTTP (Hypertext Transfer Protocol) to make requests of remote servers
- ✔ Uses hypertext to provide for interaction with the information on the Web

Web browsers are clients because in the client/server nature of the Internet, one computer (the client) requests services or data, or both, from another computer (the server). Browser clients facilitate the request and retrieval of Web documents from remote servers, display the document, and then manage the interaction of links to other Web documents.

And the winners are . . .

Numerous browser versions are available today, some general and some specific. Most users use one or both of the big two: Microsoft's Internet Explorer and Netscape's Navigator. Some of the more popular ones are (in alphabetical order to avoid showing a preference):

- ✔ **Internet Explorer** (www.microsoft.com/ie5): One of the big two.

- ✔ **Lynx** (lynx.browser.org): A text-only browser.

- ✔ **Mosaic** (www.ncsa.uiuc.edu): The original GUI browser from the National Center for Supercomputing Applications (NCSA).

- ✔ **Navigator** (www.netscape.com): The other of the big two browsers, now included in the Netscape Communicator client suite.

- ✔ **WebTV** (www.webtv.com): Although not exactly the same as the others, WebTV systems are used to browse the Web using your television set.

Don't worry about memorizing this list for the test. I only mention them in case you see one of these names in a question, so you'll know what it is and does.

Browsing for fun and profit

You should know the mechanics of browsing and how the various protocols are used to support the request, retrieval, display, and interaction of Web documents. I won't go into all the details of how each protocol works specifically here (see Chapter 12 for more detailed information on protocols).

Each time you want to view a Web document, a series of processes takes place, assuming, of course, that you have already connected to an Internet source:

1. The browser software creates a workspace and display area for viewing and interacting with the documents you tell it to retrieve. Figure 7-1 illustrates a browser's workspace displayed on a PC monitor using Internet Explorer.

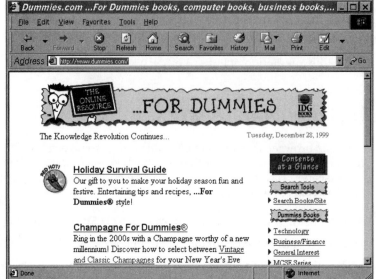

Figure 7-1:
The Internet
Explorer
browser.

2. The URL (Uniform Resource Locator) you enter in the Address or Location box of your browser or choose from the browser's history tells the browser where to find the document you want to display. See Chapter 3 for more information on URLs and Chapter 12 for a discussion on exactly how the server is located on the Internet.

3. If the requested document is found and you are permitted to download it, the document is transferred over the Internet to your computer and opened and displayed by the browser. Your browser then chooses from a variety of viewers used to display the document according to the HTML instructions embedded in it.

4. If, while you are viewing the document, you click a hypertext or hypermedia link, the URL document retrieval process begins again back at Step 2. Repeating Steps 2 through 4 over and over constitutes the activity commonly known as "surfing the Net."

5. The browser maintains a history of the pages you have viewed so that you can navigate backward and forward in sequence through the documents retrieved in this browsing session. Usually, visited documents are held in a cache, which eliminates the need to retrieve them from their source should you want to see one again. See Chapter 4 for more information on caching.

6. If you are not permitted to view a document (see Chapter 15 for information on site security), or if the URL is a bad address, an error message or error page is displayed. You must go back to the previous document or enter another URL to continue the session.

In summary, a browser interprets the commands, formatting, and hypertext links embedded in Web documents to give its user the ability to access information and move about the Web.

Browsers have also turned the Web into a multimedia delivery system through browser plug-in extensions that allow for sound, music, and voice communications, video, 3-D and virtual reality animations, and online teleconferencing. Other add-ons, such as Java applets, allow a wide array of applications to be distributed over the Web to local computers, providing the beginning of application-on-demand.

I think I'm going to URL

A Web document is referenced through its URL (Uniform Resource Locator). The URL contains either a direct reference to a specific document (a filename included in the URL) or none at all, which is actually an indirect reference to the site's default page.

The collection of documents on a server makes up a Web site. Within a Web site, a particular page — known as the home or front page — is displayed by default when the site is addressed indirectly. A site's home page typically contains links to the other documents on the site and serves as a de facto table of contents. Browsers generally recognize certain filenames, such as `index.html`, `default.html`, or `welcome.html` as a site's default page.

A URL has three primary components:

- ✔ The transfer protocol
- ✔ The server's fully qualified domain name (FQDN)
- ✔ An optional reference to a specific Web site document

Here's an example:

```
http://www.dummies.com/i-Net+/cheatsheet.html
```

In this URL, the first element is the protocol used to transfer the site's files to your computer (`http://`). The second element is the domain name of the Web site (`www.dummies.com`), followed by the optional directory name (`/i-Net+/`) and filename (`cheatsheet.html`) that contains the Web document to be displayed.

The URL is a composite of the transfer protocol, the FQDN of the server, and the optional reference to a specific file.

Moving the data on the Net

If you want a lengthy discussion on protocols, you should take a look at Chapter 12, but in the context of how a browser works, you should be familiar with the following Internet protocols and technologies:

- ✔ **FTP (File Transfer Protocol):** The TCP/IP protocol used to transfer a document from one computer's storage to another without displaying its contents during transfer.

- ✔ **Hypertext:** (also known as *hyperlink* and just plain *link*) The mechanism used to embed the URL of one Web document, graphic, or other object into another. See Chapter 9 to find out how you add a hyperlink to a Web document.

- ✔ **HTTP (Hypertext Transfer Protocol):** The TCP/IP protocol that is used to transfer documents containing hypertext links over the Internet and the World Wide Web.

- ✔ **HTML (Hypertext Markup Language):** The coding scheme used to designate how a document is to be displayed that is interpreted by the browser to reproduce the document as intended.

Most browsers in use today are *multiprotocol,* which means that they support a variety of different protocols including those listed in this section. Because they support multiple protocols, they can work with different types of servers to transfer and display information.

Taking in the view

From all outward appearances, browsers contain all the software needed to display every kind of font, color, graphic, and animation that any Web document can possibly include. I'm sorry to burst your bubble, but browsers contain only a few of the tools used to display an HTML document.

By default your browser can display text in a few common fonts, any color in its color palette, a couple of graphic types, and only the most basic of animations. To reproduce all that really snazzy stuff you've been downloading, such as dancing diapers, bouncing babies, virtual reality worlds, and interactive games, you need special-purpose software tools that go by a variety of names, including *viewers, helper applications, plug-ins,* and *add-ons.* You can download and add a wide range of these tools and add them to your browser's arsenal. If the browser did contain all the viewers required to display anything you might encounter on the Web, it would be much too large to run on even the most powerful personal computers.

For the i-Net+ exam, you should be aware of at least some of the more common browser add-ons in use. I've organized the most common tools into four groups: readers, images, sound, and actions, which are explained in the following sections. The fit in some cases may be a little forced, but I think you'll see the pattern and relationship of each viewer in the groups.

Reading the display

I include the document and other static display viewers in this group. Many of the viewers in this group are built into the browser itself. On the other hand, several document types require special viewers that you must download before you can view the document. Built-in or not, each of the following is a browser viewer:

- ✔ **HTML viewers:** This is a tricky one — the most commonly used types of HTML viewers are the most commonly used browsers. Huh? Navigator, Internet Explorer, Opera, Mosaic, and Arena are all HTML viewers.

- ✔ **Readers:** This type of browser add-on enables you to view and read entire documents online, including sales materials, brochures, and product specifications. Document viewers are becoming increasingly popular on the Web, with specialized readers now available from several special-purpose and format document packaging software programs. Probably the most popular document reader in use, and on the test, is Adobe Acrobat, which is used to create and view PDF documents.

- ✔ **SGML (Standard Generalized Markup Language):** This is a data type definition (DTD), or metalanguage, that defines how a language used to mark up a document, such as HTML, should do so. Panorama is a freebie SGML viewer for Windows.

There are too many different types of viewers, helper applications, and add-on modules for you to try to memorize each one and what it does. Your time will be better spent if you are familiar with the concept and function of browser viewers and helpers mentioned in this and the following sections. Browse over the list of viewers by type so that you can recognize a particular viewer's name and function should it appear on the exam.

Visit the Defense Sciences Engineering Division's Web site at the following URL to see and test most of the most popular viewers, readers, and add-on helper applications. If you do not have a particular viewer, you can download it to your system. This site lists each viewer by type, along with a test to demonstrate or display its function:

```
http://www-dsed.llnl.gov/documents/WWWtest.html
```

Using images to spruce up a site

Although the Web has quite a few really boring sites that contain only text, graphic images are used quite extensively to spruce up the Web. Still images are a large part of what makes up a Web document; they're included to decorate, illustrate, and very often to provide a linkage to other documents or images. I don't want to get into any qualitative judgements here — after all, beauty is in the eyes of the person looking at your Web pages. What you need to know is that graphics can be embedded in a Web document, and your choices for the graphics file format are fairly limited.

Generally, Web browsers contain viewers for only the GIF (Graphics Interchange Format) and JPEG (Joint Photographers Expert Group) formats. Other graphic types can be displayed using the appropriate viewer. Here are some of the more commonly used graphic types (see Chapter 11 for more information on both graphic and audio file formats):

- ✔ **GIF:** This format has become one of the two de facto standard image formats. GIF viewers are built into most browsers.

- ✔ **JPEG:** This format is the other de facto standard for images. Like the GIF, nearly all browsers include a JPEG viewer.

- ✔ **TIFF (Tag Image File Format):** This type of graphic file is commonly used in desktop publishing, faxing, 3-D applications, and medical imaging applications. TIFF files can be displayed with a helper application, such as Paint Shop Pro or LView.

- ✔ **CGM (Computer Graphic Metafile):** This type of graphic image file is used to display vector graphics. CGM's commonly used viewers are Ralcgm and ulview.

- ✔ **PNG (Portable Network Graphic):** PNG is an approved graphic standard by the World Wide Web consortium to replace GIF. The most popular browsers support the PNG graphic format with a built-in viewer.

Sounding out a better page

Sound is becoming a common part of the Web page sensory experience. Unfortunately, I believe that in way too many cases, sound is added to a page only because it can be. I guess for many people, a toy piano version of "Smoke on the Water" or an over-synthesized Scott Joplin rag really adds that something special to the experience and overall effectiveness of any personal Web page.

Several common audio file formats are used on the Web, and each has its own particular viewer (hearer?) or helper application:

- ✔ **MP2 and MP3 (Motion Picture Layer 2 and 3, respectively):** Although developed as a multimedia format, they are also used to store and play back sound only. MP3 files are small and can be easily transferred over the Internet. This file format requires that a browser plug-in be downloaded, such as the Microsoft Media Player or Real's RealJukebox.

- ✔ **RA (Real Audio):** This sound format creates near FM-stereo quality sound. RA files require an add-on player (also called a plug-in), such as the older RealAudio or the newer RealPlayer. Support for RealAudio files is built into the most popular browsers.

- ✔ **WAV (Windows Audio/Visual):** The helpers for audio, and video, files are also called players. The player for WAV files is available in most of the popular browsers. WAV files must be completely downloaded before they can be played back.

Other audio formats used on the Web include:

- ✔ **AU (Audio):** This is the most common file format for sound files on UNIX computers and in Java programs.

- ✔ **AIFF (Audio Interchange File Format):** The sampled sound standard for Macintosh computers. Files in this format also use the AIF and IEF file extensions. AIFF files are not compressed and can be quite large.

Taking action on a Web page

There are essentially two basic types of actions on a Web page: the action of passing data among elements of the page and the *interaction* of the user (viewer) with the interactive elements of the page.

There are a variety of ways to pass data between elements of a page or between the user and a server, but the two you need to know are:

- ✔ **CGI (Common Gateway Interface):** A program that transfers data between a Web server and the user. A very common type of CGI element is a form on a Web page, which uses a CGI program to process the data when the user clicks on the submit button. Many different programming languages can be used to create CGI programs, including C, Perl, Java, or Visual Basic.

- ✔ **Java and Javascript:** Portable pieces (objects) of programming that are downloaded to perform part, or all, of an application. Javascript elements provide many of the mouse-over effects that are becoming quite popular on Web pages. Java programs, called applets (which don't come in a box with other candied fruit — this term refers to small applications), are used for a growing variety of user-program interactions.

You shouldn't confuse CGI with Java or Javascript elements, which are client-side elements that are downloaded and executed on the viewer's computer. CGI elements are strictly server-side programs that run on the Web site's server.

Including multimedia in a Web page is a dramatic way to really sell an idea or product, or to just entertain the reader, provided the reader has the proper viewer. This is one of those awkward semantic moments that occur frequently in the computing world: *Reader,* as used here, means the person looking at the Web site, as opposed to the software used to view or display the page. Check out Chapter 11 for some additional information on multimedia.

Be sure when you encounter words like "reader" or "viewer" on the exam, that you take the time to understand how it is being used.

Multimedia combines multiple media (Wow, Captain Obvious) into a single file for simultaneous playback. There are really no rules dictating that multimedia must include video or animation, or that music or narrative must be included. *Multimedia* simply means that more than one form or media has been combined into a single playback.

Here are the multimedia formats you are likely to see on the i-Net+ exam:

- ✔ **AVI (Audio Video Interleave):** This file format was originally developed on Microsoft's Video for Windows standard. Because an AVI file does not require any special playback hardware, it is commonly used to provide multimedia objects to a wide range of users.

- ✔ **MPEG (Moving Picture Experts Group):** Generally a better-quality video than AVI and other competing formats, such as Indeo and QuickTime. MPEG files, which are highly compressed, store only the changes in the image between frames, rather than the whole frame itself. MPEG files are decoded with special hardware or, more commonly, software.

- ✔ **QuickTime:** An audio/video recording and playback system developed by Apple Computer that is built into the Macintosh operating system. QuickTime is also available for the PC using a plug-in "driver.html" helper application.

- ✔ **Flash and Shockwave:** These two Macromedia tools are used to create flashy, compact interactive and animated elements for Web pages. Flash objects, which are created using Flash drawing tools or from imported vector graphics, include navigation interfaces, technical illustrations, long-form animations, and more. Shockwave embeds multimedia objects in a Web page that can only be viewed with a plug-in browser.

Virtually amazing

Although widespread popularity for virtual reality probably still lies in the future, a wide array of virtual reality worlds are available for your viewing pleasure and amazement on the Web. These "worlds" are created within a programming (actually, a modeling) language called VRML (Virtual Reality Modeling Language). Viewing a VRML world enables you to view an object from all sides or move about a simulated world as if you were virtually one with it, and of course requires specialized viewers. Some of the more popular VRML viewers are Quicktime VR, CC Pro, Cosmo Player, WebFX, WorldView, and Fountain, for Windows computers, and Whurlwind and Voyager for the Macintosh.

For more information on VRML and to download a viewer, visit
`www.vrml.org`.

Saving with the large economy sizes

I am including a brief discussion on universal clients and all-in-one browsers because these topics appear in the list of objectives for the i-Net+ exam. Today, all the popular browsers almost qualify as universal clients, in that they contain pretty much all the protocols, readers, and add-on applications you need to view the majority of content on the Web. Back in 1996, a lot of trade magazine columns were devoting space to the pie-in-the-sky notion that someday, browser clients would encompass and come preloaded with all the software you need to access the Web, without the need to download a helper application every time you started a download.

Today's browsers are not quite universal or all-in-one clients in that the viewers packaged in the browser must be restricted to those absolutely needed by the majority of Web pages to keep the size reasonable and performance fast. But, maybe someday, in the hopefully not too distant future . . . .

Tools for the Really Important Stuff

For the i-Net+ exam, you need to know the various tools — in the form of protocols and technologies — that are used to move data across the Internet. These tools include MIME, which is used to encode document attachments so they can travel safely over the Net, and FTP, which is used to transfer entire documents between computers, the various e-mail protocols that move electronic mail messages across the Internet and to your computer, and ICQ, which is used for online Web chats.

What's MIME is yours

You really need to know what MIME is for the i-Net+ exam. No, this doesn't mean you paint your face white and pretend to be trapped in an invisible box or pull on a non-existent rope; it means you need to understand that MIME (Multi-Purpose Internet Mail Extensions) is no longer just an e-mail protocol. MIME is now used to exchange many different types of file formats over the Internet, including audio, video, images, and application programs, as well as ASCII data in e-mail messages. MIME is an extension of the SMTP (Simple Mail Transport Protocol) and enables Web clients and servers to detect and transfer data other than the straight ASCII data of a typical e-mail file.

Here's how it works:

1. A server places a MIME header at the front of a Web document being transmitted.

2. The client receiving the document uses the header to apply the appropriate viewer for the type of data indicated in the header.

Moving the big stuff around

Sometimes it makes more sense to transfer files over the Internet intact, straight from one computer to another, without interpreting their contents. Uploading a new Web page file from a desktop computer to a Web server does not require that the HTML code in the file be analyzed, it is only necessary to move the file from one computer to another. For this task, an FTP (File Transfer Protocol) client works very nicely.

FTP: Moving up and down the Internet

FTP is a TCP/IP protocol used to download and upload files over the Internet and the Web. This is the most commonly used protocol for downloading or uploading files via the Internet. *Downloading* refers to the process of transferring files from another computer down to your computer, and *uploading* refers to copying a file from your computer up to a server or host system.

Unlike HTTP, the primary protocol of the World Wide Web, FTP does not require a file to be in any particular format or structure to be transferred. FTP transfers any kind of file, including text, images, application-specific (like Word, Excel, and so on), compressed or bundled files, and programs. FTP does not care what the file format is; the file will be transferred intact. An FTP client is included in most browsers, but only a few also contain an upload feature.

Serving your clients

FTP is composed of two parts: the FTP client and the FTP server. The *FTP client* is the software running on your local computer that you use to receive or send files. The *FTP server* is the software running on the remote host (server) computer processing your requests. All of the more popular Web browser software packages (such as Microsoft Internet Explorer, Netscape Navigator, and Opera) have embedded FTP clients.

To ensure that a file arrives intact with all of its parts, FTP clients and servers actually carry on a dialog. The details of the dialog aren't important for the i-Net+ exam, but two of the major commands of this dialog are. The key command sent from an FTP client to an FTP server to download a file is `get`. The command used to upload a file is `put`.

Using the best mode for the best results

There are also a number of dedicated FTP clients that can be used to move files up and down the Internet, including BulletProof, CUTE, Fetch, and WS-FTP. An important part of using a dedicated FTP client is ensuring the appropriate transfer mode is used for the down or upload.

Files are transferred using one of three transfer mode settings:

- ✔ **ASCII transfer mode:** Effective for transferring text files.

- ✔ **Binary transfer mode:** Transfers non-text files, including executable programs, word processing documents, spreadsheets, databases, graphics and sound files, and the like.

- ✔ **Auto Detect transfer mode:** Transfers a file using Binary mode unless the file's extension is listed in an extensions list. If the file extension is listed, the file is transferred in ASCII mode. Whatever you enter into the list will be compared to the files you select to transfer using the Auto Detect mode. Extension samples are .LST, .TXT, .ME, README, and TEXT.BETA.

Trivial, but not just for small files

TFTP (Trivial File Transfer Protocol) is an alternative to regular FTP; you know — the non-trivial one. TFTP is simpler than FTP, but it is also less capable. TFTP can be used when some of the security requirements of FTP are not necessary, such as user authentication and directory visibility.

One other distinction you may want to note is that TFTP uses UDP (the User Datagram Protocol), and FTP uses TCP (the Transmission Control Protocol).

Sending messages over the Net

Sending Aunt Sally an e-mail across the Internet is a very simple proposition, no? Simply compose the message and click the Send button. "What?" you may ask, "You mean there's more to it?" Yes, there is, and you should know the process involved and the protocols used for the i-Net+ exam.

Simplifying e-mail

The primary protocol and servers used to get an e-mail message over to dear old Aunt Sally are:

- ✔ **IMAP4 (Internet Mail Addressing Protocol):** A mail server that holds incoming e-mail messages until the addressee logs on to the server, when the messages are uploaded to the addressee's computer and retained on the server, or not, at the user's discretion. IMAP has much more capability than the simpler POP3; it can archive messages in folders, share mailboxes, and allow a user to access multiple mail accounts. Stop wondering about the 4 — it is only the latest version.

✔ **POP3 (Post Office Protocol 3):** A mail server commonly used on the Internet. Forget about the 3; don't think about it; blot it out of your mind; it is totally unimportant! A POP3 mail server stores incoming e-mail messages until the addressee logs on to the server, at which point it uploads the messages to the user's computer and removes them from the message store.

✔ **SMTP (Simple Mail Transfer Protocol):** The TCP/IP protocol for sending and receiving e-mail. SMTP defines both the e-mail message format and the message transfer agent (MTA), which is the tool used to store and forward e-mail messages. SMTP is commonly used along with either the POP3 or the IMAP protocol to overcome its inability to queue received messages. Although designed to carry only text messages, MIME and other encoding schemes are used to attach documents, graphics, and program files to e-mail messages.

Notice in these three e-mail tools that SMTP is the protocol that carries e-mail messages across the Internet and that both IMAP and POP are mail servers that accept SMTP messages and their attachments and store them for the recipient.

ICQ and you seek me

ICQ (which stands for I Seek You) is an Internet conferencing program developed in Israel that has become the standard tool for interactive chat over the Internet. ICQ also provides for e-mail and file transfers, and scans the Internet and lets you know when a friend, relative, or somebody from your buddy list is online so you can chat them up.

To use ICQ, you must first download an ICQ client and receive a user identification number (UIN), also called a chat ID number. ICQ also allows IRC (Internet Relay Chat) sessions for voice or video-voice interactions or to play games with other ICQ users.

Connecting to remote networks

Most TCP/IP protocols enable you to download files and access information on remote servers, but the Telnet protocol goes one better – it enables you to log on to a remote server, provided you have been given permission. Permission to log on to a remote computer usually comes in the form of an account name and a password. With these two keys, access to the Internet, and the Telnet protocol, a remote computer is virtually at your fingertips.

Telnet is a terminal emulation protocol commonly used over the Internet and other TCP/IP-based networks. It enables you to log on to a remote computer and pretty much do whatever a local user would.

Lab 7-1 shows you how to access a remote computer by using Telnet.

Lab 7-1	Using Telnet to Access a Remote Computer

1. **On a Windows computer, enter the Telnet command using the Run dialog box, as shown in Figure 7-2.**

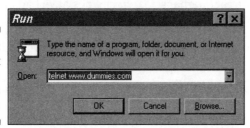

Figure 7-2:
Using Telnet
on a
Windows
computer.

The Telnet command is fairly simple in construction, as you can see in the following examples:

```
telnet www.dummies.com
telnet 172.16.100.1
```

Each of these Telnet commands connects you to a remote system, providing the remote system accepts remote log on requests. Just to save you the time, these sites are not actual telnet sites.

2. **If you were able to connect to the remote computer, you are presented with a logon request at which you can enter your prearranged account name and password.**

Provided you enter the proper account name and password, you now have the full run of the remote computer, or at least as much as its administrator has allowed you.

Why would you use Telnet? This protocol is used most often by programmers and system administrators who are setting up or maintaining a remote computer, or by users who need to access a particular application on a particular computer.

The Never-Ending Search For . . .

Before the search engine as it exists on the Web today, finding something on the Internet involved first-hand knowledge of where it might actually be and being on a first-name basis with Archie, Jughead, Veronica, and the rest of the gang.

Different search tools for different searches

Today's search engines, or *search indexes* as they are officially called, are powerful tools. The amount of content available on the Web is mind boggling, and the case can be made that perhaps search engines have had more than a minor role in the explosive growth of the Internet and the Web. Do you think you would continue to use a resource on which you could not reliably find and access the information you need? Of course not — that would be too much like finding something on my desk, and who needs that?

There are essentially three different types of search engines available for use:

- ✔ **Full text index:** This type of search engine is typically used in situations where entire text documents have been archived on a network, whether it be on the Internet or an intranet. The documents in the database are scanned to determine whether they contain any, or all, or even parts, of the words entered in the search criteria box. Legal databases, medical databases, and even university holdings often use this type of search tool to assist researchers.

- ✔ **Keyword index:** This is probably what most people think of as a search engine. Keyword indexes use creepy sounding programs like worms, crawlers, and spiders that move about the Web gathering keyword data from Web sites. Different indexes gather different data from Web sites. Some gather the meta keywords (hence their name), but others gather text from the page title or from the body of the page. People have tried to gain an advantage in the index by repeating keywords, and even including popular search words in their meta tags that have nothing to do with their Web page at all.

- ✔ **Static catalog index:** This type of search engine is really just a catalog of sites that have been submitted to it by users. The cataloged sites are sorted into preset categories or subjects that are arranged in a hierarchy, which is why catalog indexes are also called site maps. Probably the most popular of this type of search engine are Yahoo!, Magellan, and LookSmart.

Some search engines use the databases of other search engines to find URLs matching the search request, such as MetaCrawler and Dog Pile. Table 7-1 lists the more popular search engines and indexes.

Table 7-1	Popular Search Engines and Indexes	
Name	**Type**	**URL**
Alta Vista	Keyword index	www.altavista.com
Excite	Keyword index	www.excite.com
LookSmart	Catalog index	www.looksmart.com
Lycos	Keyword index	www.lycos.com
Magellan	Catalog index	www.magellan.excite.com
Web Crawler	Keyword index	www.webcrawler.com
Yahoo!	Catalog index	www.yahoo.com

Finding the data you want

What you include in the phrase you entered into the search engine's search criteria box has a direct bearing on how efficiently you find the information you are seeking. The following are some tips on how to locate the most specific information available:

1. Use what is called natural language, which means typing in the exact question you want answered. For example, if I want to locate information on holidays, I might enter: "Do they have a Fourth of July in England?"

2. To locate Web pages that contain an exact phrase or combination of words, enter the phrase or words in quotes, such as "Walla Walla Sweets."

3. Include a plus (+) or minus (-) sign to indicate whether you want to limit the search to specific references within your topic or exclude specific references from the information found. For example, if you wish to find information on buffalo, you might enter "buffalo+bison-Bills" to find information on buffalo, especially bison, excluding the professional football team in Buffalo.

4. You may also use an asterisk wildcard to indicate you wish to include any letter combinations that include the letters preceding it. For example, to find information on auto, autos, automobiles, and automatic, you could enter "auto*." The problem with using a wildcard is that you may find more variations of word parts than you expected.

An excellent site for learning more about improving your search phrases is the help pages of the AltaVista search engine at http://doc.altavista .com/help/search/search_help.shtml.

To Cookie, or Not to Cookie; That Is the Question

Either you love cookies or you hate them. The only people that don't feel one way or the other about cookies probably don't know what they are or what they do. I'm not talking snicker-doodles here; I'm talking about Web cookies. For the i-Net+ exam, you need to know what a cookie is, what's good and bad about it, and how and why you would set a cookie.

Baking up a new batch

A *cookie* is a small file of information that a Web server sends to a Web browser to be stored on the local computer, so that it can later be accessed and read from that computer through the browser. In other words, a cookie is information stored on your computer by your browser following instructions from a remote Web server.

Like the crumbs from Hansel and Gretel's cookie (or whatever it was), a cookie leaves an information trail that can be used later for a number of purposes, some of which are actually useful:

✔ Remembering a password and user ID

✔ Storing preferences for start pages and other personalized displays

✔ Buffering online transactions

✔ Tracking which part of a Web site readers are accessing or not

✔ Building reader profiles for likes and dislikes to target on-screen advertising

There are no bad cookies; only misunderstood ones

Depending mostly on your role in the use of a cookie, that of the cookie-*er* or the cookie-*ee*, your view of whether a cookie is a good thing or a bad thing can vary.

From the server's perspective (in other words, that of the company placing the cookie), the cookie can provide the user a better experience on a Web site by collecting information about what the user clicks on, spends time viewing, interacts with, or types in a form. The information in the cookie can be used to dynamically alter a Web page's display to suit the needs, tastes, and preferences of the viewer. Cookies can also remember passwords or data entered into a form. Why would anyone object to such personal service?

From the client's perspective (that of the person surfing the Web), taking down information about you so it can be used to alter your experience may seem way too much like Big Brother looking over your shoulder while you participate in what you thought was anarchy at play. Remembering your password on a controlled access site is one thing, but to show you underwear ads each time you visit is quite another. Especially since you really didn't mean to click on that pink negligee in the first place.

The debate of good versus bad will continue, with both sides being both right and not-so-right at the same time. Just about every browser includes a mechanism for turning off cookies, but you will miss the good with the bad. Here's a really great site with information all about cookies of the Web kind:

```
http://www.cookiecentral.com/
```

And here's another really great cookie site:

```
http://www.cookierecipe.com/
```

The inner workings of a cookie

If you are designing a Web site and want to be able to differentiate between hits, you could set a cookie on each visitor. This would enable you to tell 25 separate users from a single person that visited 25 times. Adding a series of statements to your HMTL code and setting the values accordingly can set up this action for each visitor to your Web page. Here is a generic example of the script you would add to your document:

```
Set-Cookie: NAME=VALUE; expires=DATE; path=PATH;
            domain=DOMAIN_NAME; secure
```

A cookie is normally set or read with a CGI script, but a Javascript statement can also manipulate it.

For the i-Net+ exam, you need to know only one of the elements in the Set-Cookie script: the expiration date. The date that a cookie expires is a Greenwich Mean Time (GMT) time and date string that specifies the date or minute that the cookie expires.

If no expiration date is specified for a cookie, it expires at the end of the Web browser session. This means that a cookie without a specific expiration date is deleted when you close your browser software.

Debunking the myths

Here are some things a cookie can be used for:

- Storing or accessing information placed on your hard disk by your browser
- Tracking your navigation on a Web site
- Remembering information entered into a form, such as a request for information or a shopping cart in case of an interruption

And here are things a cookie cannot do:

- Access data from your hard drive
- Get your e-mail address
- Steal sensitive information about you, such as your address, shirt size, birthday, or phone number

Breaking the cookie

Browsers are generally set up to allow cookies, but you can change the browser's settings to ask you before accepting a cookie, accept cookies only from trusted sites, or to just say no to all cookies — something I have always had trouble doing.

Figure 7-3 illustrates the cookie options that you can set in Internet Explorer. Netscape Navigator, and nearly all other browsers, have similar settings to control how cookies are handled in your browser.

Browsers include the ability to limit the amount of space cookes can use on your hard disk. For example, Netscape Communicator limits the number of total cookies that can be stored on your hard disk to 300. When number 301 arrives to be stored, the least-used cookie will be deleted to open a spot. Internet Explorer places cookies into the Temporary Internet Files folder on your hard disk. You control how much of your total disk can be used for this temporary file, up to the total size of your hard disk. The default value for the size of this folder is 2% of your hard drive. When this fills, once again the least-used cookies are deleted to make space for the new entries.

Cookies range in size from 50 to 150 bytes in length.

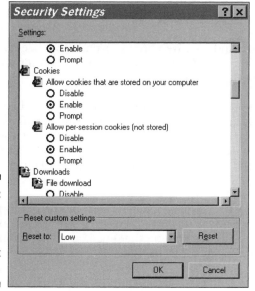

Figure 7-3:
Setting
cookie
options in
Internet
Explorer.

The Up- and Downsides of Upgrading Clients

Keeping your Web server and clients up to date with the latest releases and versions of the software in use ensures that your site and its visitors can experience the fullest browsing experience using the latest technology. On the other hand, not every piece of software is always completely compatible with every other piece of software. Walking the tightrope between updating and the possible disruptions that can be caused requires careful preparation and planning.

Getting help before you need it

If you search on the Web and in the newsgroups, you can find several cautions and error reports that relate how loading one version of a software tool can cause another unrelated piece of software to malfunction or even stop running altogether. One example of this from the past is that after Netscape 3.5 was loaded on a computer that had been running the Eudora e-mail client, the Eudora software would no longer function.

Vendor sites can be a very good source of potential installation problems and troubleshooting tips. Newsgroups that focus on a particular software application are good places to check out before proceeding with your installation. If you are in a large city, you may even find user groups for certain Web server based applications, such as Cold Fusion, IIS, and Apache.

Proceeding with caution

To avoid problems when updating Web browsers and other client software, it is recommended that you turn off your anti-virus protection software until after you have installed the update.

To have the very latest in Web page technology on your Web site may seem very cool, but if nobody can read it or if the viewer or helper application is not readily available, you may have just chased everyone away from your site. You need to ensure that your Web pages remain compatible with the audience for which they are intended and the browsers and other tools your readers may be using.

I recommend that you test all updates and new software on a computer other than your Web server before taking it live. The test server should duplicate the active server as much as possible, so that you know whether an update or installation is safe and ready for prime time.

Prep Test

1 Which of the following are characteristics of a browser? (Choose all that apply.)

A ❑ Functions as a client

B ❑ Uses HTTP

C ❑ Interprets DDL

D ❑ Supports hypertext

2 Which of the following are not components of a URL? (Choose two.)

A ❑ The transfer protocol

B ❑ The client computer's FQDN

C ❑ Document filename reference

D ❑ IP address of target document

3 Common names for the tools used by and with browsers to display Web page components include which of the following? (Choose all that apply.)

A ❑ Reader

B ❑ Viewer

C ❑ Helper application

D ❑ Plug-in application

E ❑ Browser add-on

F ❑ Applet

4 The language used to create three-dimensional worlds on the Web is _____.

A ○ HTML

B ○ XML

C ○ VRML

D ○ DHTML

5 The acronym MIME refers to _____.

A ○ Mail Internet Message Exchange

B ○ Multi-purpose Internet Mail Extensions

C ○ Multi-purpose Internet Message Exchange

D ○ Mail Interchange Message Extensions

6 Transferring a file from your local computer over the Internet to a remote computer is called _____.

A ○ Uploading

B ○ Downloading

C ○ File transfer

D ○ MIME

7 The mail server that transfers mail messages to the user's computer and then removes them from the mailbox is _____.

A ○ PPP

B ○ IMAP

C ○ SMTP

D ○ POP3

8 The type of search engine that creates a database of data taken from the meta tags of documents on the Web is a(n) _____.

A ○ Catalog index

B ○ Keyword index

C ○ Full-text index

D ○ All-in-one index

9 The small information file sent to a browser by a server to be stored on the local computer is a(n) _____.

A ○ Oreo

B ○ Cookie

C ○ Bookmark

D ○ Brownie

10 Which of the following are good sources for information on the effect of upgrading or installing software on a working Web server? (Choose all that apply.)

A ❑ Vendor Web site

B ❑ Newsgroups

C ❑ Search engine

D ❑ Other users

Answers

1 *A, B, and D.* A Web browser is a client application that uses HTTP to transfer HTML documents that are interconnected via hypertext coding across the Internet. DDL is a document description language and not a characteristic of a browser. *See "Why do they call it browsing?"*

2 *B and D.* Okay, so it is a trick question. The FQDN that is referenced in the URL is that of the server on which the document is located. The IP (Internet Protocol) address of the site can be used in the URL, but is typically not considered a part of it. *Check out "I think I'm going to URL."*

3 *A, B, C, D, E, and F.* Yes, all of these are names used for the software tools used with, by, and as a part of browsers to display components and objects embedded in or associated with Web pages. *Review "Taking in the view."*

4 *C.* The Virtual Reality Modeling Language (VRML) is used to create worlds on the Web that users can navigate as if they are a part of that world. *Take a look at "Virtually amazing."*

5 *B.* E-mail that is MIME-compliant is able to transfer file formats other than ASCII text in a message. If you have ever received one of those gobbledygook messages that go on forever, chances are the sending (or receiving) mail server is not MIME compatible. *See "What's MIME is yours."*

6 *A.* When you send a file up the Internet to another computer, you are uploading it. The reverse is when a server sends a file down the Internet to you, which is downloading. *Review "FTP: Moving up and down the Internet."*

7 *D.* POP mail pops up to your computer and then is removed from your mailbox on the server. IMAP, on the other hand, keeps your mail on the server, if that's what you want. *Check out "Simplifying e-mail."*

8 *B.* The meta tag that is sought out by the spider of a keyword index is the `Keyword=` tag. *Look over "The Never-Ending Search For . . . ."*

9 *B.* The cookie can be refused, or selectively accepted, depending on the settings indicated in the browser's setup. *See "To Cookie, or Not to Cookie; That Is the Question."*

10 *A, B, C, and D.* All of these choices can be excellent sources for information on a software upgrade or installation and its effect on your system. *Check out "The Up- and Downsides of Upgrading Clients."*

Chapter 8

Developing Internet Content

● ●

Exam Objectives

▶ Defining common Internet application programming terms

▶ Differentiating between client- and server-side programming languages

▶ Distinguishing between relational and non-relational databases

▶ Identifying the technologies used to integrate a database with a Web site

● ●

*W*eb sites exist for a purpose. In many cases, the purpose is not much more than: Everyone else has a Web page, so why shouldn't I? That's a purpose of sorts, I guess. To belong to the subculture of society that has a Web page is as much a reason to publish on the Internet as the Congress of the U.S. saying, "Me too!"

Regardless of the reason or purpose behind a Web site, it should say something beyond "Count me in." There should be a message — information that a visitor takes away and benefits from. To say that all Web sites do this is a very liberal definition of "information," but every Web site is just perfect for someone. Most Web sites are simple, made up of HTML documents that include some graphics and hypertext. However, a growing number of sites are beginning to develop the full potential of the Web by incorporating interactive user elements.

The best way to develop a Web site's purpose, objective, or mission is to provide meaningful content. In many cases, the purpose and message of a Web site can be developed and delivered using only limited HTML and a few animated GIFs. However, for a growing number of Web sites, this is not enough. Many sites require extensive development using application programming tools and database interfaces to deliver their message. These Web-borne magazines require the use of application development skills, and this is where the real Web developers are separated from the markup language pretenders.

As an Internet professional, you must know the tools and techniques used to develop Web sites. The i-Net+ exam measures your knowledge of the tools used to develop Web applications, including when to use a database and the role it plays in delivering content over the Internet and Web. In this chapter, I explain the Web site development topics you need to know for the i-Net+ exam.

Quick Assessment

Defining common Internet-application programming terms

1 _____ programs are the most commonly used Web application development standard.

2 The processing of the data entered into an HTML form begins when the user clicks the _____ button.

3 The two HTTP methods used to send HTML form data to a server are _____ and _____.

4 The acronym API stands for _____ _____ _____.

5 The two ways that library modules can be linked into a program are _____ linking and _____ linking.

Differentiating between client- and server-side programming languages

6 _____ scripts run on a user's computer and not a server.

7 _____ is a programming language that is interpreted and executed on the server.

Distinguishing between relational and non-relational databases

8 _____ databases are the most common type used with Web applications.

Identifying the technologies used to integrate a database with a Web site

9 The most commonly used language for retrieving data from a database in a Web application is _____.

10 _____ is the set of standard database APIs used to interact with common databases.

Answers

1 *CGI.* See "Interfacing with functions."

2 *Submit.* Review "Processing user data."

3 *Get, Post.* Take a look at "Getting the post."

4 *Application Program Interface.* Check out "Interfacing with application programs."

5 *Dynamic, static.* Look over "Applying dynamics to your programming."

6 *Client-side.* See "Representing the client."

7 *Perl.* Review "Taking a walk on the server-side."

8 *Relational.* Check out "Relating to the database."

9 *SQL.* Take a look at "Interfacing with databases."

10 *ODBC.* See "Integrating a database into a Web site."

Internet Programming Basics

Most of what you see on the Web is the result of some fairly basic HTML coding. You don't need much in the way of special skills to produce a Web page with colored backgrounds, varied fonts, tables, horizontal rules, and a few other page effects. However, creating the really cool stuff — the interactive CGI, Shockwave, Java applets and full-blown database applications — requires both skill and special software, in the form of programming languages.

For the i-Net+ exam, you need to know some of the more common terminology of programming applications for the Web. Don't try to learn each of the programming languages or application development tools included in this section, instead just concentrate on understanding the terms presented, as well as how and when each would be used to develop an Internet or Web application.

Interfacing with functions

The programming language most commonly used to develop programs on the Web is CGI (Common Gateway Interface). Don't confuse this CGI with the Computer Graphics Interface, a language used to display and print graphics, or the Computer-Generated Image, which is a graphic created on a computer. The programming CGI — the one you need to know — is actually a standard or specification that defines how information is to be transferred between a Web server and a CGI program.

A CGI program is any program that accepts and sends data in a way that conforms to the CGI standard. Get it? Well, hang in there — you will. CGI programs can be written in virtually any programming language, but the most common languages used are C, Perl, Java, and Visual Basic.

CGI programs are in use all over the Web to interact with the data entered and the requests made by users. Each time you fill in a form on an HTML page, you are engaging in perhaps the most common use of a CGI program: processing the data entered into a form on an HTML page. When you click the submit (or however it is labeled) button on the page, the CGI program, normally called a CGI script, is started.

Processing the form

A CGI script must be able to read data from a standard input source (called STDIN in most programming languages), write output to a standard output (called STDOUT), and read and test variables set by HTTP (Hypertext Transfer Protocol) or other programs (referred to as environment variables). A program that can do these three functions is eligible to be placed in the special folder or directory reserved on a Web server for its CGI programs, usually named "cgi-bin."

A CGI script designed to process the data in an HTML page's form typically performs the following steps:

1. Reads the data the user has entered into the form (the STDIN, in this case).

2. Does tricks with the data.

3. Outputs the results or the response, as the case may be, in HTML format to whatever is designated as the STDOUT (in the case of a form, this is generally an e-mail message).

Processing user data

If you have never designed an HTML form, you should review Chapter 9 before continuing here. For those of you who have, and those of you too stubborn to read up on HTML forms, you should know that form elements, such as a TEXTAREA, a SELECT list, or an INPUT tag, have names assigned to them. When the user clicks the submit button on a form, the CGI script receives the data that the user entered as a series of name and value combinations. For instance, if you enter **John Doe** in the Name field of a form and then click the submit button, the following data string is passed to the CGI script:

```
Name=John Doe
```

If form fields are also included for address and city, the CGI script receives the following data string:

```
Name=John+Doe&Address=123+Main+St&City=Reno
```

The script needs to *parse* (separate) the single long data string into its individual names and values.

Decoding the string

If you have ever noticed data included in a URL, you have seen data in what is called *URL-encoded* format. If you want to see what this looks like, just use a search engine and enter three or four words in the search criteria. All of those %hh characters (where the hh is some hexadecimal value) are included to enable you to use special characters, such as equal signs, percent signs, and plus signs, in your Web page address.

The reason I bring this up is because the data string passed to the CGI script is URL-encoded. Here is a sample data string:

```
Name=John+Doe&Address=123+Main+St&City=Reno
```

To *parse* (I love this macho programmer talk) this string, you would do the following:

1. Split the fields on the ampersand (&) characters.

2. Split the field name from the data value on the equal (=) sign.

3. Change all the plus (+) signs to spaces.

If the user included some special characters in the data, such as a number sign (#) in the address, you should scan the data strings for these characters, converting any %hh characters to their ASCII equivalents. For example, a %23 is a number (#) sign, and a %2D is a hyphen (-) or dash.

Getting the post

The CGI program gets the data string in one of two ways, depending on the HTTP method used with the submit button on the HTML page. The HTML code used to define a form is

```
<FORM ACTION="http://www.dummies.com/cgi-bin/get-put.cgi"
        METHOD="POST">
```

The following line signals the end of the form:

```
</FORM>
```

The two ways data can be sent to a CGI script are

- ✔ **POST:** This HTTP method sends the data string to the STDIN, where it can be read into the CGI script. The length of the entire data string is stored in the predefined environment variable CONTENT_LENGTH.

- ✔ **GET:** This HTTP method writes the entire data string into the environment variable QUERY_STRING. This method is recommended for short forms whose strings are not likely to be very long.

Responding to the user

After you have your way with the data, you may want to respond back to the user, just so he or she doesn't get impatient and click the submit button again. Whenever the user clicks the submit button, the entire process begins again as if it had never run in the first place.

Before you can send data to the STDOUT, you need to condition it to the type of data you will be sending. In most cases, you would send the following line and then a blank line, followed by the HTML page or message you want to send to the user:

```
Content-type: text/html
```

When the script ends, the message or page is sent to the user.

Knit one, Perl two . . .

The most common programming language used for CGI programs is Perl (Practical Extraction and Reporting Language). Perl is a programming language, very much like the C programming language in look and structure, that is well suited to the extraction and manipulation of text data.

Just for your information and to satisfy your curiosity about what a CGI program would look like, here is a sample Perl program. This script reads data from an HTML form and parses it as described in the "Decoding the string" section earlier in this chapter:

```perl
#!/usr/bin/perl
print "Content-type: text/html\n\n";
read(STDIN,$input,$ENV{'CONTENT_LENGTH'})
foreach (split(/&/, $input))
{
    ($NAME, $VALUE) = split(/=/, $_);
    $NAME =~ s/\+/ /g;
    $NAME =~ s/%([0-9|A-F]{2})/pack(C,hex($1))/eg;
    $VALUE =~ s/\+/ /g;
    $VALUE =~ s/%([0-9|A-F]{2})/pack(C,hex($1))/eg;
    print "$NAME : $VALUE <BR>\n";
}
foreach (split(/&/, $input))
{
    ($NAME, $VALUE) = split(/=/, $_);
    $NAME =~ s/\+/ /g;
    $NAME =~ s/%([0-9|A-F]{2})/pack(C,hex($1))/eg;
    $VALUE =~ s/\+/ /g;
    $VALUE =~ s/%([0-9|A-F]{2})/pack(C,hex($1))/eg;
    print "$NAME : $VALUE <BR>\n";
}
```

Don't worry about memorizing this program and its commands. For the i-Net+ exam, you should know the concepts of how the HTTP methods are used to direct a CGI script or program to process the data from an HTML form. Chapter 9 covers the elements of designing a form in more detail.

Interfacing with application programs

Back when I had to walk uphill both ways to the computer room, barefoot, through the snow, and under the back-breaking burden of my card deck, programmers had to write their own interfaces to input and output devices and the operating system. Today's programmers have it made. They can use any number of API (application program interface) modules. APIs predefine the interactions between programs and the operating system in order to accomplish specific types of tasks. Much like a protocol defines the rules of a certain type of communications, an API defines the specific ways in which an application program can interact with the operating system, another application program, or certain input and output devices. For example, if you wished to create the new definitive e-mail reader, all of the routines, icons, objects, and data types you need are included in the Mail Application Program Interface (MAPI).

An API is made up primarily of DLLs (Dynamic Link Libraries) which can be linked to programs to take advantage of its library of existing functions and procedures.

MAPI, SAPI, TAPI, NSAPI, ISAPI, Happy, and Sneezy

For the i-Net+ exam, you need to know the role an API plays in the development and function of an application program. In particular, you should be familiar with the APIs used with application programs that run or interface with the Internet and the Web. Specifically, you should know about the following APIs:

- ✔ **ISAPI (Internet Server API):** Designed by Microsoft, this is a high-performance interface for Web server applications that can be used in place of CGI for interactive applications.
- ✔ **MAPI (Messaging Application Program Interface):** This API contains program objects that enable an application program to open a mail client to send e-mail or attach a document to an e-mail message.
- ✔ **NSAPI (Netscape Server API):** The Netscape version of the ISAPI, which support applications running on a Netscape Web server.
- ✔ **SAPI (Server Application Program Interface):** This API contains objects to help a programmer interact with a Web server.
- ✔ **TAPI (Telephony API):** This program interface includes the objects that an application program can use to let a user talk over a telephone or a video phone to someone anywhere in the Internet world.

Applying dynamics to your programming

When writing programs for the Internet, you must decide on the approach you want to use for including standard functions in your program. You have the choice of linking library elements into your program using either a dynamic or a static approach.

Before I go on, let me stop and briefly define *library elements* to you. This is not essential knowledge for the test, but it may help you understand *dynamic linking* and *static linking,* which are. If you have ever used Microsoft Word, Excel, or any other of the Microsoft Office applications, you have witnessed first hand the use of dynamic program elements. As shown in Figure 8-1, when you save a file in any of these applications, the same dynamic program, in the form of the Save As dialog box, is used. This dynamic program is actually a small program stored in a special file called a *dynamic link library* (DLL).

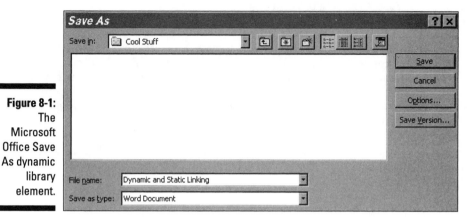

DLL files are usually grouped together in an API. Each DLL is a set of small programs that can be used with your application program to accomplish a specific task. DLLs are also found outside of APIs. If you were to search the hard disk of your Windows computer, you would certainly find a few DLL files not in an API.

DLLs are program objects that can be called by an application program when their particular function is needed in the program. They are not actually a part of the application program. They are instead a ready resource available to be plugged in if and when needed. For example, when Microsoft Excel wants to print or save a file, the particular DLL used to print or save files is called, loaded to RAM, and executed. The action of calling dynamic libraries when they are needed is referred to as *dynamic linking,* something you need to know for the exam.

Remaining static and inflexible

Another, and much older, way to create an application program is to build library routines right into the program at the time it is compiled — that is, when it is converted from human-readable text to computer-readable binary code. This is called *static linking.*

The good side of static linking is that you know exactly what your program will do. A statically linked program is not dependent that the correct version of a DLL is loaded on some unknown computer that downloads it. The problem with static linking is that you can never be absolutely sure that all the routines you have included in your program will be compatible with every system. On the Internet, there is no way to know what kind of hardware or operating system a program will encounter. Another problem is that statically linking runtime functions into your program can increase its size, which can cause download delays.

Programming from All Sides

Just like there are two sides to every story, there are two sides to Internet programming: the client-side and the server-side. Generally, application programs run on the client-side, but some do run on the server-side as well, such as a CGI script. Briefly, client-side programming runs on the client, and server-side programming runs on the server; this may sound obvious, but you need to know this!

As a programmer deciding which approach to use in developing a Web application, you must consider a number of different aspects of the finished product:

- The size of the program
- The number of processing steps or calculations involved
- The amount, format, and location of the data to be accessed
- The security required

If the size of the program is small, requiring few steps on data entered directly by the users, chances are that a client-side interpreted language, such as JavaScript, is suitable. However, if the data is retrieved from a remote server database, and security is a concern for both the data and the program's code, then a server-side compiled solution may be a better choice. One note: Remember that client-side scripts are available to anyone who displays the source of your HTML page.

If you are unfamiliar with programming Web applications, Bilkent University in Turkey hosts this excellent site:

```
http://stars.bilkent.edu.tr/
```

Representing the client

Client-side programming, or *scripting* as it is commonly called, requires creating programs (scripts) that run on the user's computer and not on a server. You can use various programming languages for client-side programming:

- **Java:** A programming language that was specifically developed by Sun Microsystems for use on the Internet. Java is very much like the C++ language, but advertised as simpler to use. Java applications can run on a single computer or be spread over several clients on a network. Java programs are portable and can be run on any computer that supports its virtual machine, or client software. Java is being used to develop interactive business applications that can be distributed over the Internet and executed locally on the client. Java is also used to create small programs, called *applets,* that can be embedded in Web pages for true client-side programming. Visit the following site for more information on Java programming:

```
http://java.sun.com/
```

✔ **JavaScript:** This scripting language was developed by Netscape. Don't confuse it with Java. JavaScript scripts are embedded in HTML documents, like Java applets, but they are interpreted only when invoked by the HTML code or the user. They are useful for shorter interactions and Web page effects, such as changing the date on a Web page, changing text or graphics when the mouse is moved over it, or calculating the total on a simple shopping cart form. Visit this URL for more information on JavaScript programming:

```
http://www.javascript.com/
```

✔ **VRML (Virtual Reality Modeling Language):** This programming language is used to define three-dimensional worlds for distribution over the Internet. Like Java, it requires client software to run. For more information on VRML, visit this URL:

```
http://www.vrmlsite.com/
```

✔ **VBScript and JScript:** Developed by Microsoft to compete with JavaScript, these two scripting languages must have client-side interpreters to run. They are both designed to work with Internet Explorer and are not supported by all other browsers. For more information on these scripting languages, visit the following site:

```
http://msdn.microsoft.com/scripting/
```

✔ **XML (Extensible Markup Language):** This is an emerging standard to be used as a way to structure data so that it can be compared, shared, or updated easily from browsers. XML is similar to HTML and uses markup symbols to structure data. However, XML's markup symbols are more descriptive. For example, a telephone number field would be defined with `<PHONENUM>` and `</PHONENUM>`. This allows for intelligent interactions with downloaded data, perhaps even dialing the telephone number. For more information on XML, visit this site:

```
http://www.xml.com/
```

Taking a walk on the server-side

Some programming languages create programs to run on the server either interactively with the user or prior to being uploaded to a client. For example, a CGI program written in Perl or C++ is interpreted and then compiled on the server before its object code is made available to the client for use. A Java application runs on a server and interacts with applets running on the client. As I discuss in the "Programming from All Sides" section earlier in this chapter, the scope, data requirements, or security of the application may deem it better to run from the server-side.

Some of the server-side programming languages you need to be familiar with include

- ✔ **Java:** Java programs can be compiled into what is called *byte-code* and can be executed either on the client or the server. Java Server Page (JSP) is a newer technology from Sun Microsystems that uses *servlets,* small programs that run on the Web server to control and structure a Web page before it is sent to the client.

- ✔ **Perl:** Perl is a server-side programming language that must be interpreted, compiled into either C or byte-code, and then executed on the server. The client interacts with the program running on the server. Because of its excellent text handing ability, Perl is a good choice for CGI applications.

- ✔ **C and C++:** C is a very powerful language used for the creation of large system software modules and operating systems. On the Internet, the C++ language, which is a superset of the C language, is very popular for creating large-scale server-side application programs too large to run on a client.

- ✔ **Visual Basic and Active X:** Visual Basic's easy-to-use GUI approach to creating applications and its expanding library of client-side controls make it very popular as a Web application development tool. Visual Basic can be used, as well as C++ and other programming languages, to create ActiveX controls, which are similar in form to Java applets.

- ✔ **ASP (Active Server Pages):** An ASP page is an HTML page with one or more small programs embedded in it. The embedded programs are pre-processed on a server before the entire page is sent to the client. ASP is a feature of the Microsoft Internet Information Server (IIS). Because an ASP page is built in standard HTML code, ASP pages are compatible with virtually all browsers, while some browsers have trouble with Java, Perl, and ActiveX.

It is far more important to remember which programming languages and technologies are client-side and which are server-side than to remember their specific functions and capabilities.

Including server-side includes

One server-side technology that you need to know about is called a *server-side include (SSI)*. An SSI functions like a limited form of a CGI application in which the CGI program is not used. Instead, the server uses only the application's CGI environment variables and responds to include statements in an HTML document to insert the value of each requested variable. The list of available environmental variables is maintained by the Web server's administrator, usually in a file with a .shtml suffix.

Server-side includes can be used for a variety of small applications, ranging from simple counters, displaying the current time, a rotating banner, or adjusting the content shown to correspond to the type of browser in use.

Extending FrontPage

One last server-side technology I want to cover for you is FrontPage Server Extensions. This is a set of programs loaded on a Web server to support the administration and browsing of a page created with Microsoft's FrontPage Web site development software. *Extensions* are additional server-side programming — primarily CGI applications and the library of Internet Server API (ISAPI) — that extend the capabilities of an HTML page created with FrontPage.

Working with Databases

To a Web programmer, there are essentially two types of databases: relational and non-relational. For the i-Net+ exam, you are expected to have some knowledge of relational databases, when you would employ one with a Web page, how a database is integrated into a Web page, and the tools that would be used to do so.

Tracing the database family tree

First, the easy one: In a *non-relational database,* none of the data is directly related to any other data. No test has been applied to see if the data in each record relates directly to the other data elements in the record. The database designer supplies any relationships in the database.

The most common form of non-relational database is a *hierarchical database.* The records in a hierarchical database are physically related in a parent-to-child manner. Each child record has at least one parent record and also has the ability to become a parent itself to other child records, just like in real life.

Hierarchical databases, and any other non-relational databases, are limited in their ability to respond to inquiries and data requests that draw on more than one data "family." Because the data itself is not related, it is difficult to tie different hierarchical trees together to present specific information. In a family tree application, an example which is naturally well-suited to this type of database, if you wanted to know how many of your ancestors on all sides of your family tree had brown eyes, you would have to traverse the trees and read each hierarchical record to test the eye color. Just a mite too input/output (I/O) intensive for a Web application. As I explain a bit later in this chapter, the relational database handles this same application very nicely.

Relating to the database

Relational databases are the most common type of database used in Web applications and the ones you'll be asked about on the test. You will read that in a relational database the data is related. Yes, I know this sounds somewhat obvious, but it is also just a little misleading as well. First of all, the term *relational* comes from some egghead math term having to do with the algorithms used to organize the data in the database. Secondly, any one data field is only related directly to the other data fields that make up its *table* (the database term for file) and *rows* (the database term for record; rows make up tables).

I don't want to go into the entire explanation of how relational databases work and what you should do to properly design and implement one — that is an entire book by itself. In fact, hundreds of books already exist on that subject. What I do want to give you is at least an overview of how a relational database is organized and then used in conjunction with a Web page.

Relational databases are organized around four basic rules:

- ✔ A database field can contain only one value. This means that if a field can have multiple values, such as course grades for a student, then each value must be in a separate table row.

- ✔ A single database field value should only be in the database one time. If at all possible (and there are exceptions), a person's name or identity number should only be in the database one time to eliminate unnecessary repetition of data (called *redundant data* in database-ese) and the chance of not updating or correcting all entries should the value change.

- ✔ Each table row has one or more fields whose values uniquely and distinctly identify it from all the other rows in a table. Of course, all rows must use the same fields in their identity (called a *key*).

- ✔ The key values of related table rows are placed in one table to point to the other. These are called *foreign keys*. For instance, the table containing the individual items on a sales order also contains a field pointing back to the sales order master record of each item. There is the parent-child thing again, but this time with a logical link based on the value of the linking fields.

Like most things having to do with the computer, there are, of course, more rules dealing with the way data is organized in a relational database, but the preceding rules are usually enough to differentiate a relational database from all the non-relational types.

Putting a Database in Your Web Site

You must deal with two major questions before inserting a database interface into your Web pages: Why? and How? Why should you insert a database? What is the purpose of providing current data to viewers of your Web site? If you know why, then next you need to consider the how question: What is the best way to provide this data? Are there tools readily available — or is this going to be a long, drawn-out, expensive project?

Why put a database on your Web site?

The experts are saying that database-enabled Web sites are the future of the Internet. From the developer's point-of-view, linking a database into a Web page frees the developer from the need to physically update the page's HTML code each time the data changes. The database link would update the data displayed each time the page is downloaded. From the viewer's perspective, the frustration of accessing a Web page that is months out of date would be a thing of the past. There is virtually no limit to the database applications that can be published on the Web.

Here are some examples that demonstrate why you would want to integrate a database into a Web site:

- **Catalog sales:** Inventory levels, price changes, and specials are posted and immediately available.

- **Student records:** Registration, grades, appointments, homework, and interactive help with assignments are available 24/7 and not just when the teacher is.

- **Research databases:** Up-to-date data available in relational databases can be extracted directly to perform analysis and statistical calculations.

- **Survey data:** Results from opinion polls and surveys are available in real-time.

I'm sure you can think of other examples; you would know your own applications much better than I. If you can answer the question, "Why use a database?" with a valid information requirement, you have all the answer you need. The overarching answer is "To share up-to-date data with my site's users."

If you want to read up on this subject, I recommend *Intranet & Web Databases For Dummies*, by Paul Litwin (IDG Books Worldwide, Inc.).

Integrating a database into a Web site

In this chapter, I discuss most of the tools that can be used to integrate a database into a Web site. In fact, most Web application programming languages have the ability in one form or another to support database interaction. Naturally, some languages are better and further developed than others, but if integrating a database into your Web pages is your goal, the tools are readily available.

Here are the database application tools you should know for the exam:

- ✔ **SQL (Structured Query Language):** SQL is the most commonly used language for interacting with databases on the Web.

- ✔ **ODBC (Open Database Connectivity):** This is a set of database APIs provided by database system vendors for client applications to use to interact with the database. ODBC prevents the need for programmers to create a different interface for different brands of databases.

- ✔ **CGI:** Perl applications are probably the most common way to show relational database data on the Web. However, a Perl program must use database programming extensions, which are normally provided by the database system.

- ✔ **Web development applications:** Applications like ColdFusion, WebObjects, and LiveWire support scripting languages to build database applications for the Web.

- ✔ **Visual Basic, C++, Java, JavaScript, and so on:** Each of the programming languages that can be used to develop server-side applications usually includes or supports tools that allow for database interaction. Included in these tools are ActiveX, SQL, and ODBC.

Interfacing with databases

One of the mainstay applications of the Internet and the Web has been seeking out information from online databases. This was true in the beginning; it is true today; and it will be true tomorrow. To this end, application developers have needed a way to request the information needed by a user from a database so a browser or application program can display it. Although not developed specifically for the Internet, SQL (Structured Query Language), a standard for interacting with databases, has emerged as a very helpful tool. SQL is not specific to any particular database software, so it has the portability required of Internet programming.

SQL is an instruction language that is used to request specific data from a database management system. Although its primary function is data retrieval, SQL can also be used for data definition and data manipulation, as well as for the management of security and data integrity controls.

SQL is an *embedded* language, which means that it is meant to be included within other programming languages and embedded in a program. For example, Visual Basic has a number of SQL commands included in its instruction set for accessing data from a database.

The primary means of retrieving data from any SQL-compatible database is the SELECT statement, which has three parts:

- ✔ The data being requested.
- ✔ The name of the database table containing the data being requested. This is the FROM clause.
- ✔ The selection criteria used to identify the specific data desired. This is the WHERE clause.

Here is an example of an SQL SELECT statement:

```
SELECT NAME FROM INET WHERE SCORE = "PASS"
```

In this example, NAME is the data being requested, INET is the database table that contains NAME, and only those entries with a SCORE equal to the value PASS are wanted. In other words, get all the names with passing scores from the INET table.

Prep Test

1 Which programming standard is the most commonly used to develop application programs for the Web?

A ○ Perl

B ○ HTML

C ○ Java

D ○ CGI

2 Which of the following is an example of a URL-encoded data string?

A ○ Name+John&Doe/Address+123&Main&St

B ○ Name&John+Doe=Address&123+Main+St

C ○ Name=John+Doe&Address=123+Main+St

D ○ Name:John+Doe&Address:123+Main+St

3 The HTTP methods that move data from the client to the server are _____ and _____. (Choose two.)

A ❑ GET

B ❑ PUT

C ❑ POST

D ❑ SEND

4 Which of the following are application program interfaces used in Web programming? (Choose all that apply.)

A ❑ MAPI

B ❑ SNAPI

C ❑ TAPI

D ❑ ISAPI

E ❑ INAPI

5 The instruction language used to request specific data from a database management system is _____.

A ○ RDBMS

B ○ SQL

C ○ MS Query

D ○ COBOL

6 The programming language used to define three-dimensional Web worlds is
_____.

A ○ VRML

B ○ HTML

C ○ DHTML

D ○ CSS

7 Which of the following are used to develop client-side applications? (Choose all that apply.)

A ❏ Java

B ❏ Perl

C ❏ JavaScript

D ❏ ASP

8 Which of the following are server-side applications? (Choose all that apply.)

A ❏ Java

B ❏ Perl

C ❏ JavaScript

D ❏ ASP

9 A Server-Side Include (SSI) responds to `include` statements in an HTML document by supplying _____ to the client.

A ○ Relational variables

B ○ Environmental variables

C ○ Extensions

D ○ APIs

10 The structural elements that make up a database are _____, _____, and _____. (Choose three.)

A ❏ Tables

B ❏ Rows

C ❏ Keys

D ❏ Repeating groups

Answers

1 *D.* CGI is not so much a programming language as it is a programming standard used for creating programs that interact between the client and the server. Perl is the most commonly used CGI programming language. *See "Interfacing with functions."*

2 *C.* This is the format used for all HTML form data. If special characters have been included in the data, they must be pulled out using hexadecimal character filters. *Review "Decoding the string."*

3 *A and C.* The `get` method is recommended for shorter forms as it loads the entire data string into a variable named QUERYSTRING. `post` places data in the STDIN area. *Take a look at "Getting the post."*

4 *A, C, and D.* I made up both SNAPI and INAPI, so don't worry about what they might really be used for. Be sure you review the common APIs and their relationship to dynamic linking and DLL files. *Check out "MAPI, SAPI, TAPI, NSAPI, ISAPI, Happy, and Sneezy."*

5 *B.* SQL (Structured Query Language) was not developed specifically for the Internet, but it is the most commonly used language for extracting data from a database. *Look over "Interfacing with databases."*

6 *A.* "Vermle," as VRML (Virtual Reality Modeling Language) is pronounced, can create some pretty snazzy three-dimensional worlds. *See "Representing the client."*

7 *A, C.* Java is used to develop both client-side and server-side applications. JavaScript is primarily a client-side tool. *Review "Representing the client."*

8 *A, B, and D.* Perl is the most commonly used programming language for CGI applications, which are server-side applications. ASP (Active Server Pages) are HTML pages with embedded programs that are preprocessed on the server. *Check out "Taking a walk on the server-side."*

9 *B.* Server-side includes are like CGI programs with only variables that are passed to the client in response to `include` statements in HTML pages. *Take a look at "Including server-side includes."*

10 *A, B, and C.* In a relational database, the objective is to eliminate repeating groups. *See "Relating to the database."*

Chapter 9

Developing HTML Documents

● ●

Exam Objectives

▶ Differentiating text and GUI editors

▶ Creating HTML pages

▶ Comprehending the use of hyperlinks

▶ Describing pre-launch testing

● ●

*O*fficially, the i-Net+ exam objectives state that 20 percent of the exam deals with how you go about developing a Web page. For the exam, you definitely need to know which HTML tags are appropriate in which instances, but you must also have an understanding how the Web functions. There is a definite relationship between the HTML tags and attributes used on a Web page and the Web protocols used to transfer and display the page.

The things you need to know to create a Web page extend well beyond just memorizing a handful of Hypertext Markup Language (HMTL) tags. You must also know some underlying concepts and technologies. I cover some of these in Chapter 2, and briefly cover them here as well, but I also include other topics here mainly because they relate directly to the task of creating an HTML document to be published on the Web.

 If you have experience creating Web pages and have been using a text editor, you may not need to review this chapter other than to skim through its topics. Chances are that you are very familiar with the usage and function of most of the HTML tags I include. However, if you have been using a GUI HTML editor to create Web documents, you may need to delve into this chapter a little deeper. Your GUI HTML editor has been doing most of the work for you, including creating and then hiding the HTML tags from you. But for the exam you must now know and be able to relate the use and function of each tag. Luckily the list of HTML tags you must know isn't too long.

Quick Assessment

Differentiating text and GUI editors

1 WYSIWYG is a function of _____ HTML editors.

2 A popular text editor used for creating HTML documents is the Windows _____.

Creating HTML pages

3 The two categories of HTML tags are _____ and _____.

4 The _____ tag set is used to enclose all the elements that define a document.

5 The tag set that encloses the portion of the document interpreted by a browser is included inside the _____ tag set.

6 You can create two general types of lists in an HTML document: _____ and _____.

Describing the use of hyperlinks

7 The mechanism used to create a link to another document is _____.

8 You can use _____ or _____ to create a link.

9 The HTML tag used to create a link is _____.

Describing pre-launch testing

10 The tool used to check HTML coding for syntax and structure errors is called a(n) _____.

Answers

1 *GUI (graphical user interface).* See "The zippy, the friendly, and the GUI."

2 *Notepad.* Review "The ol' tried and true."

3 *Unary, binary.* Check out "First, some tag basics."

4 *<HTML>...</HTML>.* Take a look at "The all-encompassing HTML tag."

5 *<BODY>...</BODY>.* See "The document body."

6 *Ordered, unordered.* Review "Order or no order — your choice."

7 *Hypertext or hyperlink.* Take a look at "Linking to the World."

8 *Text, a graphic image.* Check out "Linking to the World."

9 *<A>...</A> or anchor.* See "Setting the anchor."

10 *HTML validator.* Review "Checking the code."

Pictures and Words, and How to Tell the Difference

For the i-Net+ exam, you need to know the basics of creating an HMTL document. Probably the most basic of HTML fundamentals is knowing the difference between a text editor and a GUI (graphical user interface) editor used to create HTML pages. This sounds obvious, but you need to be aware of a few differences, besides the text and graphics thing.

As I discuss later in this chapter, creating an HTML document mostly involves inserting the appropriate HTML tags into a document so that a browser will display it the way you intended. I'd even be so bold as to say that about 80 percent of creating an HTML document involves properly placing the HTML tags that achieve your desired result.

If you have never created a Web document, I recommend that you do so using the HTML tags I describe in this chapter (and those in Chapter 10 as well). I also recommend that you use the Web to find one or more HTML tutorials to give you different perspectives on using the most common HTML tags.

The ol' tried and true

Here's where text and GUI HTML editors differ: Using a text editor means *tag, you're it*. Which is to say that you must enter each and every tag yourself with only trial-and-error to test, and most likely debug, the results. Many stubborn old HTML coders, like myself, still prefer the old tried and true methods, and the glorious self-punishment of using a text editor to create HTML pages. One of the more popular text editors used for HTML development is the Windows Notepad.

Just between you and me, word processors with GUI interfaces, such as Microsoft Word, will produce HTML documents, using the handy and oh-so-tempting Save As HTML menu choice. However, you still need to use a text editor to undo much of the unnecessary overhead created in the document. Regardless of the type of HTML editor you use, keep a text editor handy for touch-ups and tweaks.

The zippy, the friendly, and the GUI

On the other hand, when using a GUI HTML editor, the WYSIWYG (What You See Is What You Get) functions of the editor generate the needed HTML tags in response to the toolbar buttons and menu choices you click. Much like the GUI word processor, this type of HTML editor hides the HTML coding used to create your document from view.

There are actually two types of GUI HTML editors: editors and helpers. The most common type is a GUI HTML editor of the WYSIWYG persuasion. Some of the more popular GUI HTML editors are Microsoft FrontPage, Adobe PageMill, Macromedia Dreamweaver, and SoftQuad's HotMetalPro. These GUI HTML editors actually go beyond creating HTML and include other functions, such as graphical editing and page publishing wizards, as well.

The other type of GUI HTML editors, *HTML helper* editors, does just about what its name implies — it helps you make sure you spell and balance your HTML tags correctly. Usually, this type of editor includes tag spelling and syntax checkers, to help you ensure that what you intended to enter is browser-ready. A helper won't go so far as to suggest what you should have entered; remember, it is only a helper, not a guide. A few of the more popular HTML helper editors are Sausage.Com's HotDog Pro, Allair's HomeSite, and Barebones' BBEdit Lite.

For an unbiased opinion . . .

For a more extensive list of HTML editors of all kinds, check out the TUCOWS (The Ultimate Collection of Windsock Software) Web site at the following address:

```
www.tucows.com
```

Creating HTML Pages That Pass Muster — and the Test

The i-Net+ exam measures your knowledge of the methods, process, and objects used to create an HTML document. About two-thirds of the questions in this area involve the basic structure, tags, and special structures that you can apply to create a well-formed and functional Web page.

You create an HTML document as a series of sections, the actual number of which depends on how you structure the document. In general, an HTML document has three larger sections, with the first of the three containing the other two. The large sections are the HTML document itself, along with its head, and its body.

There are some other smaller sections of an HTML document, but you should focus on the HTML tags used to construct a generic Web document.

First, some tag basics

Just a few quick notes about some HTML tag concepts and terms I use in this chapter. Tags open with a < symbol and close with a > symbol. Some HTML tags use only one tag, and are called *unary* tags. An example of a unary tag is the <META> tag, which does not use a closing tag. Many HTML tags are really tag sets, called *binary tags*, that require the use of two tags to enclose the information or instruction. The second tag in a binary set, which is called the closing tag, repeats the tag being closed with a slash (/) in front. For example, the <BODY> tag opens the body of an HTML document and its binary tag partner </BODY> is used to mark the end of the document body.

Here is an example of each of these tag types:

```
Unary tag: <META name="author" content="Ron Gilster">
Binary tag: <HEAD> ... </HEAD>
```

In the meta tag example, notice that other information is included after the tag identifier (META) but before the closing mark (>), which in the example are the two values name and content. This data is referred to as *attributes*. Attributes are used to provide additional data for a tag or tag set. The attributes in the first meta clause of the example create a Name field and then assign the value "Ron Gilster" to it. Not all tags have attributes and generally the values assigned by attributes are optional.

Tags are used to issue formatting commands and to create structures on the Web documents such as tables, forms, paragraphs, the document's heading, and the document's body, and so on. On the other hand, attributes are used to supply the specifics for the display of the tag's object, such as font, color, size, alignment, and so on.

Document type

One of the smaller sections that can be included in an HTML document is the document type, which should be the first statement in any HTML document. The <!DOCTYPE> tag specifies the version of HTML that was used to create the document, and must appear before the <HTML> tag (see "The all-encompassing HTML tag" later in this chapter). This tag helps browsers, validation tools (see "Checking the code," later in this chapter), and editors interpret and function with the page. The <HTML> tag used to indicate the document type is

```
<!DOCTYPE HTML PUBLIC version-name URL>
```

where HTML identifies the language used to create the document as HTML (duh!). PUBLIC means that the specification for the HTML version used is not proprietary. The version name usually contains the long, official name for the version used. For example, the reference for HMTL Version 4.0 is

```
-//W3C//DTD HTML 4.0 Transitional//EN
```

The URL is the Web address of the public document that contains the specification of the version used, just in case someone really wants to look it up.

The all-encompassing HTML tag

The `<HTML>...</HTML>` tag set is used to enclose all the tags and elements used to define the HMTL document. Everything between the opening and closing tags is considered to be a part of the document to be interpreted by the browser. The HTML tags are

```
<HTML> ... </HTML>
```

Disregarding the `<!DOCTYPE>` tag, these tags are usually the first and last tags of your document.

The document head

The header block of an HTML document contains descriptive information about the page, including the document title, key words and terms for search engines to use, a pointer to the next page, and perhaps even links to other HTML documents. The HTML container tags used to enclose the header block are

```
<HEAD> ... </HEAD>
```

with the information to be included placed between the two tags. Both tags must be used or either no header is defined or everything in the page is considered a part of the header block. The `<HEAD> ... </HEAD>` tag set is placed inside the `<HTML> ... </HTML>` tag set.

Meta data definitions

Some of the more important tag sets you can use, especially if you want your page to be listed on a search index and found by the spiders and robots roaming the Web, are the meta tags. The `<META>` tag, which is placed inside the `<HEAD>...</HEAD>` tag set, encloses the attributes that identify key words, phrases, or topics. Here is an example of all of the stuff that can be included in a `<META>` tag:

```
<HTML>
<HEAD>
<META HTTP-EQUIV="content-type"
        CONTENT="text/html;charset=iso-8859-1">
<META HTTP-EQUIV="Resource-type" CONTENT="document">
<META HTTP-EQUIV="Description" CONTENT="IDGBooks, Inc.">
<META HTTP-EQUIV="Keywords" CONTENT="i-Net+, internet,
        certification, books, networking, www, email">
<META HTTP-EQUIV="Distribution" CONTENT="global">
</HEAD>
</HTML>
```

The HTTP-EQUIV attribute is used to bind a value to existing HTTP response headers that are provided to spiders, robots, and even browsers when the header information is requested for a page.

Page title definition

If you want a really eye-catching title for your page to show up on the search engine and across the top of the browser, you need to define a <TITLE> ...</TITLE> tag set. This binary tag is placed inside of the <HEAD>...</HEAD> tag set. Here is an example:

```
<HTML>
<HEAD>
<META HTTP-EQUIV="Description" CONTENT="i-Net+ Certification
        For Dummies">
<TITLE>i-Net+ Certification For Dummies: Certification for
        the Rest of Us!</TITLE>
</HEAD>
</HTML>
```

The document body

The next major section of an HTML document is the body, which actually kind of makes sense. At the top of the page is the head and then below that is the body. (If you are looking ahead, there are no legs, but there is a kind of footer.)

The <BODY>...</BODY> tag set encloses the part of the HTML document to be displayed. This tag set can also include a number of attributes that set default values for the entire body of the document — for example the color of the links and page background, or to designate a URL for a graphic to be used as the background. Here is an example of the body tag with two attributes:

```
<HTML>
<HEAD>
...
</HEAD>
<BODY background="http://www.dummies.com/covers/inet.jpg"
           text="0a0b0c">
...
</BODY>
</HTML>
```

In the preceding example, the opening tag for the body of the document also defines a graphic to be used for the document background, or *wallpaper,* as some people call it. The tag also sets the page's text color to a certain RGB (Red, Green, and Blue) value (see Chapter 11 for more information on RGB). An ending </BODY> tag is required.

The preceding sample code shows all that is necessary to create a Web page, albeit one that doesn't do anything beyond display a title on the browser's title bar and some weird color on the screen. In fact, all you absolutely really need to include in a document are the <HTML><HEAD></HEAD><BODY></BODY></HTML> tags to create a Web page.

Formatting to make your point

I doubt seriously that you want to have a blank Web page. Normally, you are going to all this trouble to share you thoughts, services, products, or resources with the whole Internet world. All that is really required is for you to type your message between the <BODY> and </BODY> tags. However, if you want a message that includes headings, links, graphics, tables, forms, or other formatting, there are tags and tag sets that you can use to achieve your desired document.

Taking a header

Using headers can be an effective way to title, section, and emphasize your document. Headers usually come in a range of six sizes, from the largest header at size 1 to the smallest at size 6. Rarely would you actually include all six header sizes in one document, but the range gives you some flexibility.

Headers are binary tags with the text that is to form the heading placed between the opening and closing tags. Headers can be placed anywhere in the <HTML>...</HTML> section of the document. For example, the following header would create a heading in large bold letters:

```
<H1 align="CENTER">i-Net+ Certification</H1>
```

Because the align attribute is included, this heading would also be centered on the page.

All that is required to create headers of different sizes is to change the number used in the opening and closing tags. <H2>...</H2> creates a level 2 heading, <H3>...</H3> produces a level 3 heading, and so forth.

Entering text

About the easiest thing to do when creating an HTML document is to enter text. Web browsers, unless told otherwise (see the "Give me a break" section later in this chapter), apply word-wrap to text without breaks or formatting. If you want to use nonstandard fonts, font size, boldface, italics, and insert paragraph or line breaks, you must insert the appropriate HTML tags.

Making the right point (size)

Each browser has a default setup for displaying text including the font and the font size. Fonts and sizes used vary from browser to browser, and you can usually change this to a font and size you prefer. Unless the HTML document being displayed has specifically set the font and its size, the browser standard is used.

To change the font used, an attribute called its *face,* you use the <FONT>...</FONT> tag set. Here is an example that changes the font to 12-point Arial:

```
<FONT FACE="Arial" SIZE="12">
```

You could also specify the font size as a plus or minus number that increases or decreases the font size relative to the browser's standard settings. For example, the preceding font tag could also be written as

```
<FONT FACE="Arial" SIZE="+2">
```

Accentuate the positive

You can use a variety of other tags to affect the display of your document. Table 9-1 includes the most commonly used tag sets.

Table 9-1	Tags Used to Format Text
Tag Set	*Effect*
<B>...</B>	**Boldfaces** text placed between the tags. <STRONG>...</STRONG> also boldfaces text.<I>...</I> *Italicizes* text placed between the tags.
<U>...</U>	<u>Underlines</u> text placed between the tags.

Tag Set	Effect
<S>...</S>	~~Strikes through~~ text placed between the tags.
<BIG>...</BIG>	Raises the font of the enclosed text two sizes. How much of an increase (or decrease) each size step represents is defined in your browser, but it is usually around two font points.
<SMALL>...</SMALL>	Reduces the font of the enclosed text one size.
<CENTER>...</CENTER>	Centers the enclosed text on the page.

Give me a break

Three tags that can be used to end lines and paragraphs are

- ✔ **
:** Creates a break to the next new line. Similar to a carriage return/line feed. Also known as a forced line break, it is used to break to a new line without creating a new paragraph.

- ✔ **<HR>:** Inserts a horizontal rule, a line across the page, at the point in the document where the ⟨HR⟩ tag is used.

- ✔ **<P>...</P>:** Creates a paragraph with two-line spacing between paragraphs. Some browsers do not require the closing tag and use this tag as a unary whenever a paragraph spacing is desired.

How am I doing so far?

Table 9-2 summarizes the HTML formatting tags you should know for the i-Net+ exam.

Table 9-2	Commonly Used HTML Tags
Tag or Tag Set	**Use**
<HTML>...</HTML>	Marks the beginning and end of an entire HTML document.
<HEAD>...</HEAD>	Marks the beginning and end of the document header that is sent ahead of the document body in an HTTP file transfer.
<TITLE>...</TITLE>	Marks the beginning and end of the document title that is listed on the browser title bar and is listed by search engines.
<BODY>...</BODY>	Marks the beginning and end of the main body of an HTML document.

(continued)

Table 9-2 *(continued)*

Tag or Tag Set	Use
<CENTER>...</CENTER>	Text placed between these codes is centered on the page.
<FONT>...</FONT>	Used to change the font face and size to something other than the browser's default.
<IMG SRC="xxx.xxx">	Requests the image file named to be displayed at its place in the document. This tag is covered in Chapter 11.
<Hn>...</Hn>	These tags assign the formatting of a number of preset header styles to the text they enclose. The most common are Heading Style 1 (H1) through Heading Style 4 (H4). Some browsers support more.
<HR>	Places a horizontal line on the page at this tag's location.
<B>...</B> or <STRONG>...</STRONG>	The text placed between either of these two tag sets is displayed in boldface.
<I>...</I>	The text placed between these tags is displayed in italic font style.
 	The equivalent of a carriage return/line feed with no additional line spacing. At the end of each line, HTML word-wraps running text to fit the page at display time. This tag or the <P> (paragraph) tag is placed where a line break is desired, however, the <P> tag adds a blank line as well.
<P>...</P>	This tag set is used to enclose a paragraph by inserting a line break followed by a blank line to create the end of a paragraph. If used as a binary tag set, attributes for font, size, color, and so on, can be included for the entire paragraph. It can also be used as a unary tag at the end of a paragraph.
<A HREF="xxxxxxxx">	This is the hypertext reference (link) anchor, which is the most common form of anchor used. The HREF entry is a file pathname, a URL, or a target within the body of the HTML file. This tag is explained in the "Linking to the World" section later in this chapter.

Lab 9-1 shows you how to create a basic Web page document with HTML.

Lab 9-1   Building a Basic HTML Document

1. **Using a text editor, such as Windows Notepad, open a new text file and enter the following code:**

```
<HTML>
<HEAD>
<TITLE>An HTML Page Sample</TITLE>
</HEAD>
<BODY>
<H1>This is My HTML Sample</H1>
<H2>Headers can be Different Sizes</H2>
<P>HTML interprets the tags used to enclose the text
        entered. This is an example of <B>BOLD</B>
        text.<BR>
<HR>
<BR>This is an example of <I>Italics</I> text.</P>
<CENTER><FONT FACE="Arial" SIZE +2>This line is centered
        </FONT></CENTER>
</BODY>
</HTML>
```

  2. **Save the file with the filename HTMLTEST.HTML.**

  3. **Start your Web browser and open the HTMLTEST.HTML file you've just created. The page should display like the example shown in Figure 9-1.**

Putting things in lists

HTML also enables you to create different kinds of ordered, indented, numbered, or bulleted lists. However, like most of the formatting specified in an HTML document, the actual appearance of the lists is often determined by the standard settings of the browser.

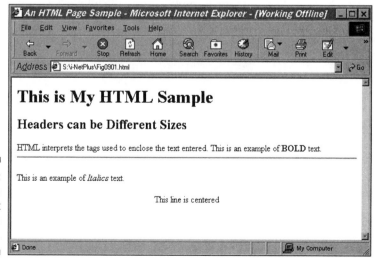

Figure 9-1:
The Web
document
created in
Lab 9-1.

Order or no order — your choice

The most frequently used HTML list makers are the ordered list `<OL>...</OL>` and unordered list `<UL>` tags. These tags enable you to create a bulleted list that is either numbered or lettered to imply an order to the list, or a list marked only by one of three standard bullet types.

The unary `<UL>` tag is the workhorse of HTML list tags, and is used to create a list in which no specific order is implied. Each entry in the list is marked either with a disc (sic), square, or circle type bullet. For example, to indicate an entry in an unordered list that is marked with filled-in square bullets, the following HTML tag is used:

```
<UL TYPE="SQUARE">
```

The binary `<OL>...</OL>` tag set is used to create a list that is either numbered or lettered. Within the ordered list tags, each list item is indicated with a unary `<LI>` tag.

You can use five different types of numerators with an ordered list:

- **1:** Arabic numbers beginning with 1
- **a:** Lowercase letters beginning with a
- **A:** Uppercase letters beginning with A
- **i:** Lowercase Roman numerals beginning with i
- **I:** Uppercase Roman numerals beginning with I

You can also affect the spacing of the table and the number or letter used for the first entry through the `COMPACT` and `START` attributes. Here's an example of a list marked with upper-case alpha letters beginning with the letter *J* that is displayed in compact form:

```
<H3>More Things to Do Before Exam </H3><P>
<OL TYPE="A" START="J">
<LI>Practice making HTML pages
<LI>Experiment with different text editors
<LI>Experiment with different GUI editors
<LI>Analyze differences
</OL>
```

Creating a definition list

Creating what looks like a glossary list or term definition list on an HMTL page involves the use of three different HTML tags and tag sets:

- **<DL>...</DL>:** This tag set encloses a collection of definition terms to create a definition list.

✔ **<DT>:** This unary tag creates a left-justified entry to be paired up with an indented definition description (<DD>) tag.

✔ **<DD>:** This unary tag is used along with a <DT> tag to create an indented definition below the entry it defines.

For example, the following HTML code creates a definition list entry:

```
<DL>
<DT>geek
<DD>a well-regarded, valuable member of society
<DT>nerd
<DD>a highly intelligent, honored, revered member of society
...
</DL>
```

Miscellaneous list types

HTML also has a few other types of lists available that can be used to create still more lists that all resemble the ones I just covered. The Directory and Menu list types convert paragraphs into an indented, bulleted list using the <DIR>...</DIR> and the <MENU>...</MENU> tag sets, respectively. As with any of the binary list tags, each item in the list is indicated with a list item <LI> tag.

An example of how a menu list is created with the Menu tag is

```
<H1>Today's Specials</H1>
<MENU>
<LI>Liver and Walla Walla Sweet Onions
<LI>Brussel Sprouts and Lima Beans
<LI>Spinach Lasagna
<LI>Whidbey Island Clams
</MENU>
```

Although more or less obsolete, the DIR command is a very handy tool for creating an unstructured list inside of a table cell. To do so, the tags are something like this:

```
<TR><TD>DIR><LI>May<LI>Kim<LI> John<LI>Linda</DIR></TD></TR>
```

Linking to the World

Another essential bit of knowledge you must have for the i-Net+ exam is the use of hypertext and hypermedia links. These are the tools, generally referred to as *hyperlinks* or just *links,* that connect one Web document to other parts of itself, its Web site, or to other documents on the Web.

Hypertext is the mechanism used to link documents by creating a link with key words or an image. Hyperlinks have become so commonplace on the Web that you probably don't even think about what is happening when you click on one to jump to another document or Web site. Hypertext was originally developed to conveniently allow documents to be easily cross-referenced and accessed online. Using key words, phrases, or images to create a hot link, documents can be related, eliminating the need to reinvent information available elsewhere.

As illustrated in Figure 9-2, a hyperlink is a clickable entry that links to the URL of the Web page or site with additional information on the related subject. Clicking the link causes the referenced document to be downloaded and displayed by the browser.

Figure 9-2:
Hyperlinks
used in text.

Hypertext, a concept developed by Ted Nelson in 1965 is used to link related documents. For example, by selecting a single word in a

Setting the anchor

You create hypertext links with an anchor (also called link anchors): <A>...</A>. You use anchors to provide the links that users click to jump around your document, Web site, or the entire World Wide Web. You include a document reference inside the anchor by using the HREF attribute:

```
<A HREF="file pathname">...</A>
```

This is by far the most common form of anchor used. The HREF entry contains a file pathname for a document located on the same Web site, a URL pointing to a document on another Web site, or a target within the body of the same HTML file.

If you boil hyperlinks down to their most basic function, they involve a preset target location that is pointed to by a hypertext reference. Hyperlinks can be on the same document or across the world. Regardless, the structure remains the same: a link pointing to a target.

Linking up and down the page

To provide hyperlinks that enable the user to move up and down on the same HTML document, you must first define the targets. At each point in a document that you plan to allow the user to link to, you must insert a <A NAME="xxxx">...</A> tag set. The name assigned to the anchor becomes a target to which you can later link. Unless you place some text between the opening and closing tags, the anchor is invisible to the user.

The anchor used to provide the link to a target includes an HREF attribute that names the target link to which the link jumps if activated. This code includes both the target and link anchors for an on-page hyperlink:

```
<A NAME="Top"></A> (placed at the target location)
...
<A HREF="#TOP">Back to Top</A> (placed wherever you want to
          provide a link to the target, more than one
          allowed)
```

The pound (#) sign inserted in the HREF target reference indicates that the link is in the same document. In fact, the next time you open a Web document that has on-page links, click one, and then look at the address or location bar of your browser. Chances are that something like #top has been appended to the page's URL, indicating the exact address of the link. I come back to this in the next section.

Intra-document links are commonly used to create a linkable table of contents for a page that exceeds a single display. You can list links from sections of the document vertically or horizontally on the page, allowing users to jump to what they are after instead of scrolling down the page.

Linking across time and space

The other type of hyperlink that you can create links users to other documents that reside either on the same Web site or on a remote host. This type of link uses the HREF (hypertext reference) attribute in the anchor tag to specify exactly the fully qualified URL of the target document. A fully qualified URL includes the transfer protocol along with the domain and document references. For example, http://www.dummies.com is a fully qualified URL.

Here are examples of the two different types of hyperlinks you can use. First, here's a link to a page on the same Web site:

```
<a href="funstuff.html">More Fun Stuff</a>
```

And here's a link to a remote Web site:

```
<a href="http://www.dummies.com">Visit the "... For Dummies"
          Web Site</a>
```

Creating an image hyperlink

You are not limited to text-only hyperlinks. You may also create a link using a graphic image. A graphic hyperlink, also called a *hypermedia link,* can point to any of the same type of links used with a text link. The only difference in creating the link is that instead of including text to display as the link, a graphic image tag is used. For example, this HTML coding turns a graphic image into a hyperlink:

```
<a href="http://www.dummies.com/books/"><img SRC="dummies-
           books.gif"></a>
```

The School of Better-Safe-Than-Sorry

On the i-Net+ exam, you will be asked about the procedure you should use before launching a Web page or Web site or when making changes to an existing page or site. You should also be prepared for questions on ways in which existing pages can be verified for accuracy and effectiveness.

If everyone in the world had the same computer with the same size and type of monitor, and they all connected to the Internet using the same data speed, then the World Wide Web would be a better place. Unfortunately, all types and sizes of computers are in use, and they connect to the Web using the full range of modem and network data speeds available, including some rates you thought had to be dead and gone. If you think everyone connects at 56 Kbps using a Pentium-class computer with a 21-inch monitor, think again.

Test, test, and test again

Before you publish your Web site, you should perform a series of tests to determine how the contents of its documents will display on the Web. Any document worth its download time should be designed to display and function properly in just about every possible situation out there.

Pre-release testing enables you to identify the problems your page encounters. Testing for every eventuality is virtually impossible, of course, but you should give it a go anyhow. Whether or not you choose to fix any performance flaws in your documents is up to you, but you should at least be aware of the problems. That way you can have your excuses ready when the complaints pour in.

Your pre-release testing should include, but not necessarily be limited to, the following items (these are the ones to know for the test):

- **Testing the links:** You should test every link on every page of the Web site, including the on-page links. Nothing is more frustrating to a user than a link that goes nowhere.

- **Testing with different browsers:** You decide which is better: a site that says it is designed only for the browser you don't have, or a site that has been set up to function equally well on the major browsers? Unfortunately, browser makers are always trying to one-up each other, and as a result browsers may stray from what are considered the standards. You should be sure to test your page with different browsers.

✔ **Testing mission-critical elements:** If your site includes forms, shopping carts, online catalogs, or other e-commerce elements that are used to place online orders or request information, your testing must ensure that these elements are functional, even if they weren't involved in changes made to the site.

✔ **Testing access and availability:** Users must be able to get to the host computer and have access to your Web pages. This sounds obvious, but you'd be surprised how many sites are launched with supervisor-only access permissions or the wrong URLs. Especially on UNIX or Linux servers, file permissions can be a roadblock if not set up correctly. Sometimes the URL that users must use is just a little different from the one you use internally on a network. Your testing should include accessing and downloading all of your Web site's documents from a remote computer.

✔ **Testing with different connection speeds:** Those really spiffy JPEG and animated GIF files you included throughout your Web pages may look great and download very fast on your Pentium III 550 MHz Xeon computer. However, to someone downloading these images at 14.4 Kbps, they are a roadblock to your page's real message. Your testing should include downloads over different connection speeds, including different dialup and direct-connection speeds, if available.

The effectiveness of your page depends on its performance issues as much as, if not more than, its text, images, and functions. This level of pre-release testing is essential for success on the Web, especially if you are working on other people's pages.

Checking the code

There are tools available (some for free!) to check your HTML coding for syntax and structure. These tools, called *validators,* scan your documents and check the HTML programming statements against the standard to help you find errors, missing tags, and other coding *faux pas*.

You can find one of the better HTML validators at the World Wide Web Consortium (W3C) Web site at this address:

```
http://validator.w3.org
```

Try using the validator on one of your own pages or those of a friend whose friendship is strong enough to withstand the wrath of the validator (sounds like an early Schwarzenegger movie, doesn't it?).

Checking up on the old stuff

Probably the biggest problem with published Web pages is neglect. As dynamic as the Internet and the Web are, it is not unusual for links that flourish today to be missing in action tomorrow. Webmasters restructure their sites to suit their own needs, and do not necessarily concern themselves with other pages that may have links to their pages. A really cool page put up by a student at a college disappears when the student graduates, and businesses go out of business or change their names. The list is endless for reasons why Web pages disappear. Web pages should be monitored frequently to ensure that their elements and links are still functional.

There are some tools available to you for checking the continued validity of any hyperlinks on your Web pages. Generically, these tools are called *link checkers*. These tools help you to avoid the dreaded 404: Object Not Found errors, the Web equivalent to the Windows Blue Screen of Death. Two popular link checkers are MOMSpider (Multi-owner Maintenance Spider) from the University of California at Irvine (www.ics.uci.edu/pub/websoft/MOMspider/) and SiteRuler from Web-King (www.thewebking.com).

More robust tools, called *all-around checkers,* are now emerging as well. These tools perform the same tasks as HTML validators (see the previous section) and link checkers, plus checking the spelling, download time, and other performance characteristics of a document. Many of these checking features are also built into the higher-end Web editors, such as Microsoft's FrontPage and Adobe's PageMill. One of the better all-around checker bundles is available from the Netscape Netcenter's Web-Site Garage at www.websitegarage.com.

Prep Test

1 The advantages of using a GUI-type HTML editor over a text editor include which of the following? (Choose all that apply.)

A ❑ Plain text display

B ❑ WYSIWYG display

C ❑ Automatically generated HTML code

D ❑ There is no apparent difference between GUI and text HTML editors.

2 The type of HTML tag that requires an opening and a closing tag — for example, <TAG>...</TAG>, is a(n) _____ tag.

A ○ Unary

B ○ Binary

C ○ Hypertext

D ○ Meta

3 The HTML tags required at minimum to define a Web document are _____, _____, and _____. (Choose three.)

A ❑ <HEAD>...</HEAD>

B ❑ <!DOCTYPE>

C ❑ <HTML>...</HTML>

D ❑ <BODY>...</BODY>

E ❑ <A>...</A>

4 The two HTML tags used to insert a new-line break or begin or end a paragraph are _____ and _____. (Choose two.)

A ❑ <P>...</P>

B ❑ <PR>

C ❑

D ❑ <NL>

5 The HTML tag used to define an ordered list is _____.

A ○ <IL>...</IL>

B ○ <UL>...</UL>

C ○ <OL>...</OL>

D ○ <DL>...</DL>

6 Which of the following can be used to create a hyperlink? (Choose two.)

A ❑ Meta data

B ❑ Text data

C ❑ Graphic image

D ❑ JavaScript

7 Hyperlinks can be created to point to _____, _____, or _____. (Choose three.)

A ❑ Target in same document

B ❑ Remote URL

C ❑ Local URL

D ❑ Itself

8 To create a hypertext link in an HTML document, you use _____.

A ○ <IMG>

B ○ <HREF>...</HREF>

C ○ <A>...</A>

D ○ <HTML>...</HTML>

9 Which of the following should be included in a Web page/site pre-launch testing procedure? (Choose all that apply.)

A ❑ Test hypertext links

B ❑ Test with different browsers

C ❑ Test access to host computer

D ❑ Test with different connection speeds

E ❑ Test on different size displays

10 Two tools that can be used to check the validity of a document's HTML code and its hypertext links are _____ and _____. (Choose two.)

A ❑ HMTL compiler

B ❑ HTML validator

C ❑ Link checker

D ❑ Hypertext spider

Answers

1. *B and C.* There are definitely advantages to these two features, which is why GUI HTML editors are so popular. Some editors also include functions to check links and download times. *See "Pictures and Words, and How to Tell the Difference."*

2. *B.* It is called a binary tag because, you guessed it, it has two tags: an opening tag and a closing tag. A unary tag has only one tag. *Review "First, some tag basics."*

3. *A, C, and D.* At minimum, you can define an HTML document with the code <HTML><HEAD></HEAD><BODY></BODY></HTML>. *Take a look at "The document body."*

4. *A and C.* The <P> or paragraph tag creates a hard return to end a paragraph or leave a blank line. The <BR> break tag adds a soft return to break to a new line. *Check out "Give me a break."*

5. *C.* That's what OL stands for: ordered list. Ordered list items are either numbered or lettered in an ascending sequence. Detail items in the list are defined using the <IL> unary tag. *Look over "Order or no order — your choice."*

6. *B and C.* A hyperlink can be created with either a text phrase (from a single character to several words) or a graphic image. *See "Linking to the World."*

7. *A, B, and C.* I guess you could actually have a hyperlink point to itself, but it wouldn't be very efficient, so I'm ruling it out. *Review "Linking to the World."*

8. *C.* The anchor tag set <A>...</A> is used to create hyperlinks in HTML. IMG and HREF are attributes used in the anchor tag. *Look over "Setting the anchor."*

9. *A, B, C, D, and E.* All of these items, plus a few others, should be included in the testing procedure of a Web site. *Check out "Test, test, and test again."*

10. *B and C.* There are also all-around checks that will do both of these jobs and more. *Take a look at "Checking the code" and "Checking up on the old stuff."*

Chapter 10

Working with Tables and Forms

Exam Objectives
▶ Using HTML to create a table
▶ Creating an HMTL form

*T*ables are the Web page designer's best friend. They provide a ready alignment tool that the designer can use to magically align text and graphics so they appear to float next to one another on the ether of the browser. Tables are also good for displaying related data in a tabular or matrix format.

Where tables are excellent for displaying information to viewers, forms are equally valuable for gathering information from viewers. If you have any experience with Web pages at all, undoubtedly you have run across a form of one type or another. The list of ways in which a form can be used to gather information is virtually endless.

The result of having these two tools available to use is key to the value of the Web itself. Information can be easily presented in a manner that is also easily read and understood. Data can be requested from the user and easily accepted, transmitted, and processed on the Web. Without these tools, the Web loses some of its ability as an information source and its value as a data gathering tool.

For the i-Net+ exam, you should know when and why a table or form should be used and the HTML coding used to create either or both. If you have never included a table or a form in your Web pages, this would be an excellent time to add one or both, just for practice.

Quick Assessment

Using HTML to create a table

1 The HTML tag used to contain the definition of a table structure is _____.

2 Each table row is defined with a(n) _____ HTML tag set.

3 Each table row cell is defined using the _____ HTML tag set.

4 A <TH>...</TH> tag set is used to define a table _____.

5 _____ sets the amount of spacing between the contents of a cell and its border.

Creating an HMTL form

6 CGI is the abbreviation for _____ _____ _____.

7 An HTML form structure is created inside the _____ tag set.

8 The two primary attributes defined for a form are _____ and _____.

9 _____ and _____ are the two methods used to retrieve or send data from a form.

10 Only _____ option button(s) may be selected at one time.

Answers

1 *<TABLE>...</TABLE>*. See "Setting the table."

2 *<TR>...</TR>*. Review "Pretty data all in a row."

3 *<TD>...</TD>*. Check out "Are you a cells person?"

4 *Header.* Take a look at "Naming the columns."

5 *Cellpadding.* See "Some facts on the table."

6 *Common Gateway Interface.* Review "So, why use a form?"

7 *<FORM>...</FORM>*. Take a look at "Forming the form."

8 *Method and action.* Check out "Forming the form."

9 *GET and POST.* Look over "Methods and actions."

10 *One.* See "Option buttons."

Getting Tabular

You can use a table in an HTML document for many reasons: to arrange data vertically or horizontally, to align text and images, or to provide a tabular, rows-and-columns display. You can also use a table to create the look of multiple columns on a page, or to place text on either side of a graphic image. Tables provide a host of formatting solutions when designing a Web page. The flexibility of a table stems from the fact that a table cell may contain any object that can be placed anywhere in an HTML document.

Setting the table

You define a table structure inside the <TABLE>...</TABLE> tag set container. The opening tag is required if you want to define a table. Likewise, the closing tag is needed to stop the definition of the table. However, if the closing tag is not provided, everything following the table is considered to be a part of it and the table displays.

Table definitions can be included inside other tables. In fact, a table can be defined inside a cell definition (see the "Are you a cells person?" section later in this chapter).

Pretty data all in a row

Inside the table tag set, you define the rows of the table using the <TR>...</TR> tag set. The actual HTML table is created through a series of table row definitions. The <TR> tag sets, each defining the cells contained in each row, define both the height and number of columns in the table. As the cells in each row align vertically, they create columns. There are no rules that say each row much structurally match each of the other rows, but it does make for a much more appealing table if they do. If table row definitions are omitted, the table definition will default to a single row table.

An HTML table definition with three empty rows looks like this:

```
<TABLE>
<TR></TR>
<TR></TR>
<TR></TR>
</TABLE>
```

Naming the columns

Each column of the table — that is, the first cell in the vertical column of cells in the same position on each row — can be assigned a header or label. This is done with a table header tag: <TH>...</TH>. Here is an example of a table that includes table headers in the first row:

```
<TABLE>
<TR><TH>Column 1</TH></TR>
<TR><TH>Column 2</TH></TR>
<TR><TH>Column 3</TH></TR>
<TR></TR>
<TR></TR>
</TABLE>
```

Are you a cells person?

You divide table rows into individual cells using the <TD>...</TD> HTML tag set. There really are no restrictions on what you can place inside a table detail definition. A cell can contain another table, a form, a graphic, text, a hyperlink, and so forth. Here is an example of a table definition that includes text in each of the three cells of a three-row table:

```
<TABLE>
<TR><TH>Column 1</TH></TR>
<TR><TH> </TH><TH>Column 2</TH></TR>
<TR><TH> </TH><TH> </TH><TH>Column 3</TH></TR>
<TR><TD>Cell 1-1</TD><TD>Cell 2-1</TD><TD>Cell 3-1</TD></TR>
<TR><TD>Cell 1-2</TD><TD>Cell 2-2</TD><TD>Cell 3-2</TD></TR>
<TR><TD>Cell 1-3</TD><TD>Cell 2-3</TD><TD>Cell 3-3</TD></TR>
</TABLE>
```

Figure 10-1 shows how a browser displays this HTML code.

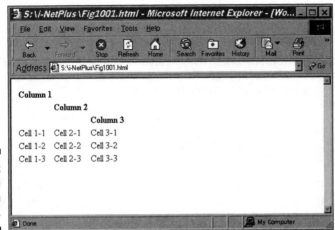

Figure 10-1:
A table
displayed in
a browser.

Defining a table with HTML

Lab 10-1 demonstrates how to insert a table in a Web page.

Lab 10-1   Inserting a Table in an HTML Document

1. **At the place in the document where you want to insert the table, enter the HTML tag** <TABLE>. **Remember that this is a binary tag for which you must later add the closing tag.**

   Each row of the table is defined by the binary tag <TR>...</TR>, and each row cell (each column on each row) is defined with the tag set <TD>...</TD>, which you insert inside the <TR>...</TR> tag set.

2. **For the first row, enter the** <TR> **tag.**

3. **You can also create a table heading by using the tag set** <TH>...</TH> **on the first row (or any other row, if you want). Enter the following code after the first** <TR> **tag:**

   ```
   <TR>
   <TH>Name</TH>
   <TH>Address</TH>
   <TH>Phone</TH>
   </TR>
   ```

4. **Now enter a <TD>...</TD> entry for each cell on the row. On each row, enter the name, address, and phone number of your friends, famous people with whom you'd like to be friends, or people who would like to be famous and aren't your friends. For example, the code for the first data row looks like this:**

```
<TR>
<TD>Bill Gates</TD>
<TD>Redmond, WA</TD>
<TD>425-555-1212</TD>
</TR>
```

5. **Continue to fill in the table rows and cells with the data for all of your very best friends. When you have completed all the entries (you may want to shorten the list for this lab exercise), complete the table with the closing tag for the table: </TABLE>.**

The HTML code that you should have at the end of Lab 10-1 should look something like this (see Figure 10-2 for how it is displayed in a browser):

```
. . .
<TABLE>
<TR>
<TH>Name</TH>
<TH>Address</TH>
<TH>Phone</TH>
</TR>
<TR>
<TD>Bill Gates</TD>
<TD>Redmond, WA</TD>
<TD>425-555-1212</TD>
</TR>
<TR>
<TD>Ron Gilster</TD>
<TD>Walla Walla, WA</TD>
<TD>509-888-1212</TD>
</TR>
</TABLE>
. . .
```

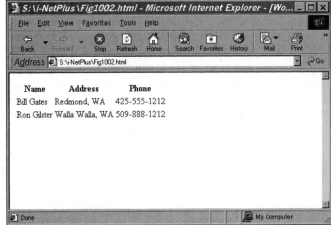

Name	Address	Phone
Bill Gates	Redmond, WA	425-555-1212
Ron Gilster	Walla Walla, WA	509-888-1212

Done   My Computer

Figure 10-2:
The table
created in
Lab 10-1.

Lab 10-2   Using a Table to Align Text and Graphics

1. **Create a three-column, two-row table definition using the steps described in Lab 10-1.**

2. **Insert a <TD>...<TD> tag in the first (top) row. Place inside the tag container any text you desire.**

3. **Immediately after the first <TD>...</TD> tag set, insert another one, placing the following string inside the tag set:**

   ```
   <IMG SRC="pathname of image on your system">
   ```

   Be sure you change the text inside the quotes to the location of a graphic file on your system.

4. **Add a third <TD>...</TD> in this row and enter any text you'd like.**

5. **Save the file and use a browser to open and display it. The text and graphics should all be on the same line.**

The table created in Lab 10-2 creates HTML code something like this (see Figure 10-3 for an example of how this would be displayed by a browser):

```
<TABLE>
<TR>
<TD>Column 1 Text</TD>
<TD><IMG SRC="doggie.gif"></TD>
<TD>See the Doggie?</TD>
</TR>
<TR>
<TD></TD>
<TD></TD>
<TD></TD>
</TR>
</TABLE>
```

Figure 10-3:
Tables can
be used
to align
text and
graphics.

Some facts on the table

Lab 10-1 shows how to create a basic table structure. You also need to know
about a few table attributes for the exam. In general, these attributes perform
the same whether they are used with a table, row, or column tag. For the
exam, you should know about the following attributes:

- ✔ **Align**= Unless you specify an alignment, the browser will left-justify any
  text or graphics in the table's cells. You can position the table to the left,
  center, or right using this attribute inside the <TABLE> tag. When used
  inside the <TR>, <TH>, or <TD> tags, this attribute indicates the alignment of the contents of the cells.

- ✔ **Border**= Used solely within the <TABLE> tag, this attribute indicates the
  width of the table's border in pixels. The valid range is 0 (no border) to
  around 6, after which the border begins to look like a fortress wall. If you
  specify a border of 0 (zero), it will make the structure of the table, that
  is, the table and cell walls, invisible and the contents impressively —
  and mysteriously — aligned.

- ✔ **Cellpadding**= Used solely within the <TABLE> tag, this attribute sets the
  amount of space between the contents of the cell and its border. Think
  of it as the padding around the cell — something I know only too well.
  The value specified is in pixels and more than 5 pixels is more padding
  than is needed to move a piano.

- ✔ **Cellspacing**= Another of the attributes for the <TABLE> tag, this one sets
  the amount of spacing inserted between cells. The default value is 1
  pixel with a value of 5 being very common.

- ✔ **Colspan**= This attribute is only used with <TD> tags to indicate that a
  particular cell spans more than one column of cells.

✔ **Rowspan=** Like the Colspan attribute, this attribute is used with the `<TR>` tag to indicate that a row's height is equivalent to more than a single row's vertical heighth in the table.

✔ **Width=** This attribute can be used with all of the table tags to set the absolute or relative width of the table. By using a width attribute of a set number of pixels, you can set the table or cell to a fixed width. If you want to keep the table width relative to the amount of display space available (a good idea on a global network with many different types and sizes of monitors), you set the width attribute to a percentage of the total space available. When the percentage width is used with cells (`<TD>` tags), the cell is set to a percentage of the table's width.

Be sure you know the HTML tags used to create a table and that you understand that any HTML tag or tag set can be entered between the tags of a table cell (`<TD>. . .</TD>`) tag set.

Working True to Form

For the i-Net+ exam, you need to know why and how a form is included on a Web page. Unless you have been away on an all-expenses paid vacation in a monastery or fulfilling your life by living as a hermit for the last three years and have never seen the Internet, then I'm sure you have encountered at least one or a hundred online Web page forms. Often, the form consists merely of a single textbox to enter your e-mail address. A form may also be multiple documents that accept text in boxes, as well as allow you to click mutually-exclusive options, or click all-that-apply check boxes. The number of variations for using a form on a Web page is probably equal to the number of people designing Web pages with forms — and that's a bunch.

So, why use a form?

First things first. Why use forms? Web page forms are commonly used on a Web site to gather information from users. The form could be registering someone to an e-mail newsletter or a listserv, taking an online order, accepting search criteria, gathering responses to a survey, or any other purpose that requires taking information from a viewer. Probably the most common use of a form on a Web page is the feedback form, which enables you to collect specifically requested data or feedback (hence the name) from a viewer.

The primary drawback to incorporating a form in a Web page, besides having to deal with the millions of responses you are sure to get, is that not all browsers support forms, and you must provide the required CGI (Common

Gateway Interface) programs to support the form. However, this is a relatively minor concern because the more popular browsers have built-in form
support and include the specialized CGI utilities required to process the
form. Figure 10-4 shows an example of a form (from the `www.dummies.com`
Web site) that includes multiple form elements.

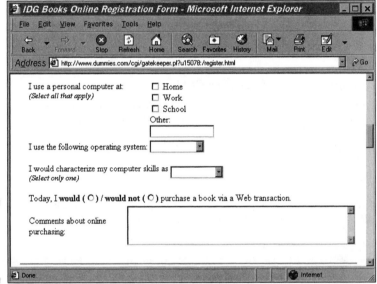

Figure 10-4:
A sample
Web page
with forms.

CGI is an Internet standard that enables an external server to process the
data entered into the form as directed by the method specified. If you have
ever been acknowledged after registering a piece of shareware, ordering a
book, or running an online demo, you have experienced an interaction with a
CGI program. Not all forms require CGI support. The more popular browsers
have built-in CGI-like functions to send form data via e-mail or to reset or
clear HTML forms.

Forming the form

A Web page form is built up inside the `<FORM>` ... `</FORM>` container. Just
declaring a form by including this tag set accomplishes absolutely nothing by
itself. You must also include the form elements and specify the action you
want to be performed when the user sends in his or her information. There is
no magic here, you must specify exactly how you want the form processed.

Methods and actions

A Web page form opens with the ⟨FORM⟩ tag and ends with the ⟨/FORM⟩ tag. Inside these tags, you insert the form elements that make up the form and their titles. The ⟨FORM⟩ tag has two primary attributes: method and action.

✔ **Method** enables you to set the form to either get data from another source (METHOD="GET") or send the data entered into the form to a separate destination (METHOD="POST").

✔ **Action** specifies the action to be taken when the user clicks on the submit button.

You must choose: E-Mail or CGI!

To have the form data sent to an e-mail address when the user clicks the submit button, the following attributes are included in the opening ⟨FORM⟩ tag:

```
<FORM METHOD="POST" ACTION="mailto:techsupt@dummies.com">
...
</FORM>
```

If the data were to be provided to a CGI program, the action would list the URL to which the form's contents are to be posted. For example:

```
<FORM METHOD="POST"
  ACTION="http://www.dummies.com/cgi-bin/form.cgi">
...
</FORM>
```

Boxes, buttons, and lists

Following are the form data elements you should know for the exam.

Text entry, hidden, and password fields

A text entry field enables the viewer to enter unformatted text data, as shown in Figure 10-1. A text entry field provides a space for text entry fields, such as names, addresses, or very short comments, which are taken as is and not edited, processed, or verified. The following HTML code is used to create a text entry field within a form:

```
<INPUT TYPE="text" NAME="user-name" SIZE="40"
MAXLENGTH="40">
```

The ⟨INPUT⟩ tag creates the text data field. Setting its TYPE parameter to text identifies the element as a text entry field.

The NAME= parameter assigns a reference name to be associated with the value entered. This is important for two reasons: It labels the data value in any e-mail messages, or it allows a CGI program to identify and process the data sent to it.

The SIZE= parameter sets the length of the field in characters so the browser knows how large to draw its container, which in this case is a text box. The "maxlength" value sets the maximum number of characters that are accepted. These last two fields can be different — for example, the field can have a size of 20 and a maxlength of 40, in which case the text box scrolls to the left after the 20th character is entered.

Two other values can be used in the TYPE field of a text entry field: hidden and password. These two data field types can be useful in creating forms that work with CGI functions.

A *hidden* field type tells the browser that the field is not to be displayed. This creates a field hidden from the user's view. These fields are handy for constants and other data values that need to be passed to a CGI program in addition to the data entered in the form.

A *password* field type tells the browser to echo every keystroke in the field with an asterisk instead of the character typed.

The following code segment shows the coding for each of these field types:

```
<input TYPE="hidden" NAME="discount% "
   SIZE="2" MAXLENGTH="2">
<input TYPE="password" NAME="password"
   SIZE="10" MAXLENGTH="10">
```

Check boxes

Users can toggle a check box data element to answer either yes (true, selected, and checked) or no (false, unselected, and unchecked). Check boxes are used when more than one choice is allowed. Here is a sample of the HTML coding used to create a check box input:

```
<INPUT TYPE="checkbox" NAME="mailing-list"
   VALUE="Yes" checked>
```

The settings for this element are very similar to those used for a text entry field. The TYPE parameter sets the element as a check box and the NAME parameter sets the field reference. The VALUE clause sets the actual value that is to be sent when the box is selected. The "checked" value at the end of the tag is included when you want the box to have a default setting, which could also be set to "unchecked."

Option buttons

Option buttons, which are also called radio buttons, are used to select a value from a list of options in which only one option may be chosen. When any one button in a group is selected, any button previously selected will automatically be unselected. The term *radio button* refers to the action of a push-button radio, like a car radio, on which only one selection can be active at a time.

To create an option button group, the buttons must be placed next to each other and be assigned the same NAME parameter. Here is an example of the HTML code used to create an option button group:

```
<input TYPE="radio" NAME="Processor"
 VALUE="Pentium" checked> Pentium
<input TYPE="radio" NAME="Processor"
 VALUE="486DX"> 486 DX
<input TYPE="radio" NAME="Processor"
 VALUE="486SX"> 486 SX
```

Combo boxes and select lists

The combo box form element, also known as a *select list,* presents the viewer with a pull-down list of values from which one value can be chosen. Where option buttons can be used effectively for short lists of items from which only one can be chosen, a longer list of items, such as states, or a list of items likely to change, is better implemented with a combo box. Select lists require less space on the Web page and are generally easier for the viewer to use. The combo box gets its name from being a combination of a list and a text entry field. Here is a sample of the HTML code used to create a combo box:

```
<P>What Country do you Live in?
<SELECT NAME="Country">
<OPTION VALUE="USA">United States
<OPTION VALUE="CAN">Canada
<OPTION VALUE="MEX">Mexico
</SELECT>
```

The <SELECT> tag opens the list definition and the NAME parameter assigns its reference identity. Each value to be included in the list is then coded in an <OPTION> tag that identifies both its selected data value and its list identifier. For example, in this example "Canada" will be displayed as a choice in the list and if selected, the value "CAN" will be sent forward.

To create a list from which more than one selection can be made, the MULTIPLE attribute is added to the <SELECT> tag. This lets users select more than one choice and, depending on the browser, they may even be able to select a range of values. The <SELECT> tag with a MULTIPLE attribute would look like this:

```
<SELECT MULTIPLE NAME="country" size=10>
<OPTION VALUE="USA">United States
<OPTION VALUE="CAN">Canada
<OPTION VALUE="MEX">Mexico
</SELECT>
```

Text areas

The <TEXTAREA> tag creates a box that enables the user to type longer text entries. For example, a text area may be used to gather general comments or opinions from users concerning how they may feel about a Web site, product, or book. The <TEXTAREA> tag creates a container that also includes vertical and horizontal scroll bars. Here is a sample of the HTML coding used to create a text area:

```
Comments: <TEXTAREA name="Comments" ROWS=5
COLS=65></TEXTAREA>
```

The attributes ROWS and COLS specify the height of the text area as to the number of lines and the width in characters. This example defines a text area as 5 lines high and 65 characters wide. The actual data is not limited to the number of rows and columns specified in the tag. These attributes only set the display size of the text box.

Submit and reset buttons

A form with only one element does not need a submit button because simply entering a value and then pressing the Enter key automatically submits the data. If the form has two or more elements, a submit button, which the user must click, is required to invoke the action specified in the <FORM> tag and transfer the data.

If you want to allow the user to clear out a form and start over, you may include a reset button on the form. The reset button clears all data entered into any of the data elements and resets them to their default values. This HTML code creates both the submit and reset buttons:

```
<INPUT NAME="Submit" TYPE="submit" VALUE="Send Request">
<INPUT NAME="Name" TYPE="reset" VALUE="Clear">
```

Prep Test

1 The _____ HTML tag is used to contain the definition of a table structure.

A ○ `<ROW>...</ROW>`

B ○ `<COL>...</COL>`

C ○ `<TABLE>...</TABLE>`

D ○ `<MATRIX>...</MATRIX>`

2 Which of the following are used within a table structure definition to define rows, cells, and headers? (Choose three.)

A ❑ `<TD>...</TD>`

B ❑ `<COL>...</COL>`

C ❑ `<TH>...</TH>`

D ❑ `<TR>...</TR>`

3 Uses for a table in an HTML document include which of the following? (Choose all that apply.)

A ❑ Displaying information

B ❑ Aligning text and graphics

C ❑ Gathering information

D ❑ Linking to other documents

4 The _____ HTML attribute controls the amount of spacing between cells of a table.

A ○ Border

B ○ Cellspacing

C ○ Cellpadding

D ○ Colspan

5 Choose the statement that best describes the condition of the following HTML table definition:

```
<TABLE><TD>Test1</TD><TD>Test2</TD>
```

A ○ A one-row table with two cells displays

B ○ Nothing displays because no rows were defined

C ○ A two-row table with one cell each displays

D ○ Nothing displays because no closing tag is defined

6 Data entered into an HTML form is processed by a(n) _____.

A ○ Form-mail utility

B ○ CGI utility

C ○ E-mail client

D ○ Form data helper application

7 Which of the following are the two HTTP methods used to process form data? (Choose two.)

A ❑ GET

B ❑ PUT

C ❑ POST

D ❑ UPLOAD

8 The following code segment defines which type of form element?

```
<INPUT TYPE="text" NAME="name" SIZE="24">
```

A ○ Hidden field

B ○ Password field

C ○ Text field

D ○ Name field

9 Between a group of check boxes and a group of option buttons, in which group can users select as many choices as they like?

A ○ Both check boxes and option buttons

B ○ Only check boxes

C ○ Only option buttons

D ○ Neither check boxes nor option buttons

10 What element is used to invoke the action specified in the ACTION attribute?

A ○ Reset button

B ○ Back button

C ○ Submit button

D ○ Cancel button

Answers

1 *C.* I know this one was just a little obvious, but they can't all be killers. Just in case you struggled with it, you may want to look over the chapter again. *Take a look at "Setting the table."*

2 *A, C, and D.* There is no HTML tag for columns, but there is a COLSPAN attribute used with ⟨TD⟩ tags. *See "Getting Tabular."*

3 *A and B.* You cannot directly accept data from the user with a table or link to another document. However, you can place a form or a hypertext link in a cell and accomplish those tasks. *Check out "Getting Tabular."*

4 *B.* Many people confuse cellspacing and cellpadding. Cellspacing is between cells and cellpadding is inside a cell. *Review "Some facts on the table."*

5 *A.* Although the HTML code is missing table rows and the closing table tag, the table will still display as a one-row table with two cell values. *Look over "Defining a table with HTML."*

6 *B.* Because the data is normally passed back to the server for processing, CGI utilities are used to process the data as directed by the method and action specified in the form definition. *See "So, why use a form?"*

7 *A and C.* You can either get data from the server or post data to the server. *Take a look at "Methods and actions."*

8 *C.* If you knew where to look, this should have been pretty easy for you. The TYPE attribute defines the type of form element defined. *Review "Boxes, buttons, and lists."*

9 *B.* Option buttons allow only one mutually exclusive choice from a group of options. Check boxes allow one, some, or all of the boxes to be selected. *Check out "Check boxes" and "Option buttons."*

10 *C.* There are two standard types of action buttons associated with forms: submit and reset. The reset button clears the form for re-entry and the submit button invokes the ACTION attribute. *Look over "Submit and reset buttons."*

Chapter 11

Working with Graphics and Multimedia

- -

Exam Objectives

▶ Defining common graphic formats

▶ Describing the uses of popular multimedia file formats

▶ Identifying popular multimedia plug-ins

- -

*N*owhere is the eye of the beholder and its fickle opinion of what constitutes beauty so critical than on the Internet and Web. Graphic images are everywhere on the Web in the form of illustrations, logos, backgrounds, animations, navigation buttons, and even the toolbars of the browsers. Graphics provide the Web with its friendly, appealing, and inviting look and feel.

Dictionary definitions for the word *graphics* refer to the art of drawing, graphic arts, and computer graphics. However, what is lost in these definitions is that graphics can take on other dimensions of significance, especially when used on the Web.

For the i-Net+ exam, you need to see graphic images and multimedia as more than just pictures and sounds. You must be familiar with the various types of graphic images used on the Web, their characteristics, where they are best used, and how they are created. You must also know the file formats in use and the compression algorithms used when capturing images, sound, and both together.

A number of different graphic formats are discussed in this chapter, but because it is printed in black and white, it is very difficult to show the resolution and image quality differences and contrasts of the different file formats. Your best bet for viewing and comparing these images is to use the Web itself.

For the i-Net+ exam, you should concentrate on the technical parts of working with multimedia, including the file formats and compression techniques used as well as the add-on and helper applications needed to view each of the various file formats.

Quick Assessment

1 The abbreviation RGB refers to _____, _____, and _____.

2 _____ decreases file sizes by reducing the number of colors used in the image.

3 A(n) _____ compression technique reduces the size of the original image without losing any of the image data.

4 The two most popular graphic file formats used on the Web are _____ and _____.

5 The file format best suited to photographs is the _____ format.

6 The _____ audio file format is the de facto format for nonstreaming audio.

7 The digital audio-visual format developed by Apple Computer that creates files with an MOV extension is _____.

8 The abbreviation PDF refers to _____ _____ _____.

9 The _____ utility is used to convert Macintosh documents into portable files.

10 The QuickTime VR application enables users to view _____ worlds.

Answers

1 *Red, Green, Blue.* See "In the land of the RGB."

2 *Dithering.* Review "Applying dithering and compression."

3 *Lossless.* Check out "Does lossless mean less loss?"

4 *GIF, JPEG.* Take a look at "Speaking graphically."

5 *JPEG.* See "JPEG images."

6 *WAV.* Look over "Lending an ear to audio-only formats."

7 *QuickTime.* Review "Seeing and hearing video and multimedia architectures."

8 *Portable Document Format.* Take a look at "Portable documents."

9 *BinHex.* Check out "BinHex documents."

10 *Virtual reality.* Look over "Multimedia applications and viewers."

Examining Graphics on the Web

There is a wide variety of graphic file formats with different color, resolution, effects, and compression characteristics. Although many of the graphic file formats in use are specific to a particular brand of computer hardware or a particular operating system, most can be converted to work with other systems. On the other hand, many are platform-independent and easily work on different types of computers.

Computer graphics are stored in many types of file formats, but, in general, there are only two primary types of image files: uncompressed and compressed. In the following sections, I provide you with some background material on how browsers display colors, or the difference between dithering and compression, along with a review of the two types of uncompressed image files: bit-map images and vector graphics. I discuss compressed graphic image files later in this chapter.

In the land of the RGB

Web browsers use the RGB (red, green, and blue) color scale to determine the color that is to be displayed. Each color is represented as three values in the RGB scale.

The six-digit RGB code is a hexadecimal number that includes three sets of two positions, with each set used to indicate the amount of red, green, and blue in the color. For instance, the color red is coded as FF0000 (only red, no green, or blue) and green is 00FF00. The RGB code for yellow is FFFF00 — that is, a mix of red and green with no blue. Table 11-1 lists a few of the color codes for some of the more popular colors.

Table 11-1	RGB Colors
Color Name	*RGB Color Coding*
Black	000000
Blue	0000FF
Brown	A62A2A
Gold	CD7F32
Green	00FF00
Grey	C0C0C0

Color Name	RGB Color Coding
Orange	FF7F00
Pink	BC8F8F
Red	FF0000
White	FFFFFF
Yellow	FFFF00

Applying dithering and compression

Two techniques are used to reduce the storage space, bandwidth, and download time requirements for a graphic image file: dithering and compression.

By replacing solid colors with patterns of two or more colors that the human eye and brain will see as similar shades, *dithering* reduces the number of colors used in the image and thus decreases the file size. For example, an area of solid 256-color amber would be replaced with a background of 16-color yellow with a pattern of orange or red dots, depending on the shading.

Compression reduces the size of a graphic file by eliminating long strings of the same color (strings of bits or bytes all representing white, or yellow, or blue, for example). The repeated string of color is replaced with a set of instructions that describes the string. Commonly, several rows of the same color appear one after the other, for instance in the background color of a Web page. If there were only two such rows in a 640 X 480-color image, over 10,000 characters can be replaced with a two- to four-byte instruction.

Sorting out lossy and lossless formats

There are two types of compressed image file formats: lossless and lossy. *Lossless formats* compress all of the original image or graphic in such a way that none of the original image data is lost and can be recreated exactly to the original image quality. A *lossy format* throws out some of the original image data as a part of its compression process when storing the image file. Usually, the discarded data is too small to be detected by the human eye and there is no discernible difference between the original and the compressed image.

Does lossless mean less loss?

When a lossless compression reduces an original image file, it uses a simple substitution method to ensure that it does not lose any data. If several parts of the image are the same, it assigns the repeating pattern a number. For example, if the sequence 1 3 5 7 9 is assigned the number 1, each time the sequence is found, it can be replaced with the number 1, saving four digits each time. A key (1 = 1 3 5 7 9) is stored in a decoding table attached to the image and used by the browser to display the image. An image file that contains expanses of a flat color may compress down to as much as one-tenth of its original file size. A complex graphic with little or no repetitive image elements may reduce by only 20 percent.

Lossy come home

Lossy compression actually discards parts of an image to reduce its file size, operating on the nobody-will-notice philosophy. The image is first divided into squares and then a mathematical algorithm, called the Discrete Cosine Transformation (DCT), is applied. DCT transforms each data square into a set of big and small image elements that fit together to make up the image. Unlike a simple substitution algorithm, a variable amount of compression can be applied. When a higher compression ratio is desired, the smallest elements of the image are eliminated, reducing the amount of data available to reconstruct the image.

Speaking graphically

The graphics used on the Web are generally raster graphics. A raster graphic represents an image as a grid of x (horizontal) and y (vertical) coordinates. The x and y coordinates represent the horizontal and vertical addresses of the pixels on the computer screen. Each coordinate addresses a set number of pixels along either axis of the display.

Two raster graphic formats dominate the Web: GIF (Graphics Interchange Format), the most popular Web image type, and JPEG (Joint Photographic Experts Group). The PNG (Portable Network Graphic) is another format that is gaining popularity as a replacement for the GIF format, which contains a compression algorithm on which a patent is held by the Unisys Corporation.

Many Web browser software packages will display only these graphic formats. Table 11-2 contrasts the two most popular formats. Remember that the information in this table is generic. JPEG file compression performs better on photographs and high-resolution raster graphics, while GIF files work better with vector and other fairly low-resolution images.

Table 11-2	GIF versus JPEG
GIF	**JPEG**
Good detail and workable file sizes. Excellent for background images.	Smaller file size and good balance between image size and resolution.
Retains the original picture's detail, which results in the best on-screen resolution.	Compresses the original image, which can result in the loss of some of the image's finer details.
Can be animated. An animated GIF contains a sequence of pictures in a single file that create an animation like an old-fashioned flipbook.	Cannot be animated.
The best option for image files under 35 kilobytes.	Useful for image files above 35 kilobytes, because the JPEG format's compression reduces the file size keeping download times reasonable.

GIF images

GIF (Graphic Interchange Format) is an 8-bit color lossless format that displays up to 256 RGB colors and is supported by virtually every browser. It is generally used for nonphotographic images with a narrow range of color, such as a company logo.

GIF images support *interlacing,* which stores the image in four passes instead of one. A non-interlaced image is transmitted one row of pixels at a time beginning with the top row and filling in from the top down. An interlaced GIF file is first displayed in full size in low resolution, and sharpens as the image's pixels are sent in the next three passes.

Two versions of the GIF format are in use on the Web: the original GIF 87a and a newer GIF 89a, which adds the ability to make image backgrounds transparent. After a color has been designated as the transparent color in the image file, a GIF 89a-compatible browser replaces every pixel of the designated color with a pixel the same color as the Web page's background. This allows the background color to show through the image in those areas.

GIF images can also be animated with a "flip-file" technique. By rapidly flipping through a series of images, a graphic object can be animated in the same way that a movie simulates motion using a series of still images. Line drawings work best, but photographs can also be used.

JPEG images

The JPEG (Joint Photographic Experts Group) format was created to enable true-color, 24-bit graphics to be contained in smaller files. JPEG is a lossy compressed image format that produces 10-to-1 space savings over a GIF file of the same image. JPEG is excellent for photographs and true-color original images, but does not work well with line art or files that contain only a few colors. JPEG files cannot be transparent and always appear rectangular on a Web page. For maximum color accuracy and a small file size, without transparency or interlacing, use the JPEG format.

PNG images

Another common raster graphic image format gaining some popularity on the Web is the PNG (Portable Network Graphics — pronounced ping) format. This is a new lossless true-color format developed to replace the GIF format. The PNG has some features the GIF doesn't, including 254 levels of transparency, more control over image brightness, and support for more than 48 bits per pixel. In comparison, the GIF format supports only one level of transparency and only 8 bits per pixel for 256 colors. A PNG file also compresses better than a GIF file, typically 10 to 30 percent smaller file sizes.

Other common graphic image formats

Some other common graphic image types include:

- ✔ **BMP (Bitmap Picture):** The standard format on DOS and Windows computers that stores images as 1-bit monochrome, 8-bit grayscale, or 24-bit color images.

- ✔ **DIB (Device Independent Bitmap):** A Microsoft Windows-based format that stores color data along with the image it affects.

- ✔ **EPS (Encapsulated PostScript):** A format developed by Adobe for PostScript printers. These files have two parts: a text description that tells a PostScript printer how to output the image and a bit-mapped PICT image for on-screen previews.

- ✔ **PICT (Macintosh Picture):** The standard format on Macintosh computers, originally developed to store 1-bit monochrome images. PICT is now capable of storing both raster and vector graphics.

- ✔ **TIFF (Tagged Image File Format):** A lossless format that provides a mechanism for storing many different types of images, including monochrome, grayscale, and 8- and 24-bit color bit-map files.

Working with your color palette

The color image you so painstakingly decide on may be all for naught, if the color is not commonly included in the color lookup table (CLUT) of the browser used to view your page. A CLUT is similar to the color-mixing chart at the paint store. A browser uses the color-coding stored in the compressed graphic image file to reference the CLUT and display the color indicated, or the closest one supported.

Although no standard color palette works equally well on all platforms, there is a 216-color palette commonly used that does not dither on most browsers. This allows you to use the colors of the palette with the assurance that the viewer will see what was intended to be displayed. Otherwise, what-you-see-is-not-necessarily-what-others-see (WYSINNWOS) takes over. More information is available on this palette at www.lynda.com.

Working with Internet Multimedia

Multimedia is the use of more than one medium (type) of sight or sound to entertain or inform. Multimedia coordinates and mixes the actions of sound recordings, still images, and moving images to create productions that make an impact on the viewer. The computer and the CD-ROM have made it possible for anyone to be a multimedia producer. The Internet and the Web have extended these possibilities by providing the ideal media over which multimedia productions can be released to a global audience.

Building multimedia with audio and video

The primary building blocks of multimedia are video and audio objects stored in files with special formatting that enables them to be transferred electronically and converted back into images or sounds. These files contain digitized images and sounds encoded into specific file formats for transmission and decoding on the viewer's computer.

In general, multimedia file formats can be separated into the following groups:

✔ Audio file formats

✔ Video file formats

✔ Multimedia (audio-visual) formats

I discuss file formats developed specifically for multimedia on the Internet and the World Wide Web in the "Multimedia documents" section later in this chapter.

Lending an ear to audio-only formats

The most common audio-only file formats in use are

- ✔ **AIFF (Audio Interchange File Format):** A digital audio file format for the Macintosh. AIFF breaks sound objects into parts called chunks. The Common chunk holds data such as the sound's sampling rate and size, and the Sound Data chunk contains the digitized sound samples.

- ✔ **WAV (waveform audio):** The de facto file format for non-streaming audio files. (For information on streaming files, see the "Streaming file formats," section later in this chapter.) WAV files are supported on nearly all platforms and require no special software beyond that normally included with virtually all sound cards. A WAV file contains a digital representation of an analog sound signal, and like most digital sound formats, the better the recording quality, the larger the file. WAV files can be very large. For example, an 8-bit recording can use as much as 1.5MB per minute of original sound, and a 16-bit recording can require 3MB per minute.

- ✔ **AU (Sun audio):** This standard, originally developed for the UNIX and NeXT platforms, is very similar to the WAV file format and fairly common on the Internet. All Windows audio players and Web browsers include support for the AU file format.

- ✔ **MIDI (Music Instrument Digital Interface):** A standard for synthesized sound reproduced by sound cards equipped with a synthesizing chip. A MIDI-capable sound card can specify the instrument originating the sound, the note being played, and the duration of the sound. MIDI is a standard adopted by the electronic music industry for controlling devices such as synthesizers, keyboards, and other devices that create music. Because a MIDI file stores only what is needed to reproduce a sound, MIDI files are much smaller than other sound data files, such as a WAV or AIFF file.

- ✔ **3-D audio:** An emerging sound playback technique used to give more depth to traditional 16- or higher-bit stereo sound, 3-D audio reproduces sound using a special device that adjusts the speaker's sound to create the impression that the speakers are further apart.

- ✔ **MPEG audio:** Compresses CD-quality sound by as much as a 12-to-1 ratio and produces reasonable playback sound quality. The MPEG audio standard has three layers (Layers I, II, or III) that increase in complexity as the layer number increases. The sound quality also increases with the layer number. Until very recently, only layers I and II are commonly used, but MP3 (as layer III is now called) is fast becoming popular as a record and playback standard over the Web.

Seeing and hearing video and multimedia architectures

Most video file formats are based on multimedia architectures. Just like you wouldn't videotape your child's birthday party with no sound, full-motion video images are rarely recorded without sound because the result would lack meaning and context. For this reason, the majority of the multimedia architectures used to store and transfer video images on the computer also store audio data as well. Combining video images with sound requires more sophisticated file formats than are required for sound only, resulting in larger, more complex files.

The three most popular multimedia file formats are:

- ✔ **AVI (Audio Visual Interleaved):** A proprietary digital audio-visual architecture developed by Microsoft that is also called Video for Windows and ActiveMovie in newer versions. AVI is actually more of an interface to a set of Windows graphic display routines instead of a video file format. Nonetheless, AVI files produce good video and sound reproduction. Drawbacks with AVI include a smaller windowpane for playback and the large file sizes it can generate. For example, a 30-second color animation AVI requires 1.4MB of storage space. DirectShow and ActiveMovie, which support playback of multimedia from the Web, CD-ROM, and DVD, are slowly replacing AVI.

- ✔ **QuickTime:** A proprietary digital audio-visual architecture developed by Apple Computer that has become one of the most popular and widely supported multimedia formats in use on any platform. QuickTime is a series of graphic display interfaces that are used to encapsulate supported audio and video file formats with instructions for playback. QuickTime creates good quality video clips in reasonably sized files. QuickTime files carry a MOV file extension.

- ✔ **MPEG (Motion Picture Experts Group):** MPEG is used for audio only, video only, as well as multimedia audio-visual files. MPEG is a nonproprietary, digital audio-visual architecture developed by the same organization that created the JPEG graphic image file standard (on which MPEG is based). MPEG was born from the desire for full-motion video on personal computers, and using MPEG, computer filmmakers have the ability to create a full-screen, full-motion video with a frame rate of 30 frames per second — the same frame rate used in television. Nearly all browsers support MPEG playback, but several add-on players are readily available for those that do not.

Using multimedia document tools

Numerous document creation and editing tools can publish multimedia documents to the Web. Among these are the member applications of Corel's WordPerfect Office, Microsoft Office, and the Lotus SmartSuite. Within these document preparation bundles, probably the best tools for producing multi-media for the Web are the presentation graphics packages (Corel Presentations, Microsoft PowerPoint, Lotus Freelance, and other freestanding packages such as Adobe Persuasion and Harvard Graphics). These tools publish documents in HTML format and often require additional editing.

Portable documents

The PDF (Portable Document Format) file format is a very common file format for documents encapsulated for viewing on the Web. A PDF file is created with Adobe Acrobat or Adobe PageMaker a convenient way for Web site owners to provide print-image documents on the Web.

Rich text documents

Another popular and highly portable document format for documents attached to Web pages is the Rich Text Format (RTF). Using this file format, you can exchange text files among different word processors running on different operating systems.

BinHex documents

BinHex (Binary/Hexadecimal) is a utility for converting Macintosh files into portable files that must be decoded at the receiving end. Netscape's Navigator browser, for one, includes the BinHex encoding and decoding capability as a standard. You can download a BinHex utility for either a Macintosh or Windows.

Web sites where BinHex utilities for both Macintosh and Windows computers can be found are:

> www.aladdinsys.com/expander/
>
> www.macupdate.com/info/33095.html
>
> www.simtel.net/

Serving up streaming file formats

Streaming audio and video, the latest developments in multimedia file formats, are experienced in near real-time. Enough of the file, maybe 10 percent of the total file, is downloaded from its source and while the remainder of the file is still downloading, the downloaded portion is played. The user can see and hear the file without waiting for the complete file to be received. The result is that you can see or hear, or both, a large streaming media file as it is downloading, rather than waiting for your 33.6 Kbps modem to download the entire file.

The alternatives to streaming data are files in a non-streaming format, such as WAV or MPEG files. Non-streaming files must be completely downloaded before playback can begin. Even the top browsers require plug-in players, such as Microsoft Media Player or RealPlayer, for each of the separate formats on the Web.

The top two streaming players are

- ✔ **RealPlayer:** Streams files from two existing technologies (RealAudio and RealVideo) over the Internet. RealNetworks, the company behind RealPlayer and related streaming media tools such as RealPlayer Plus and Real Jukebox, supports both live interactive and on-demand video and is the dominent streaming media company in the marketplace.

- ✔ **Windows Media Player:** Streams live and recorded broadcasts over the Web. Windows Media Player 6.0 is included in the full installation of Microsoft Internet Explorer 5.0, but on the Windows version only.

Multimedia applications and viewers

There are perhaps 50 different software tools that develop multimedia content for delivery over the Web. In most cases, an add-on or helper application is required to view multimedia files downloaded or streamed over the Web.

On the i-Net+ exam, you should know when each type of multimedia application would be used. Focus especially on Flash, Shockwave, and QuickTime (including QuickTime VR).

Here are some of the more popular add-on applications:

- ✔ **Macromedia Flash:** Although not actually a playback option, this tool is used to create small and compact animations and other motion effects for the Web. Flash objects are viewed through Flash-compatible applications such as Shockwave, RealPlayer, and others. More information is available at `www.macromedia.com/software/flash/`.

- ✔ **Macromedia Shockwave:** Shockwave users can deliver and experience interactive multimedia, graphics, and streaming audio on the Web. Shockwave elements are created and played back with Shockwave players that can be added to nearly every browser. Some of the latest browser versions include Shockwave viewers. To see some Shockwave demonstrations and get more information on how it's used visit `www.shockwave.com/`.

✔ **QuickTime and QuickTime VR:** These streaming media tools from
Apple Computer enable you to listen to and watch more than 30 video
and audio file formats running on a wide range of platforms. The
QuickTime VR tool also lets you view three-dimensional virtual reality
(the meaning of the VR) worlds in a 36-degree point of view also through
a streaming media format. Look for this one on the exam! If you have
never experienced a virtual reality world, you really owe it to yourself to
visit Apple's VR site at `www.apple.com/quicktime/qtvr/`.

✔ **RealPlayer:** This client enables users to listen to streaming audio, watch
streaming video, and view animations either live or on-demand. You can
get more information on RealPlayer at `www.real.com`.

✔ **Windows Media Player:** This multimedia and animation development
tool requires no programming skills to create and publish animations to
the Web. Liquid Motion objects are displayed on any browser that supports Java, running on any platform.

Jazzing up a site with Flash

Macromedia Flash produces sites that are flashier than sites using what some
would categorize as traditional Web technologies. Through Flash a site can
deliver to its visitors such attention-grabbing and entertaining elements as
music tracks, sound effects, animations, and other interface innovativations.
Flash includes an array of drawing tools, but any vector-based graphics can
be imported. In addition to its flashiness, Flash also implements streaming
technology so that sites begin playing in full-screen animated images as they
download. The Flash Player, a browser add-on application, is the most widely
distributed streaming multimedia viewer in use. In December, 1999, over 230
million copies of Flash and Shockwave had been distributed.

Shocking multimedia developments

Macromedia's Shockwave player has become a Web standard for playing multimedia content over the Web. Shockwave lets users interactively view Web
objects, such as games, slide presentations, animations, and multimedia-
enhanced banners and other advertisements through their Web browsers.
Some interesting sites to visit to see Shockwave elements in actions are
`www.disney.go.com`, `www.cartoonnetwork.com`, `www.candystand.com`
(for both Shockwave and Flash elements), and for you more serious types,
checkout `www.clevermedia.com/`.

The primary difference between Flash and Shockwave is that Flash is a
streaming media tool and Shockwave is not.

Moving about the Web in QuickTime

Apple Computer produces its QuickTime streaming multimedia tools in two
flavors: the popular QuickTime and the virtual reality version QuickTime VR.

QuickTime supports a number of file formats for playback, including MP3 (MPEG) and MIDI audio, and JPEG, BMP, PICT, PNG, and GIF image file formats. QuickTime also supports several formats of digital video and streaming formats such as AVI and MPEG. Some QuickTime streaming media sites you can visit for demonstrations are:

```
www.cnn.com
www.nickelodeon.com
www.mtv.com.
```

Quicktime VR, which reproduces virtual reality worlds that display a panoramic 360 degree view from a fixed view-point, is also a streaming media tool. For demonstrations on Quicktime VR, there are a variety of applications listed at www.apple.com/quicktime/qtvr/.

Looking up some good review sites

Some very good sites for reviewing your multimedia terminology and concepts is:

```
http://computingcentral.msn.com/category/multimedia/
http://directions.simplenet.com/hobbes/
http://hotwired.lycos.com/webmonkey/multimedia/
http://dutiem.twi.tudelft.nl/projects/MultimediaInfo/
```

Prep Test

1 Which of the following best describes lossy file compression?

A ○ All of the original image is compressed using simple substitution.

B ○ Parts of the original image are discarded to reduce the file size.

C ○ Only solid black or white areas are discarded during compression.

D ○ Only a potential exists for data loss during decompression.

2 Graphics on the Web are generally of which type?

A ○ Vector

B ○ Dithered

C ○ Raster

D ○ Half-raster

3 What are the two most popular graphic file formats on the Web? (Choose two.)

A ❑ BMP

B ❑ TIFF

C ❑ GIF

D ❑ JPEG

4 Which of the following are audio file formats used on the Web? (Choose three.)

A ❑ AIFF

B ❑ WAV

C ❑ QTVR

D ❑ MPEG

5 Web documents can be made portable in which of the following formats? (Choose two.)

A ❑ A presentation graphic slide show

B ❑ A PDF document

C ❑ A BinHex document

D ❑ A Microsoft Word document

6 The technology that enables a user to begin playback of a multimedia file before the entire file has downloaded is called _____.

A ○ Bit-mapped
B ○ Non-streaming
C ○ BinHex
D ○ Streaming

7 Which audio-only file format or technique adjusts the sound so that speakers sound like they are farther apart?

A ○ AU
B ○ MIDI
C ○ 3-D audio
D ○ MPEG

8 Which audio-only file format or technique is the standard for synthesized sound?

A ○ AU
B ○ MIDI
C ○ 3-D audio
D ○ MPEG

9 Which of the following statements relate to multimedia? (Choose all that apply.)

A ❑ More than one medium of sight or sound to entertain or inform
B ❑ Coordinates and mixes media from several sources
C ❑ Can be transferred electronically
D ❑ Only one medium can play back at a time

10 What is the primary difference between the GIF 87a and GIF 89a image standards?

A ○ Only 89a supports interlacing
B ○ Only 89a supports 256 colors
C ○ Only 89a supports transparent backgrounds
D ○ There are no differences

Answers

1 *B.* Lossy file compression loses part of the image data as it compresses it. Usually, unless the compression is very high, the loss is not noticeable by the human eye. *See "Lossy come home."*

2 *C.* Although more and more vector graphics are showing up, raster graphics are the current standard. *Review "Speaking graphically."*

3 *C and D.* Until such time as PNG or another format can unseat one of these two, they will likely remain the graphic file format champs. *Take a look at "Speaking graphically."*

4 *A, B, and D.* QTVR (QuickTime Virtual Reality) is not an audio file format; all the others are. *Check out "Lending an ear to audio-only formats."*

5 *B and C.* Presentation graphics files, such as Microsoft PowerPoint, and word processing documents usually require an add-on viewer on non-native platforms. *Look over "Using multimedia document tools."*

6 *D.* Streaming technology begins playback before the entire file has been downloaded. *See "Serving up streaming file formats."*

7 *C.* 3-D audio is useful if the speakers are very small or close together — for example, mounted on the side of a monitor. *Review "Lending an ear to audio-only formats."*

8 *B.* MIDI (Music Instrument Digital Interface) is the standard adopted by the electronic music industry for controlling keyboards, synthesizers, and other music source or playback devices. *Look over "Lending an ear to audio-only formats."*

9 *A, B, and C.* Multimedia can play back multiple media sources at once in a coordinated stream. *Check out "Working with Internet Multimedia."*

10 *C.* GIF 89a allows the background colors of an image to be replaced with another color, allowing graphics to appear to blend with Web page backgrounds. *Take a look at "GIF images."*

Part IV
The Internetwork

The 5th Wave   By Rich Tennant

"SINCE WE GOT IT, HE HASN'T MOVED FROM THAT SPOT FOR ELEVEN STRAIGHT DAYS. ODDLY ENOUGH THEY CALL THIS 'GETTING UP AND RUNNING' ON THE INTERNET."

In this part . . .

Twenty-five percent of the test is comprised of questions regarding the overall infrastructure of the Internet and its core components. You need to know about each of the current Internet's components and how they relate to each other. You should also be able to describe such things as domain names, DNS, and the nature, purpose, and operational essentials of TCP/IP protocols.

A majority of Internet users connect using some form of remote access. Therefore, you really need to understand the purpose and usage of the most common remote access protocols, and just a little about the basics of modem operations. Be sure you know how the various protocols or services apply to an e-mail system, the World Wide Web, and the file transfer system.

The Internet's infrastructure is made up of a variety of connectivity hardware and software. Be ready to answer questions about the various types of hardware, bandwidth technologies (link types), and the role played by the various servers found on the Internet.

You should also have a good understanding of Internet security concepts, including access control, virus protection, encryption, authentication, and VPNs, and know how to identify the various types of suspicious activities and the actions taken in each case.

Chapter 12

Internetworking

● ●

Exam Objectives

▶ Describing the relationship of the Internet's core components

▶ Explaining domain names and DNS

▶ Defining the TCP/IP protocols and their functions

● ●

*T*he logic behind the statement, "You don't need to know the inner workings of an internal combustion engine to know how to drive a car," doesn't hold for the Internet. In order to truly know how to use the Internet, you really must know its inner workings.

As an Internet professional, you cannot possibly troubleshoot a user's problem without knowing how the Internet's pieces fit and work together. By and large, users aren't interested in knowing how this all works. They just want it to work each and every time. Your ability to quickly discern the root of the problem, which usually has something to do with the IP address in one manner or another, is your key to successfully supporting Internet users.

What, you don't want to do customer support? You only want to be a Web designer and the i-Net+ is your first step? Well, I'm sorry to burst your bubble, but you still need to know this stuff. The core technologies of the Internet and IP addressing are required fare for any type of Internet professional. At least until they create the job of professional Internet surfer, and you'll have to get in line behind me for that position.

Quick Assessment

Describing the relation-ship of the Internet's core components

1 A modem or a NIC is the _____ that interacts with the communications protocols to connect you to the Internet.

2 An ISP connects to the backbone through a(n) _____.

3 The _____ refers to the high speed lines that carry Internet data between regional gateways.

4 An Internet interconnection point is called a(n) _____.

Explaining domain names and DNS

5 The _____ is a series of interrelated databases that provide host name to IP address resolution services.

6 The six top-level domains are _____, _____, _____, _____, _____, and _____.

7 Countries outside the United States use a _____ for their top-level domain code.

8 The Internet name that combines a host computer name with its domain name is a(n) _____.

Defining the TCP/IP protocols and their functions

9 An IPv4 address uses _____ three-digit numbers separated by periods.

10 The IP addressing device that is used to identify the network ID in an IP address is the _____.

Answers

1 *Network adapter.* See "Starting from home."

2 *POP.* Review "The ISP waystation."

3 *Internet backbone.* Take a look at "Time-out for definitions."

4 *NAP.* Check out "I sure could use a NAP."

5 *DNS.* Look over "Covering the DNS world."

6 *com, edu, gov, mil, net, org.* See "So, what's a domain?"

7 *Two-letter code.* Look over "Domains around the world."

8 *FQDN.* Check out "A fully qualified domain name."

9 *Four.* Review "A quick refresher of interesting IP address facts."

10 *Subnet mask.* Take a look at "Separating networks from hosts."

Assembling the Internet: Backbones and NAPs

As defined in Chapter 2, the Internet is really just a set of interrelated communications protocols that enable users to send e-mail, view and transfer documents, and — coming soon to an ISP near you — telephone-quality voice, full-motion video, and more. The Internet isn't a thing so much as it is a concept. I know that is hard to grasp for some people. I use it; therefore, it exists. Yes, the software you use does exist and the protocols supporting that software exist, but it is the cooperation of the software and protocols that creates the Internet, and whether that exists or not is for you to decide.

The part of the Internet that exists without a doubt is the physical infrastructure that provides the physical transport mechanism for the Internet — whatever that may be. For the i-Net+ exam, you need to know the components that make up the Internet's infrastructure and how they work together. Likely it will be easier for you to visualize the maze of cable and devices that make up the Internet's physical infrastructure if I start on the outside edge and work my way to the heart of the system.

Starting from home

First and foremost, the Internet is a network — actually a network of networks, but a network nonetheless. If you use a modem, either inside your computer or external, to connect to the Internet, the modem serves as your network adapter. If you happen to connect to the Internet on a local area network, your network adapter is inside your computer in the form of a network interface card (NIC). In either case, your network adapter — modem or NIC — interacts with the appropriate communications protocols so that you can network with the Internet. Although your modem or NIC network adapter is a very important link in the Internet network, it is not a part of the Internet's infrastructure; it is only one of the links you use to connect to the infrastructure.

The ISP waystation

When you connect to the Internet through your network adapter, you or your company establishes a connection to an ISP (Internet service provider). As I explain in Chapter 2, an ISP provides a range of Internet and communications-related services. However, connecting you to the Internet backbone is by far its most important service. In fact, this is the core reason for an ISP to exist. All of its other services are supplemental to the basic action of providing you with a connection to the Internet infrastructure and backbone.

ISPs either have direct connections to an Internet backbone or purchase access to the backbone from other higher level ISPs. Be careful with the levels: A higher-level ISP works at a lower level of the Internet infrastructure. The ISP serves as a buffer between the high-speed Internet backbone and your relatively slow-speed telephone or LAN connection by providing routing services to get your Internet traffic onto the Internet backbone.

The ISP connects to the backbone through a _POP_, or point of presence. The POP provides a local center and connection point to the high-speed backbone for the ISP. A POP usually serves several ISPs, other communications companies, and even some large businesses.

Time-out for definitions

I need to clear up a few of the terms I've been throwing at you: Internet infrastructure, Internet backbone, and POP:

- **Internet infrastructure:** The cabling, hardware, and software that together provide the underlying physical core of the Internet. The infrastructure of the Internet is made up of all the various backbone services that interconnect through regional gateways and local points of presence (POPs).

- **Internet backbone:** In general terms, the high-speed lines that carry Internet data between the regional gateways and local POPs. The Internet actually has more than one backbone system and several backbone providers, each with its own network of cabling (usually fiber optic cabling), routers, and POPs.

- **Point of presence (POP):** The connection point to the Internet backbone and infrastructure. Usually, a POP is a local or regional network router to which ISPs can route their Internet traffic.

I sure could use a NAP

At the highest levels of the Internet infrastructure are very high speed interconnection points, called network access points (NAPs). There are 12 major NAPs in the U.S. and several others around the world. The interconnections between these links create the spine of the Internet's backbone.

In 1995, when the Internet became commercial, four official NAPs were created: three were run by regional telephone companies in San Francisco (Pacific Bell), Chicago (Ameritech), and New York (Sprint Communications), and the fourth in Washington, D.C., which was setup by Metropolitan Fiber Systems (MFS) and was known as MAE-East (Metropolitan Area

Exchange-East). Since then, five more MAEs (MAE Chicago, MAE Dallas, MAE Houston, MAE Los Angeles, and MAE NewYork) have been added and have become de facto NAPs. In addition, two Federal exchanges and one called the Commercial Internet Exchange (CIX) have been added.

There are 12 major exchange points within the U.S. Visit the Web site for WorldCom, Inc., at `www.mfst.com/MAE/doc/maedesc/maedesc1.html`, or Ameritech at `http://nap.aads.net/main.html` to get more information on the services of a NAP.

The backbone connects to the backbone

Like all else in computing terminology, the term *backbone* is used a couple of different ways. There are LAN backbones, the cabling that interconnects buildings on a university campus for example, and there are WAN backbones, the kind that make up the Internet. So, it is not unheard of for a (LAN) backbone to connect to the (WAN) backbone.

How fast is fast?

I need to spend some time on line speeds before I go much further. If you connect to the Internet via a dialup modem, you can connect with speeds of up to 56Kbps. If you use DSL or cable modems, you have speeds of up to 1.54 Mbps, or about the speed of a T1 line (see Chapter 2). If you connect to the Internet over a LAN, your network connects to your ISP by either a dialup or perhaps a T1 line at 1.54 Mbps.

I mention these speeds to illustrate the dramatic difference in bandwidth between whatever means you use to connect to your ISP and the bandwidth of the Internet backbone, which may have speeds of 155 Mbps or higher. With its large bandwidth capacities, the backbone system of the Internet is capable of carrying the traffic from your ISP and its POP combined with all the other ISPs and POPs in the infrastructure.

The fiber-optic backbone

The backbone of the Internet — that is, all the various infrastructure backbone segments combined — is created from fiber-optic cabling (see Chapter 2). In the United States, fiber-optic cable uses the communications standard Synchronous Optical Network (SONET) and in Europe, it uses the Switched Digital Hierarchy (SDH) standard. These standards allow the fiber-optic networks (backbones) of the various carriers and NAPs to interconnect and interoperate with one another, thus creating the Internet's infrastructure and backbone.

The Internet backbone currently operates at 155 Mbps bandwidth — its next evolution, the vBNS (very high-speed Backbone Network Service) will operate at around 622 Mbps.

Finding Your Way Through the Internet Domain

In the preceding sections of this chapter, I describe the Internet in physical terms — as a network of cabling, NAPs, ISPs, and user connections. However, the Internet also has a softer side: the Internet domain structure. For the exam, you need to be very familiar with how the Domain Name System (DNS) is used to translate URLs and e-mail addresses into numerical IP addresses so that you can reach a remote host computer to download or deliver a message. You should also know the structure of the DNS, the types of entries that make up the DNS databases, and the different types of high-level domains in use. That's all!

Covering the DNS world

The Domain Name System (DNS) is a series of interrelated databases that provides the name-to-address resolution service for the Internet and the Web. In general, the DNS contains individual records that relate the domain name of a host computer, such as www.dummies.com, to its IP (Internet Protocol) address (206.175.162.18), or vice versa.

What's your authority?

The databases of the DNS are organized into a hierarchy based on their authority. The level of authority is actually a level of responsibility, derived from how much of the domain is included at any one level. Responsibility increases at the higher levels of the DNS hierarchy, just as in a company, the higher-ups have more responsibility than the poor working stiffs below them. Just like in a company organization structure, more responsibility usually carries more authority. Authority over what? The higher the authority a DNS level has, the broader its ability to resolve domain names into IP addresses. In other words, the more authority the DNS table has, the more entries it has.

Okay, so what this really means is that the DNS databases located closer to the Internet servers in its region have less authority and as a result have fewer entries (primarily those of the servers in its region). The next higher DNS database has authority over all of the DNS tables beneath it, and likewise has more entries, and so on all the way to the top, where the "Big Kahuna" of

DNS tables exists with the highest level of authority, and by far the most entries. Since a server in a remote region begins searching at the top of a domain regional structure, it makes sense that the highest level should have the most entries. Servers from within a region then need go only as high as necessary to find servers in their region. Got it?

Dividing up the task

DNS consists of databases that are divided up into domains and zones, and then distributed around the globe so that the DNS tables are focused on serving a certain domain within a particular region of the world. For any one database to hold all the domain names and IP addresses for every host computer connected to the Internet around the world would be virtually impossible.

So, what's a domain?

A DNS domain is all of a certain type of Internet accounts organized regionally into their levels of authority. Okay, but what's a domain? Long ago (actually back in the ARPANet period of Internet development), the powers-that-were established six top-level domains in the United States and one for each of the networked countries of the world to try to organize the rapid growth of the network.

The Internet DNS is organized so that all of the commercial companies are together, all of the educational institutions are together, all of the sites in China are together, and so forth. Table 12-1 lists the six major domains.

Table 12-1	Top-Level Domains
Domain	*Organization Type*
.com	Commercial entities
.edu	Education institutions
.gov	Branches of government
.org	Non-commercial and non-profit organizations
.mil	Branches of the military
.net	Internet service providers

Within any of the domains listed in Table 12-1, there are host computers within the domain. For example, dummies.com is in the .com domain, and all of the .gov hosts are organized into the .gov domain.

The DNS database tables are divided and distributed around the Internet onto what are called *name servers.* A name server processes requests from DNS clients for domain name resolutions. If one name server cannot process a request (which means in DNS talk that it has no authority), the request is passed on up the hierarchy to the next highest name server.

Domains around the world

Because the United States: 1) invented the Internet, 2) believes it owns the Internet, and 3) controls the Internet world, it also hogged up all six of the cool top-level domains. All the other countries in the world have to get by using only a two-letter top-level domain code that is generally based on the country name. For example, w-s-k.de is a German ISP; its top-level domain is .de (short for Deutschland, which is German for Germany), placing it in the German domain.

Table 12-2 lists some of the international country domains used (this is hardly a complete list, visit http://www.nu2.com/codes.html to see a complete list.

Table 12-2	Country Domain Codes
Country Code	*Country*
.al	Albania
.ca	Canada
.cn	China
.de	Germany
.fr	France
.gr	Greece
.jp	Japan
.mx	Mexico
.uk	United Kingdom
.us	United States

Yes, even the United States has a two-letter country code. Recently, each state in the U.S. was assigned a two-letter code as well. For example, the domain wa.us represents Washington State.

At the root of it all

The top-level domains exist in the hierarchy on what is known as a *root domain.* This level of the hierarchy is serviced by the DNS root servers, a system of 13 file servers. The central server contains the master list of top-level domains. Each day, the master domain list is copied to the 12 other file servers that are geographically dispersed around the world and managed by a variety of other agencies. The central root server and the master list are managed by Network Solutions, Inc., the company that currently manages domain name registrations.

Getting in on the fun

If you want to create a presence on the Internet by launching a Web site, you must first register the domain name you want to use. Your domain name is like your Internet handle or alias, but it is also the lookup address used to find your IP address.

If I wanted to publish a Web site under the domain name www.dummies.com, I would first perform a WHOIS search to see if it was already in use. I would not be allowed to register an already existing and registered domain name. However, if I can come up with a domain name that is not already being used, I can register it. My ISP assigns me an IP address and then completes the process by registering both the domain name and its IP address with the proper authority, currently Network Solutions, Inc. (www.networksolutions .com).

Now, my new domain name (www.yourdomainnamehere.com) is added to the appropriate DNS database so that my Web site can be accessed by Web surfers with exceptional taste and sophistication, as well as by my friends.

DNS table entry types

Some of the commonly used types of records in a DNS table are:

- ✔ **A (address) resource record:** Lists the address for a given machine.

- ✔ **CNAME (canonical name) resource record:** Specifies an *alias,* or nickname, for the official, or canonical, name.

- ✔ **HINFO (host information) resource record:** Contains host-specific data. The HINFO records list the hardware and operating system that are running at the listed host.

- ✔ **MB (mailbox) resource record:** Lists the machine where a user wants to receive e-mail.

- ✔ **MG (mail-group member) resource record:** Lists members of an e-mail group.

- ✔ **MX (mail exchanger) resource record:** Specifies a list of hosts that are configured to receive mail sent to this domain name.

- ✔ **NS (name server) resource record:** Lists a name server responsible for a given zone.

- ✔ **PTR (domain-name pointer) resource record:** Allows special names to point to some other location in the domain.

- ✔ **RP (responsible person) resource record:** Identifies the name (or group name) of the responsible person(s) for a host.

- ✔ **SOA (start-of-authority) resource record:** Designates the start of a zone and must appear at the beginning of every DNS *hosts* file.

- ✔ **WKS (well-known services) resource record:** Describes the well-known services supported by a particular protocol at a specified address.

A fully qualified domain name

Within a domain there can be several computers or hosts. Each domain name is unique, and within each domain each host also must have a unique name. The Internet name that includes both the host computer name and its domain name is called a *fully qualified domain name* (FQDN), because it specifies, or *qualifies,* a specific host in the named domain. Say that ten times fast! And please don't try to pronounce FQDN in mixed company, it just goes by its initials.

The FQDN www.dummies.com identifies the host computer www in the domain dummies.com. In the .com domain, dummies.com is a subdomain. So, the computer www is located on the dummies.com subdomain in the .com domain.

IP: The Other Address

The other side of the domain name is its IP address. Humans like the domain name, but computers just love the IP address. In fact, the computer absolutely must have the IP address because it is easier to use in digital form.

For the i-Net+ exam, you need to know a few things about how TCP/IP and IP addressing work, including:

- ✔ The basic principles of IP addresses

- ✔ IP address classifications (and how to tell one from another)

- ✔ How an IP address is decoded into its network part and its host part

- ✔ Which IP addresses are public (Internet) and which are private (intranet)

A quick refresher of interesting IP address facts

Before I get too deep into TCP/IP and its dependence on IP addressing, here are a few IP facts you should be aware of for the i-Net+ test:

✔ There are two versions of IP addresses, one in use (IPv4) and one in discussion (IPv6):

- IPv4 (IP version 4) is the version that you need to know for the test and to function in today's Internet world. In this book, anywhere I refer to *IP addressing,* I am referring to IPv4.

- IPv6 (IP version 6) is still under discussion. It is a 128-bit IP address that uses 8 sections of 16-bits each, which obviously provides a much longer and more complex addressing scheme. Now you have at least heard of it.

✔ IP addresses consist of four up-to-three-digit numbers separated by periods.

✔ IP addresses are 32-bits in length, consisting of four 8-bit numbers.

✔ Each of the four 8-bit numbers in an IP address is called an *octet.*

✔ The IP address for the domain name www.dummies.com is 206.175.162.18. You really don't need to know this address for the test, but I highly recommend it for excellent certification study guides.

Classes, networks, and hosts

IP addresses are divided into five classes, four of which are actively used on the Internet, and a fifth that is being held in reserve. The five IP address classes are lettered from highest to lowest as A to E.

One thing you should remember as I explain IP addressing is that the folks that devised this scheme never thought the Internet would grow beyond a few thousand networks of a few thousand users each. The IP network classes were devised originally to meet the needs of large, medium, and smaller networks, and not the Internet behemoth of today.

Table 12-3 summarizes the characteristics of the five IP address classes. Each class of IP address has a set number of networks and hosts per network, as well as a set range of IP addresses. There are also some IP addresses set aside for special purposes (see the "Special addresses" section later in this chapter).

Table 12-3	IPv4 Address Classes	
Class	*Number of Networks*	*Address Range*
A	126	1.0.0.0 to 126.255.255.255
B	16,384	128.0.0.0 to 191.255.255.255
C	2,000,000	192.0.0.0 to 223.255.255.255
D	0	224.0.0.0.0 to 239.255.255.255
E	Class E addresses are reserved for future use	

Class A addresses

There can be only 126 Class A networks on the entire Internet, but each of these networks can have a little less than 17 million uniquely addressed host computers. Accordingly, Class A addresses are only awarded to very large networks.

Class A addresses range from 1.*xxx.xxx.xxx* to 126.*xxx.xxx.xxx*, where the number indicates a network and the *xxx*'s identify a server or networked computer. There are 126 possible Class A networks, each with as many as 4 million nodes. Class A networks account for 50 percent of all IP addresses in use.

38.170.216.18 is an example of a Class A IP address.

Class B addresses

Class B addresses are assigned to medium-sized networks. There can be 16,000 Class B networks of more than 65,000 hosts each. Class B networks account for around 25 percent of all IP addresses on the Internet.

168.14.201.10 is an example of a Class B IP address.

Class C addresses

Class C networks are much smaller and there are around two million of them on the Internet, accounting for about 12.5 percent of all available IP addresses. Each Class C network can address a maximum of 254 computers.

204.16.223.5 is an example of a Class C IP address.

The lower classes

Class D addresses are set aside for network multicasting, which sends network packets to groups of host computers, generally located on different networks. Class E addresses are reserved for future use.

Special addresses

Network addresses that are all zeros (0.0.0.0), all ones (111.111.111.111), and network addresses beginning with 127 are special network addresses. All zeros indicates the current host, all ones is used to send a broadcast message to the local network or network segment, and 127.*xxx.xxx.xxx* addresses are used to perform loopback testing, which sends a signal out to the network that is bounced back to the sending station. Loopback testing is used to test network adapters and connections.

There are also three IP address ranges set aside for network managers to use on internal networks and intranets not connected to the Internet. The IP addresses in these ranges are called private addresses. Any addresses not in these address ranges are public addresses. Private addresses are not routable, but public addresses are routable.

The private IP address ranges are

- ✔ 10.0.0.0 through 10.255.255.255
- ✔ 172.16.0.0 through 172.31.255.255
- ✔ 192.168.0.0 through 192.168.255.255

Separating networks from hosts

An IP address identifies both the identity of a network and one of its host computers. After a domain name is translated into its associated IP address, the message or Web site is located on the Internet by identifying the network portion of the IP address. In order to pull the network ID out of an IP address, a filter is applied that masks out the bits not used in the network address, thus highlighting the network's address. This filter is called a subnet mask.

Here's how the subnet mask is used:

1. In order to route an IP address to its destination, it must be determined if the address is on the local network or a remote network.

2. The subnet mask extracts the network ID from the IP address, and the network ID is compared to the local network ID.

3. If the IDs match, the destination is on the local network. If they don't, the address must be routed outside of the local network.

A subnet mask is a binary bit pattern that when added to the binary bits of the IP address filters out non-matching bits. The bits of the local network will yield the local network address, and the bits of a remote network do not produce the local network address. This filtering action is called Boolean algebra.

A quick lesson in Boolean algebra

Boolean algebra uses binary logic to yield binary results. There are four basic principles in Boolean algebra:

- ✔ 1 and 1 = 1
- ✔ 1 and 0 = 0
- ✔ 0 and 1 = 0
- ✔ 0 and 0 = 0

The only way to end up with a 1 is to combine two 1s. Everything else results in a 0. Another way to look at this is that if 1 indicates a true condition and 0 a false condition, then only true and true can make true. Any combination of true and false (or false and false) result in false.

If I were to line up two rows of binary numbers, the first being a value being tested and the second a truth filter, only those positions where both numbers have a one (true), would yield a one in the resulting condition number produced by combining them with Boolean algebra. In this example

```
Test number:      101011101
Filter number:    100000101
Result number:    100000101
```

only where the test number and the filter number both have a one in a column will a one appear in the result number. ***Words to live by:*** only true and true make true.

Class masks

Each IP address class has a default subnet mask that is used to identify the network ID in any address of that class. Table 12-4 lists the standard IP class subnet masks.

Table 12-4	Standard Subnet Masks
Address Class	*Standard Subnet Mask*
Class A	255.0.0.0
Class B	255.255.0.0
Class C	255.255.255.0

Putting on your mask

Here is an example of how the subnet mask is applied:

1. A destination IP address of 206.175.162.18 has a binary equivalent of 11001110 10101111 10100010 00010010. (Don't worry — you won't be asked to convert decimal numbers into binary on the test.)

2. The common Class C subnet mask is 255.255.255.0. Its binary equivalent is 11111111 11111111 11111111 00000000

3. When these two binary numbers are combined (see "A quick lesson in Boolean algebra" earlier in this section), the network ID is identified as 206.175.162.0. The host ID (18) is stripped away.

4. The resulting network ID is the same as the IP address of the local network, which indicates that the host with the original IP address is a node on the local network.

But I Still Can't Connect

There are reasons why you may not be able to connect to remote servers over the Internet; it may be your own doing or it could just be the fates evening the score for your past deeds. Regardless, for the i-Net+ test, you need to know the kinds of problems you can run into with e-mail, Web sites, and, everyone's favorite, the slow server.

Making the e-mail connection

There are two primary reasons why you cannot connect to an e-mail server: your configuration is wrong and, well, your configuration is wrong.

Whether you are dialing up an ISP or connecting over a LAN, if your e-mail client is not configured properly, you won't make the connection. Here are some common e-mail bugaboos:

✔ **Cannot create network connection, unable to locate host:** This error can have a number of causes. Two common causes are that you are not connected to your ISP when trying to send e-mail, or that you are trying to connect to the wrong server or service. Check your dialup connection settings.

✔ **Unable to find the SMTP host or POP3 server:** Most likely the SMTP (Simple Mail Transport Protocol) or POP (Post Office Protocol) designation in your account settings is not correct. Verify it with your service provider or LAN administrator and then enter the correct setting; it should be something like mail.*isp*.net or pop.*isp*.net.

✔ **The password entered is incorrect, please re-enter your password:** Okay, you are positive you have repeatedly entered the correct password. So, humor me, check the Caps Lock key. If all is well, contact your mail administrator to see if the password file has been corrupted.

✔ **Unable to find DNS server:** The most common reason for this error is that the TCP/IP settings are either wrong or failed to connect. Check and verify your TCP/IP settings and, if they are as they should be, contact the ISP or network administrator.

✔ **Sent mail is not delivered to addresses:** This is an indication that the mail server designation in your network settings is not the local POP or SMTP server. You need to check the settings for the account to which you are trying to connect. These settings are usually set in your e-mail client.

Taking the slow boat

There is nothing so frustrating as a slow e-mail or Web site server. Your half-gigabyte of RAM and 500 Mhz processor have absolutely no impact on a slow remote server on the Internet.

The primary cause of a server being slow is either a general lack of resources (RAM, processor speed, and slow disk drives) or a server with ample resources spreading them too thin to too many users. The solution for the server's users is simple; if it takes eons, don't go there. However, the only remedy for the site owners is to either increase the resources or limit the number of concurrent accesses. In either case, the goal has to be an increase of available resources to each user accessing the server.

Your problem could also be that the remote server only appears to be slow. The backbone may be busy or overloaded, or the site is requesting a reverse DNS and the DNS tables are incorrectly set for your server. If the backbone is near or at capacity, you can only wait and try again later. However, if you do have a reverse-DNS problem, your ISP must resolve this problem working with the Network Solutions, and possibly ARIN (American Registry for Internet Numbers – the agency that assigns IP addresses) people to correct the DNS tables. Reverse-DNS problems occur when a remote server cannot translate your IP address back into your e-mail account and domain-name-server ID.

Testing the connection

You can track down where on a network a problem may exist by using the PING and TRACERT commands to test whether the remote server or site is valid or responding properly.

To run either of these TCP/IP utilities on a Windows computer, choose Start⇨Run. In the Run dialog box that's displayed, enter either the **ping** or the **tracert** command, followed by a URL or IP address you want to test. Here's a sample Run dialog box entry:

```
tracert www.dummies.com
```

Prep Test

1 Which of the following are parts of the Internet infrastructure? (Choose three.)

- A ❑ POP
- B ❑ Regional gateways
- C ❑ Backbone
- D ❑ NIC

2 Each of the major interconnection points on the Internet backbone is called a(n) _____.

- A ○ POP
- B ○ PPP
- C ○ ISP
- D ○ NAP

3 The Domain Name System (DNS) is _____.

- A ○ A Windows-based tool used to translate MAC device addresses into IP addresses.
- B ○ A series of interrelated databases organized in a hierarchy that is used to translate domain names into IP addresses.
- C ○ A UNIX-based local file that is used to translate computer-names into their IP addresses.
- D ○ A series of connecting points on the Internet backbone.

4 Which of the following are valid top-level domains? (Choose all that apply.)

- A ❑ .net
- B ❑ .org
- C ❑ .bus
- D ❑ .uk
- E ❑ .ca
- F ❑ .wa.us
- G ❑ .stu

5 Requests from DNS clients for domain resolution are processed by _____.

- A ○ Name servers
- B ○ Web servers
- C ○ Browsers
- D ○ WINS servers

6 The Internet name that combines the host computer name with its domain name is called a(n) _____.

A ○ URL

B ○ Socket

C ○ FQDN

D ○ IP address

7 Which two characteristics apply to the IP address 101.101.101.010? (Choose two.)

A ❑ IPv6 address

B ❑ IPv4 address

C ❑ Class C address

D ❑ Class A address

8 Each of the address segments in an IP address is called a(n) _____.

A ○ Sextet

B ○ Quartet

C ○ Quartile

D ○ Octet

9 IP addresses in the range 10.0.0.0 to 10.255.255.255 are _____.

A ○ Public addresses

B ○ Private addresses

C ○ Restricted addresses

D ○ Routable

10 If your customer repeatedly gets the "Unable to locate host computer" error message when trying to check his or her e-mail, what action should you recommend?

A ○ Ensure the connection is active when the e-mail client is trying to send or receive mail.

B ○ Ensure the password is valid.

C ○ Check the DNS settings.

D ○ Check the TCP/IP settings.

Answers

1 *A, B, and C.* The Internet infrastructure is made up of all the components, cabling, connectivity devices, software, protocols, and so on, involved in carrying and delivering packets over the network. *See "Assembling the Internet: Backbones and NAPs."*

2 *D.* Okay, POP is arguably a correct answer as well, but a POP is not really considered a MAJOR connection point on the Internet backbone, while a NAP is. *Review "I sure could use a NAP."*

3 *B.* Answer A describes WINS; answer C describes a local hosts file; and answer D describes the NAPs. DNS is a hierarchy of interrelated databases that are used to convert domain names into IP addresses and sometimes the reverse. *Take a look at "Finding Your Way Through the Internet Domain."*

4 *A, B, D, E, F.* `.net` refers to network service providers; `.org` is used for non-profit and non-commercial organizations; `.uk` is the top-level for the United Kingdom, and `.ca` is the one for Canada; `.wa.us` is used for the Washington State domain, just like `.ca.us` is used for California. *Check out "So, what's a domain?" and "Domains around the world."*

5 *A.* The DNS is a client/server world with host software clients requesting domain name resolution from DNS name servers. *Look over "So, what's a domain?"*

6 *C.* The fully qualified domain name (FQDN) includes the name of the host computer (`www`) along with the domain name (`dummies.com`). The URL includes the FQDN along with the transfer protocol and an optional reference to a specific document. *See "A fully qualified domain name."*

7 *B and D.* IPv4 addresses, the ones actually in use currently, have four up-to-3-digit numbers separated by periods (dots). Class A addresses are in the range of 1.0.0.0 to 126.255.255.255. *Review "A quick refresher of interesting IP address facts" and "Classes, networks, and hosts."*

8 *D.* Not to be confused with a singing group, each IP octet represents a single 8-bit number. *Look over "A quick refresher of interesting IP address facts."*

9 *B.* There are three ranges of private and non-routable IP addresses that can be used for networks behind a firewall or intranets that do not connect to the Internet. *Take a look at "Special addresses."*

10 *A.* This message usually means that the wrong server is in use for the service being requested or that there is no connection made to the server at all. *Check out "Making the e-mail connection."*

Chapter 13

Connecting to the Internet

● ●

Exam Objectives

▶ Describing the operation of a modem

▶ Explaining remote-access protocols and services

▶ Identifying hardware and software-connectivity tools

▶ Describing Internet-bandwidth technologies

▶ Defining server types

● ●

*M*ost users (including me for sure, and very likely you) use remote access to connect to the Internet. To gain access to e-mail, to browse the Internet and the World Wide Web, or to download or upload files, users typically employ a combination of plain old telephone service (POTS), a modem, and some form of point-to-point protocol. To experienced Internet users, this process hardly deserves thinking about, because it happens so automatically. However, to an inexperienced or technically-challenged user, this is a daunting experience, somewhat akin to navigating the fiery, life-threatening Internet maze of hell.

I don't know about you, but I, for one, am guilty of taking remote dialup access for granted. I subconsciously hum along to the song of the modem's handshake, while I daydream about the cool stuff I'll see when the connection is made. How many times have you given serious thought to what exactly is going on? I suggest you pay attention the next time you connect to your ISP and really think about what's going on in this process.

For Internet-support technicians, you can bet your browser that the majority of questions you field are about modem dialup, remote access (configuration, logon, and so on), and connectivity and transport protocols. Surfing the Net is the easy part, because it uses tools (browsers, mouse, and keyboard) that a 4-year old can easily operate. The problems lie in the modem, telephone, and protocols — the parts that were designed, in a continuing effort to maintain job security, to be set up and operated only by technical support people.

The general topic of remote access is included on the i-Net+ exam in the Networking section, which amounts to 20 percent of the test. Just how much of the test involves remote access, connectivity, and protocol issues is hard to say, but you should figure on seeing at least five or so questions on this topic.

Quick Assessment

Describing the operation of a modem

Explaining remote access protocols and services

Identifying hardware and software connectivity tools

Describing Internet bandwidth technologies

Defining server types

1 A modem converts _____ signals into _____ signals.

2 All computer modems communicate through a _____ port.

3 The most common tunneling protocol is _____.

4 The two protocols used for establishing a point-to-point connection are _____ and _____.

5 A(n) _____ is the physical device that enables one hardware or software interface to interconnect with another.

6 A(n) _____ is the entrance and exit to and from a network.

7 A(n) _____ carrier transmits 24 channels of data at 64Kbps.

8 The carrier service that handles bursty network WAN traffic very well is _____.

9 A(n) _____ server saves Web pages and FTP files downloaded by users to eliminate unnecessary bandwidth usage.

10 A continuously running program that handles client requests is a(n) _____.

Answers

1 *Digital, analog.* See "Converting signals."

2 *Serial.* Review "The port."

3 *PPTP.* Look over "Tunneling through the Net."

4 *PPP, SLIP.* Check out "The Protocol of Remote Access."

5 *Adapter.* Take a look at "The Stuff Connections are Made From."

6 *Gateway.* See "The Stuff Connections are Made From."

7 *T1.* Check out "The Bigger They Are, The Faster It Flows."

8 *Frame relay.* Take a look at "The Bigger They Are, The Faster It Flows."

9 *Cache.* Review "Cache server."

10 *Daemon.* Look over "HTTP server."

What You Should Know about Modems

Most users connect to the Internet through the public telephone system — the plain old telephone service (POTS). In a kind of oil-and-water comparison, POTS is an analog signal system designed to carry sound waves, and the computer and the Internet are digital systems designed to transmit binary data. Analog and digital can be converted one to the other, but they do not mix, which is why a device to perform the conversion is needed.

Converting signals

The conversion of digital signals to analog signals so that they can be transmitted over the POTS, which by the way is called the public-switched telephone network (PSTN) in the context of the Internet, is called *modulation*. After the signal has traversed the PSTN and arrived at its destination, a process called *demodulation* converts the analog signal back into a digital format for use on a computer or network.

Modem standards

You have probably heard or read about the "V" standards. Table 13-1 lists the "V dot" modem standards you are likely to come into contact with on the job and possibly on the i-Net+ test. The bits-per-second numbers listed in Table 13-1 are the maximum rates supported by each of the modem standards.

How modulation and demodulation works

Modulation is the conversion of digital computer signals (you know like on and off, high and low, yes and no, 1 and 0) into analog audio-frequency (AF) tones. Binary ones (digital high values) are converted into a specific constant audio tone. Binary zeroes are transformed into a different constant tone. It is these two sounds that are transmitted over the telephone line between two modems, the modulator and the demodulator.

If you listen to the output of a modem, it sounds like static in a kind of hissing roar. This is the result of thousands of the two different audio tones being transmitted each second.

At the destination modem, demodulation reverses the conversion process, changing the audio tones back into their digital-signal equivalents for the computer, printer, or whatever digital device is attached to the modem. As its name implies, a modem can perform both modulation and demodulation depending on which end of the process it is in any transmission.

Internet users, with computer equipment new and old, use a variety of modem standards for remote connectivity. You should be familiar with the various standards, especially V.34 and V.90 (hint, hint).

Table 13-1	The V.x Modem Standards
Standard	*Bits per Second (bps)*
V.32	9,600
V.32bis	14,400
V.34	28,800
V.34bis	33,600
V.42	57,600
V.90	56,000+

The word *bis* is a French term for "second," and is used to indicate a second version of a standard. You may also see standards that have *terbo*, a third, but not necessarily faster version.

Here's the latest

The V.90 standard, the latest modem standard, transfers data to the modem using a technology that lets the data bypass modulation at a speed of 56 Kbps. However, when uploading data, a V.90 modem transfers data at a speed of 33.6 Kbps that must be modulated.

Connecting a modem

Modems are attached to a computer either internally or externally. The internal modem has become basically a standard feature of most of the newer computer models. However, some people prefer the external modem. In my case, I just like to watch the lights! A can of diet soda pop and modem lights — now that's quality entertainment! Okay, so I need to get out more.

An internal modem is installed in either an ISA (Industry Standard Architecture) or a PCI (Peripheral Components Interconnect) expansion bus slot on the computer's motherboard. The internal modem usually has a small speaker attached so that you can hear the series of sounds played during the connection (handshake) process.

A quick note on the sounds you hear during the connection process: These sounds are purely for your benefit. In the computer system, the only component with ears is you. These sounds let you know something is happening. Experienced modem users can also tell if something is wrong by listening to the sound sequence.

An external modem connects to your modem using a serial port. External modems are not as common as they once were, but they are still in use.

The plug

Regardless of whether the modem is internal or external, it is attached to the PSTN with an RJ-11 plug, a smaller version of the RJ-45 connector used with Ethernet networks (see the "The Stuff Connections are Made From," section later in this chapter).

The port

All computer modems communicate through serial ports. A serial port transmits its data one bit at a time in a single-file line, or in a series (in contrast to a parallel port that transmits its data many bits at a time side by side). Most computers have at least one serial port, which is designated as COM1. *COM* refers to communications or serial port. The computer can have as many as four serial ports, which would be designated as COM2, COM3, and COM4.

Configuring a modem

Usually, a modem requires very little configuration. Most modems are preset to general communications standards and are compatible with nearly all PC types. There are a variety of ways to configure a modem that does require some setup, including software, built-in commands, or DIP switches or jumper blocks on the modem.

Actually, two phases are involved in setting up a modem connection: configuring the modem, and setting up the dialup network properties. Just for practice, use Lab 13-1 to set up a modem on a Windows computer.

Lab 13-1   Configuring a Modem on a Windows Computer

1. **To set up the modem on a Windows 98 computer, use the Install New Modem wizard, shown in Figure 13-1. Access the Install New Modem wizard by double-clicking the Modems icon in the Windows Control Panel and then clicking Add in the Modems Properties dialog box that's displayed.**

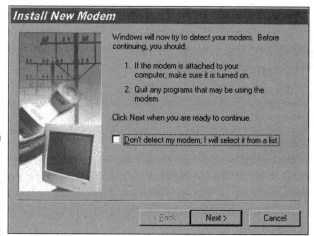

Figure 13-1:
The Install
New
Modem
wizard.

The system can detect the new modem (assuming it is already installed into an expansion slot or connected to a serial port) or you can pick it from the list of supported modems (my recommendation). Figure 13-2 shows the list of modems supported in Windows.

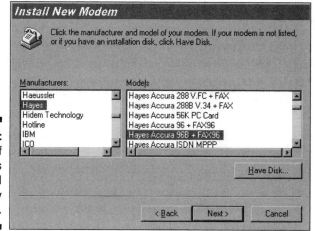

Figure 13-2:
The list of
modems
supported
by
Windows.

Modems are often pre-installed and configured on new computer systems. You can check the configuration settings of an installed modem by clicking the Properties button in the Modems Properties dialog box. Figure 13-3 shows a modem's connection properties.

U.S. Robotics 56K Voice Win Prope... ? ×

General | Connection | Distinctive Ring | Forwarding |

Connection preferences
Data bits: 8
Parity: None
Stop bits: 1

Call preferences
☑ Wait for dial tone before dialing
☑ Cancel the call if not connected within 60 secs
☐ Disconnect a call if idle for more than 30 mins

Port Settings...   Advanced...

OK   Cancel

Figure 13-3:
A modem's
connection
properties.

2. **To complete the modem configuration, you need to configure the dialup network settings. This configuration is centered around the dialup destination. Double-click the Dial-Up Networking icon in the My Computer window, as shown in Figure 13-4.**

🖳 *My Computer*   _ □ ×

File Edit View Go Favorites Help

Back Forward Up Cut Copy Paste Undo

Address 🖳 My Computer

My Computer

Dial-Up Networking
System Folder

Use Dial-Up Networking to gain access to shared information on another computer, even if your computer is not on a network. The computer you are

3½ Floppy (A:)   (C:)   (D:)   Removable Disk (S:)

Printers   Control Panel   Dial-Up Networking   KODAK DC260 Zo...

Scheduled Tasks

🖳 My Computer

Figure 13-4:
The Dial-Up
Networking
icon in the
My
Computer
window.

In the Dial-Up Networking window is an icon labeled Make New Connection and possibly some existing connections. Double-clicking the Make New Connection icon opens the Make New Connection wizard, shown in Figure 13-5, that guides you through steps to create a new dialup destination.

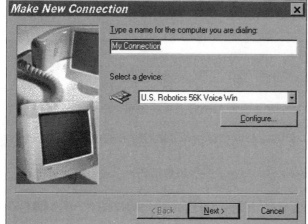

Figure 13-5:
The Make
New
Connection
wizard.

The secret language of the modem

Deep inside your modem is a set of secret commands that most computer and modem users never see, even though this secret code set is common to nearly all modems. The AT command set is used to set up, command, and operate the modem. Your computer performs these operations automatically using the commands in the AT command set.

The AT command set gets its name from the fact that most of the commands are preceded by the code AT, which stands for attention. For example, the command to dial 555-1212 is ATDT5551212, which is interpreted as AT (attention), DT (tone dial), and the phone number.

Table 13-2 contains a few of the common AT commands.

Table 13-2	Modem AT Commands
AT Command	**Action**
, (comma)	Pause
/ (slash)	Wait for connection

(continued)

Table 13-2 (continued)

AT Command	Action
*70	Turn off call-waiting feature on telephone line
A	Answer incoming calls manually
DT	Dial using touchtone mode
&F	Reset modem to factory settings
H	Hang up
Z	Reset and reinitialize modem

I've heard that some telephone systems may use 70# or other key combinations to turn off the call-waiting feature. That's fine, but for the exam, remember *70.

Other members of the modem family

There are modems that are used to connect to carrier types other than the PSTN, including DDS, ISDN, DSL, and cable TV transport media.

Review the following transport media and connection types so that you understand what each is and the benefits of each. You will definitely see these on the test.

In other words, there are different modems for different transport technologies:

- ✔ **Analog:** This is the modem I have been talking about so far, and the one with which you are probably the most familiar. Analog modems are used to connect to the POTS and PSTN.

- ✔ **Cable modem:** This device enables your PC to receive and send data signals over your cable TV system at around 1.5 Mbps. A cable modem is actually more like a coaxial cable network adapter than a normal computer modem.

- ✔ **DDS (Digital Data Service):** This type of line, also called a dedicated or leased line, provides a direct point-to-point dial up connection usually between two points of the same organization. A DDS line does not use modems, using a CSU/DSU (customer service unit/data service unit) at each end of the line instead. The primary benefit to the DDS line is that it is dedicated. It is still a dialup line with dialup speeds, but offers a clear end-to-end channel for the user.

✔ **DSL (Digital Subscriber Line):** This is an emerging technology that delivers high-bandwidth to homes and businesses using their ordinary POTS copper telephone lines. You may see DSL referred to as xDSL, where the x represents the various flavors of DSL being offered, including ADSL (Asymmetric DSL), HDSL (High bit-rate DSL), VDSL (Very high data-rate DSL), and others. If you live close enough to a telephone company's central office, you could soon be able to receive data at as much as 6.1 Mbps. DSL modems use one of three modulation techniques: Discrete Multitone Technology (DMT), Carrierless Amplitude Modulation (CAP), or Multiple Virtual Line (MVL).

✔ **ISDN (Integrated Systems Digital Network):** ISDN is another standard for transmitting digital signals over POTS copper wire, and other media as well, at speeds of up to 128 Kbps. There are two types of ISDN service: Basic Rate Interface (BRI), which is commonly used for home and small businesses; and Primary Rate Interface (PRI), for larger companies for high-bandwidth usage. ISDN service requires an adapter, called an inverse multiplexor, at each end of the transmission.

The Protocol of Remote Access

When you connect to the Internet using a modem, you are most likely using the PPP (Point-to-Point Protocol) or perhaps even the SLIP (Serial Line Internet Protocol). PPP connects one computer to another network and handles any network protocol translation problems encountered. In effect, PPP turns the modem into a network adapter, enabling your connection to the remote network.

Getting the point-to-point

PPP (point-to-point protocol) is the de facto protocol standard for point-to-point connections, providing interconnection to a host of networking protocols, including TCP/IP, NetBEUI (NetBIOS Extended User Interface), AppleTalk, and IPX. PPP seamlessly connects your computer to the remote network and its network protocol regardless of the network protocol in use locally. PPP also supports data compression and error checking, making it fast and reliable.

Giving it the SLIP

SLIP (serial-line Internet protocol) is a legacy protocol common to UNIX systems, where it is used for establishing dialup connections to the Internet. SLIP provides no addressing, and is used only to connect to TCP/IP networks.

Tunneling through the Net

The most common tunneling protocol is PPTP (Point-to-Point Tunneling Protocol), which tunnels PPP over an IP network to create a network connection. In other, and hopefully clearer, words, *tunneling a protocol* means a protocol, such as IPX or AppleTalk, is routed inside packets of another protocol, like TCP/IP. In this way, two networks can connect and communicate, each in its native protocol, such as AppleTalk, while their communications are transmitted using a TCP/IP format.

PPTP allows packets from a variety of protocols (IP, IPX, or NetBEUI) to be encapsulated inside of IP packets for transmission. Like plain brown shipping cartons, the IP outer wrapping is discarded at the receiving end and the original packet is then forwarded on to its destination over its native protocol.

PPTP creates a virtual connection for a remote user. To users, it appears that they are directly connected to the network, as if they were local to it. This PPTP connection creates what is called a *virtual private network* (VPN). See Chapter 15 for more information on VPNs.

The Stuff Connections Are Made From

Connections are actually built on hardware and software that allow two devices to communicate without losing function or data. There are many different types of hardware and software that can be used to establish a connection.

Here are the hardware and software you should know for the i-Net+ exam:

- ✔ **Adapter:** This is any physical device that allows one hardware or software interface to interconnect with another. As relates to the Internet, the adapter for most PCs is either its modem or its NIC, or both.

- ✔ **Bridge:** A bridge is a device used to connect two local area networks (LANs) that use the same protocol, such as two TCP/IP networks. A bridge looks at each message sent over the network, taking action on those that need to be bridged over to a different network.

- ✔ **Firewall:** A firewall, which is usually software but can be a special piece of hardware, protects private networks from unauthorized access by outside users. A firewall is configured with a set of permitted and denied users, domains, or ports that are allowed or not allowed to pass through to the internal network.

- ✔ **Gateway:** A gateway is the entrance and exit to and from a network. A gateway is usually a router on the network through which messages for outside destinations are sent outward and messages for destinations on the internal network are permitted to pass.

✔ **Hub:** Hubs are used to interconnect parts of networks and are quite common on Ethernet networks. There are passive and active hubs that receive and route signals received on one of its ports to one or all of its other ports. Hubs are used as clustering devices to connect several devices to a single network cable.

✔ **Internet-in-a-box:** This is a catch-all name that describes a catch-all product type. Internet-in-a-box devices include everything a small office needs to connect to the Internet securely, which may include connections for dial up, DSL, ISDN, and other transport types, a proxy server, a firewall, and extra storage in the form of *cache-in-a-box* — dynamic storage that may be accessed by all users on the inside network.

✔ **Network interface card (NIC):** This is a special kind of expansion card that servers as an adapter and allows a computer to be connected to a network.

✔ **Network operating system (NOS):** An NOS is the system software designed to manage and support the client workstations and other devices connected to a LAN. Novell NetWare and Banyan Vines are commonly used NOSs. Windows NT, while actually a multipurpose operating system and not technically an NOS, is usually referred to as an NOS.

✔ **RJ-45 connector:** This plug and receiver set look very much like the RJ-11 connectors used with your telephone system. The RJ-45 is the standard connector for UTP (unshielded twisted pair) cabling and uses 8 wires, or 4-pairs. The "RJ" stands for registered jack.

✔ **Router:** A router can be either hardware, software, or both. A router decides the next location to which a message traveling on the network is to be sent. Routers are located at all of the network intersections of the Internet and provide the routing that gets a message from its source to its destination.

✔ **Switch:** A network switch is a sophisticated hub that operates much like a router, but usually within a single network. A switch examines a message to determine its route, and then switches it on to only the best route to its destination.

✔ **UTP (Unshielded Twisted Pair):** When used as Ethernet 10BaseT wiring, this cable uses four-twisted pairs of copper wire.

The Bigger They Are, the Faster It Flows

In addition to the various pieces of hardware and software used to establish a connection (see the previous sections in this chapter), another consideration is the bandwidth technology or link type used to carry the data. These technologies may or may not affect the data itself, but they definitely have an impact on its speed (bandwidth) and the linkage used to connect to the transport media.

For the i-Net+ exam, you need to know about the following bandwidth technologies and link types:

- ✔ **T1/E1:** A T1 carrier transmits 24 channels of data at 64 Kbps each, for a total data speed of 1.54 Mbps. A T1 can be fractionalized a number of different ways to provide a varying number of circuits at different data rates ranging from 56 Kbps, 384 Kbps (quarter T1), 512 Kbps (half T1), or 768 Kbps (three-quarter T1). The approximate equivalent of a T1 in Europe is the E1 carrier, which provides a rate of 2.048 Mbps over 32 channels.

- ✔ **T3/E3:** A T3 carrier transmits 672 channels (the equivalent of 28 T1s) for a total bandwidth of 44.74 Mbps. The E3 carrier is its European equivalent which consists of 16 E1 carriers with a bandwidth of 34.368 Mbps.

- ✔ **Frame relay:** This carrier service handles bursty (intermittent transmissions as opposed to a constant stream of data) network WAN traffic very well using a variable length packet called a frame, and is usually provided over either a full or fractional T1 carrier. Frame relay offers a service between ISDN on the low end and ATM on the high-end.

- ✔ **X.25:** This standard network protocol allows computers on different public networks, like the Internet, to communicate through an intermediary computer, such as CompuServe or America Online. X.25 protocols provide physical and data-link layer support across networks.

- ✔ **ATM (asynchronous transfer mode):** No, not the machine you get money from, ATM is fixed connection cell-switching technology that transmits cells at speeds of either 155.52 Mbps or 622.08 Mbps. With newer technologies, such as SONET (Synchronous Optical Network), ATM networks can carry bandwidth of nearly 10 gigabits per second.

- ✔ **DSL (digital subscriber line):** This technology uses the copper cabling of the POTS to transmit data at around 1.5 Mbps.

Servers, Servers Everywhere, but Not a Byte to Eat

Moving about the Internet, you will encounter several different types of servers. The different types of servers found on the Internet, and on the i-Net+ exam are:

- ✔ Application servers
- ✔ Cache servers
- ✔ Certificate-authority servers
- ✔ Directory (LDAP) servers

- ✔ DNS Servers
- ✔ E-commerce servers
- ✔ FTP servers
- ✔ HTTP (Web) servers
- ✔ List servers
- ✔ Mirror servers
- ✔ News servers
- ✔ Proxy servers
- ✔ Telnet servers

Each server type processes a discrete variety of messages, functions, or activities for its clients on either local or remote networks.

Let me clear up one thing before I go on: A server is not necessarily hardware. In fact, a server of the Internet kind is most often a specialized type of software, and many software servers can run on a single computer. Okay, so the computer on which a server runs is a server, but don't say I didn't try to save you from yourself.

In the following sections, I describe the features and functions of the various servers you need to know for the i-Net+ exam. Bear in mind that in each of these cases, I am describing one or more computer programs.

I wouldn't exactly memorize the following server types, if I were you, but I do recommend that you study each one so that you know the specialized function it performs.

Application server

There are usually three levels to a Web-enabled application: the GUI (graphical user interface) server, the application (or logical processes) server, and the database server. An application server is the part of this structure that processes the data that is displayed by the GUI server, and is stored or retrieved by the database server.

Cache server

A cache server eliminates unnecessary trips to the frequently visited Web sites or FTP servers by saving (caching) Web pages and FTP and other files downloaded by its users. When a cached page is requested, it is provided from the cache server rather than from the Internet. A cache server function is commonly a part of a proxy server (see the "Proxy server" section later in the chapter).

Certificate authority server

A certificate authority (CA) server issues and controls the security information (public and private keys) used to both encrypt and decrypt messages sent over internal (LANs or intranets) and external networks (the Internet and extranets). Chapter 15 discusses encryption processes in more detail.

Directory server

Directory servers are built around the Lightweight Directory Access Protocol (LDAP), a protocol that enables you to search for organizations, individuals, files, and devices on the Internet or an intranet. Directory servers are also called LDAP servers.

A directory server uses a hierachical or tree format with levels for the root, countries, organizations, departments, and finally units (people, files, and printers and other shared resources). LDAP directories are commonly distributed across several servers, with each having its own duplicate copy of the entire directory hierarchy.

DNS server

DNS (Domain Name System) servers are arranged in a hierarchical structure around the Internet. Each DNS server contains a regional portion of the entire DNS database so that the FQDNs (Fully Qualified Domain Names) used by humans to address Internet locations can be translated into their IP address equivalents. An FQDN contains both the network and host IDs of a site, and at the lower-levels of the DNS architecture, both of these parts are used to locate the IP address of a host computer. However, at the upper-levels of the DNS hierarchy, the network portion of the FQDN is less-important and only the domain is used to locate in which DNS domain structure the address is likely to be found.

For example, if you wish to download a page from the *For Dummies* folks, you issue a request to the FQDN of `www.dummies.com`. If you are in the same geographical region as the `www` server at IDG Books Worldwide, Inc., and are also within a `.com` network yourself, then the combination of the host (www) and the network (`dummies.com`) is very likely to be found at the levels of the DNS closest to your server. However, if you are located in another region, say halfway around the world, and are at a `.edu` network, your DNS request must navigate out of your regional .edu hierarchy, up to the highest level (global) `.com` structure (where the regional location of the network is looked up) and down through the `.com` database of the appropriate region until the host ID is also found.

You can expect a question on the test concerning the level of the DNS hierarchy on which host information is or isn't likely to be found.

E-commerce server

E-commerce servers perform many different tasks and are actually a combination of programs that support business-to-customer and business-to-business functions. Common functions on an e-commerce server are shopping carts, credit card processing, EDI (Electronic Data Interchange), and other sales, customer support, and data collection activities. Chapter 17 discusses most of the activities Internet capitalist pigs include on their e-commerce sites, which are supported by e-commerce servers.

FTP server

FTP (File Transfer Protocol) is used to transfer files from one computer to another over the Internet. The functionality of FTP is provided by the protocol, plus an FTP server and FTP client. The FTP client connects to the FTP server and, after clearing security, downloads the desired file. The FTP server acts as a form of gatekeeper on the FTP site, allowing only authorized clients to access its resources.

HTTP server

An HTTP (Hypertext Transfer Protocol) server, which is commonly called a Web server, processes requests from HTTP clients (a.k.a. browsers) through an HTTP daemon, which is usually abbreviated HTTPd. A *daemon* is a continuously running program that handles requests from clients. The HTTPd waits for HTTP requests and then processes them as they arrive.

List server

There is a special mailing list type called a *listserv* that users must join through subscription and exit by unsubscribing to the list. A listserv is managed by a *list server* — software that manages requests from subscribers and sends out new messages and postings from the list's members to the list of subscribers. A list server is not a mail server, although they both process e-mail.

Mirror (site) servers

A Web site that contains duplicate copies of files from another Web site is a mirror site. The purpose of a mirror site is to provide a secondary, and hopefully closer, site to computer users who want to download files from the original site. A mirror site is an exact duplicate of an original site. There is no specific software for mirroring a site, and the server software found on one is reflective of the functions on the original site.

News server

A news server hosts Internet (USENET) newsgroups and local discussion groups. NNTP (Network News Transfer Protocol) is the protocol used by news servers for managing the messages posted to newsgroups. An NNTP server contributes management services to the network to help organize and list the messages sent to USENET newsgroups. Most ISPs provide a news server for their subscribers' use.

Proxy server

A proxy server sits between local network clients and the Internet to provide security, caching, and administration support to the network. A proxy server — a device whose functionality is constantly growing — can provide a variety of services, including connectivity, routing, gateway, and signal conversion services to a network.

Telnet server

A server to which you can connect using the Telnet protocol is a Telnet server, which is also known as a *host server.*

Prep Test

1 Which of the following abbreviations refer to the public telephone system? (Choose two.)

A ❑ PSTN

B ❑ PTS

C ❑ RBOC

D ❑ POTS

2 Computer modems connect over which type of port?

A ○ Parallel

B ○ Serial

C ○ ISA

D ○ PCI

3 A modem is configured on a Windows computer using which built-in software tool?

A ○ Network Connectivity wizard

B ○ Install New Modem wizard

C ○ Make New Connection wizard

D ○ TCP/IP Properties window

4 Which of the following are types of computer modems? (Choose all that apply.)

A ❑ xDSL

B ❑ ISDN

C ❑ LMDS

D ❑ Analog

5 The de facto protocol standard for point-to-point connections is _____.

A ○ PPTP

B ○ VPN

C ○ PPP

D ○ SLIP

6 The _____ protocol is used to tunnel PPP over an IP network.

A ○ VPN

B ○ SLIP

C ○ TTPT

D ○ PPTP

7 The device used to allow a computer to connect to a network is a _____.

A ○ NIC

B ○ Gateway

C ○ Hub

D ○ Router

8 The device that provides a network's entrance and exit point to and from the Internet is a _____.

A ○ NIC

B ○ Gateway

C ○ Hub

D ○ Router

9 The _____ protocol standard allows computers on different public networks to communicate through an intermediary computer.

A ○ ATM

B ○ DSL

C ○ X.500

D ○ X.25

10 The type of server that manages and services mailing list subscriber requests is a(n) _____.

A ○ List server

B ○ FTP server

C ○ Newsgroup server

D ○ E-commerce server

Answers

1 *A and D.* The public switched telephone network (PSTN) and the plain old telephone system (POTS) are common names for the standard public telephone system. *See "Converting signals."*

2 *B.* Modems, both internal and external, connect to a computer through a serial port. *Review "The port."*

3 *B.* You access this tool through the Modems icon in the Windows Control Panel, and it talks you through the process of configuring a new modem on the computer. *Take a look at "Configuring a modem."*

4 *A, B, and D.* These modems and the others listed in the chapter should impress upon you that POTS modems aren't the only kind in use. You should know for the test that there are other transports and that some use modems to connect to the computer. *Check out "Other members of the modem family."*

5 *C.* PPP (point-to-point protocol) is the most commonly used dial up protocol for connecting one computer to another. PPP is the protocol used to connect your computer to your ISP. *Look over "Getting the point-to-point."*

6 *D.* The Point-to-Point Tunneling Protocol (PPTP) encases the "native" protocol inside of a PPTP packet for transport over the IP network. *See "Tunneling through the Net."*

7 *A.* A NIC (network interface card) is a type of adapter used to connect a computer to a network. A NIC is installed inside the system unit in an expansion slot. *Review "The Stuff Connections are Made From."*

8 *B.* A gateway is usually located on the router placed at the edge of the network where it interfaces with the Internet. *Look over "The Stuff Connections are Made From."*

9 *D.* X.25 is one of the oldest protocols around, and is still very commonly used to connect remote devices to networks. *Check out "The Stuff Connections are Made From."*

10 *A.* A list server manages a subscription-based e-mail service most commonly known as a listserv. *Take a look at "List server."*

Chapter 14

Dealing with Internet Problems

Exam Objectives

▶ Using diagnostic tools

▶ Identifying and resolving Internet problems

● ●

I say with only the very smallest amount of sarcasm that should a problem *ever* occur with an Internet connection, address, or remote site, that as an Internet professional you must know the tools to use to properly diagnose the problem and identify its source. The question isn't one of *whether* a problem will happen; but rather a matter of *when*. Every Internet user should be forced to say the Internet Pledge of Understanding each and every time he or she connects to the network:

> *I pledge understanding to the net, of the entire global community, and to the anarchy for which it stands, one network with no gods, undefeatable, with chaos and performance on occasion.*

The i-Net+ exam recognizes that your ability to isolate and fix a problem with an Internet connection, site, or address is an essential skill for an Internet professional. In this chapter I go over the types of Internet problems you may encounter both in life and on the exam. I also include the files or software that can cause these problems, and the tools you use to resolve them. There is no way that I can cover every possible problem that customers may have and their remedies, so I'm concentrating on those you are likely to see on the exam. But, one thing's for sure, never again will you be able to say without guilt, "I don't know what the problem is; try rebooting your computer."

Quick Assessment

Using
diagnostic
tools

1 The _____ utility is used to verify that an IP address is valid.

2 The utility that can be used to display a computer's TCP/IP configuration is _____.

3 _____ is a Windows utility used to identify a computer's network interconnections.

4 The utility that can be used to identify possible trouble on the path from a computer to a remote IP address is _____.

5 A(n) _____ is a device that evaluates a network's condition by analyzing its traffic.

6 To list statistics about the active server, you would use the _____ utility.

7 On a Windows NT computer, the utility that is used to display the computer names cache is _____.

8 The protocol that can also be used to maintain the address resolution protocol cache is _____.

Identifying
and
resolving
Internet
problems

9 There are three general types of problems you can encounter when connecting to the Internet: _____, _____, and _____ problems.

10 If a URL results in an error page, the problem may be in the _____ settings.

Answers

1 *PING.* See "Hello. Are you there?"

2 *IPCONFIG.* Review "Displaying the IPCONFIGuration."

3 *WINLPCFG.* Take a look at "The Windows IP configuration tool."

4 *TRACERT.* Check out "Tracing the route."

5 *Network or protocol analyzer.* Look over "Other troubleshooting tools."

6 *NETSTAT.* See "Checking network statistics."

7 *NBTSTAT.* Review "NBT statistics."

8 *ARP.* Look over "ARP: Not the beer or the seniors' club."

9 *Connection, addressing, hardware.* Check out "Problems of the Internet Kind."

10 *WINS server, DNS server, or default gateway server.* Take a look at "Addressing your problems."

Internet Troubleshooting and Diagnostic Tools

The Internet does not have the luxury of a single unifying force, being bound as it is only by participants swearing to abide by the rules and protocols set by its self-appointed leaders. The guidelines and rules of the Internet are globally and generally accepted, but standards, rules, and guidelines are open to interpretation and can result in uneven application.

Another problem-causing problem on the Internet is that many of the software servers and clients may have been rushed to market, and in many cases are not much more than beta versions anyway. The software doesn't even need to be on your computer to cause you trouble, it could be that a request sent by your client to a remote server may be the one thing the software developers thought you would never do. The TCP/IP protocol suite includes several utilities that you can use to validate and troubleshoot performance problems or errors on the Internet. Some of these tools are standard protocols and are available on all systems, while others are unique to certain operating environments. In the following sections, I define the usage and products of the TCP/IP utilities you should know for the i-Net+ exam.

Validating the network

The best first step of troubleshooting a problem is to validate a destination address or perhaps the configuration of the local and remote networks. The standard TCP/IP utilities PING, IPCONFIG, and NBTSTAT are tools that can be used to determine if an address is a good address as well as display a computer's current network configuration.

Hello. Are you there?

PING is a standard TCP/IP utility used to verify that an IP address is a good address and that messages you send from your computer can reach it. PING, which stands for Packet Internet Groper, sends out ICMP (Internet Command Message Protocol) echo request packets that request destination addresses to reply. If the destination address is a good one, the remote host or server should answer back with an ICMP echo response packet. If the first packet is not answered, the request times out with the assumption that the destination address is either invalid or is not functioning. Figure 14-1 shows a sample PING session.

Figure 14-1:
The PING
utility in
action.

Displaying the IPCONFIGuration

IPCONFIG (Internet Protocol Configuration) is another standard TCP/IP utility that is very useful for displaying a computer's TCP/IP configuration. IPCONFIG can display the following information:

- ✔ Host name
- ✔ DNS (Domain Name Server) servers
- ✔ Node type
- ✔ MAC (Media Access Control) address
- ✔ DHCP (Dynamic Host Control Protocol) status
- ✔ IP address
- ✔ Subnet mask
- ✔ Default IP gateway

Figure 14-2 shows the display from the IPCONFIG utility.

Figure 14-2:
The
IPCONFIG
utility's
display.

The Windows IP configuration tool

WINIPCFG is the IP configuration tool unique to Windows operating systems, and is executed from either an MS-DOS or Windows NT command line or it can be executed in the Windows Run dialog box using Start⇨Run and entering **winipcfg**.

Figure 14-3 shows how the display from this command identifies the network interconnections for a computer, including its adapter type, MAC (adapter) address, IP address, default gateway, and the subnet mask used on its network segment.

Figure 14-3:
The IP
Configuration
window
displayed by
WINLPCFG.

```
IP Configuration                                  _ □ X
┌─ Ethernet  Adapter Information ─────────────────────┐
│                        ┌─────────────────────────┐  │
│                        │ PPP Adapter.          ▼ │  │
│                        └─────────────────────────┘  │
│        Adapter Address    44-45-53-54-00-00         │
│             IP Address    207.53.185.54             │
│           Subnet Mask     255.255.255.0             │
│        Default Gateway    207.53.185.54             │
│                                                     │
│      ┌──────OK──────┐  ┌─ Release ─┐  ┌─ Renew ─┐   │
│      └──────────────┘  └───────────┘  └─────────┘   │
│      ┌─ Release All ─┐ ┌─ Renew All ┐ ┌ More Info >>┐│
│      └───────────────┘ └────────────┘ └─────────────┘│
└─────────────────────────────────────────────────────┘
```

NBT statistics

On Windows NT computers, NetBIOS creates a computer names cache that it uses to forward packets over a network. The Windows utility NBTSTAT (NetBIOS over TCP/IP Statistics) can be used to display the computer names cache so that the MAC and IP address of a computer can be verified. NBTSTAT can also be used to troubleshoot problems in the LMHOSTS (LAN Manager Hosts File) and other HOSTS files.

ARP: Not the beer or the seniors' club

The Address Resolution Protocol (ARP) is another tool that can be used to verify the network's status. ARP is also the protocol used to convert MAC addresses into IP addresses on some computer and router systems. ARP uses a table, called the ARP cache, that can be modified (add, change, or delete) or displayed using ARP protocol commands.

The Apple Computer version of this command is the Apple Address Resolution Protocol (AARP), which can be confused with the senior citizen's organization which uses the same acronym. However, I doubt that the AARP (the club) is able to change routes as quickly as the computer one.

TCP/IP troubleshooting tools

The TCP/IP protocol stack also includes troubleshooting utilities that can be used to determine if a problem exists, as well as where on the network the problem may be. Some of the utilities discussed in the previous section, such as PING and NBTSTAT, can be used for troubleshooting, but TRACERT and NETSTAT are TCP/IP utilities used solely for troubleshooting and isolating network problems.

Using a computer, practice with each of the PING, NETSTAT, and TRACERT utilities and the others listed in this and the previous section, until you know exactly what they do and the format and contents of their displayed results.

If you need a target for PING and TRACERT, use the following FQDN and IP address:

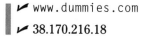

- ✔ www.dummies.com
- ✔ 38.170.216.18

Tracing the route

The TRACERT (Trace Route) utility is a widely used tool for pinpointing problems along the route to a remote host or domain across the Internet. TRACERT operates something like the PING utility in that it sends out a series of ICMP echo request packets to each hop (router) along the route used to get to a specific IP destination. The results are displayed along with the time interval of each response. A packet that times out or takes an unusually long time to respond may indicate a problem point in the route used.

Checking network statistics

Available on both Windows and UNIX systems, the NETSTAT (Network Statistics) command is used to list a range of display options to show several different sets of statistics for the active network. Among the more commonly used of these options are the active TCP/IP connections on a network, the status of the Ethernet connections, or the current contents of the system's routing table.

Other troubleshooting tools

In addition to TCP/IP utilities, there are a number of different types of troubleshooting and analysis tools that can be used to diagnose, isolate, and perhaps even repair a network problem. Here are brief overviews for the different network tools you should know for the exam:

✔ **Network monitors:** These are software packages that track and report all or a portion of a network's traffic, including separating the traffic by packet type, type of error, or direction (in or outbound). Examples of network monitors are McClaren's Big Brother, a name you had to expect (http://maclawran.ca/), Freshwater Software's SiteScope (www.freshtech.com), and IPSentry (www.ipsentry.com).

✔ **NOS (network operating system) event and alert logs:** Most network operating systems (NOSs) record log files for system events and alerts preset by the administrator, as well as provide a reporting tool to display the contents of the log. For example, the Windows NT Event Viewer shows you the system and application logs.

✔ **Physical media testers:** Hardware such as digital voltmeters (DVM), time-domain reflectometers (TDR), oscilloscopes (no abbreviation or acronym), and advanced cable testers can be used to find and isolate problems on the physical media of the network.

✔ **Protocol analyzers (also known as network analyzers):** These devices help you to evaluate a network's condition by monitoring and analyzing network traffic. These tools are commonly used to determine if problems are occurring in the physical media, hubs, bridges, or routers.

Problems of the Internet Kind

So what kinds of problems can you expect to find on Internet systems? The list is endless, and most of the problems in the list are user-centric. However, there are a few types of problems that can be generically categorized into three groups. Some of the categorical problems you can experience when connecting, or attempting to connect, to the Internet:

✔ **Connection problems:** Your modem won't connect, or if it does it won't stay connected. Or, if you are on a LAN (local area network), you can access local network resources, but not the Internet.

✔ **Addressing problems:** The URL is correct, but you either timeout or get an error message.

✔ **Hardware problems:** I don't mean hardware problems with your personal computer, although that would certainly impact your ability to use the Internet. What I mean is hardware problems on the network beyond your control, such as with a router or firewall.

Failing to make your connection

Here are a few of the problems you may encounter when trying to connect to the Internet:

✔ **Your modem is dialing, the other end answers, but the connection is never actually made.** This problem indicates that one of the modems — yours or the ISP's — is not configured properly for the connection being made. I'll give you one guess on whose modem is likely the culprit. Check the configuration and setup of your modem and if needed contact the technical support staff of your ISP to verify its settings. If you have connected in the past, this should fix the problem. However, if you are connecting for the first time, and the problem persists, and the ISP is able to swear that the problem is not theirs, your modem may be incompatible with switching equipment (the telephone company's or the ISP's) in the connection. In the latter situation, you should try a different modem (from a different manufacturer) with a different V.xx specification. Your ISP should be able to recommend which devices are compatible with their equipment. After all, they must have some customers connecting to them.

✔ **The ISP's dialup number is busy.** You either need to retry at a later time, ask the ISP for a different number to use, or find an ISP that has more incoming lines available during peak times.

✔ **Your modem connects but disconnects right away.** This indicates a settings problem, most likely in the protocols. Verify the settings you should have with the ISP's technical support staff and correct your configuration.

✔ **After being connected for a while, the modem disconnects for no apparent reason, Part I.** This is a common problem, known as a *drop out,* which is caused by other devices sharing the same line as the modem. Phones store called numbers in memory that is charged by a small capacitor that must be kept charged. About every 15 minutes or so, the capacitor draws power away from the telephone itself. This commonly causes the modem to sense the change in the line voltage which causes it to think that the line has been dropped and so it disconnects. About the only remedies available are to either get a separate telephone line for your modem or a different telephone that does not have internal memory functions.

✔ **After being connected for a while, the modem disconnects for no apparent reason, Part II.** Another reason for this recurring problem theme is the call-waiting feature on the telephone. On phones with this feature, an incoming call triggers a series of short beeps that interrupt the data and signals flowing over the modem. This interruption as well as the call-waiting beeps are interpreted by the modem to mean that the line should be disconnected. There are two levels of remedy for this. One is to enter the call-waiting disconnect command (usually *70) in your modem startup script. The other remedy is to cancel the call-waiting feature. You could, I suppose, get a separate line for the modem, or have I already mentioned that? Don't forget to put the call-waiting connect command (*71) in the end-of-session script in the modem configurations to turn the call-waiting back on when you're finished with the modem.

Addressing your problems

Here are a few common URL and IP addressing problems:

- ✔ **The URL downloads the wrong site.** Behind every failing electronic system you will find a human fully capable of making data-entry errors. DNS and HOSTS file entries can be entered incorrectly. If you experience a situation where you are very sure you have the right URL (say, www.dummies.com), but download Needlepoint R Us every time you enter that URL, chances are that there is a DNS problem somewhere upline. Contact your ISP to notify them of the problem. If you are the ISP, then notify Network Solutions (www.networksolutions.com) of the problem, after verifying it, of course.

- ✔ **The URL you entered never appears or it results in an error page.** Ruling out that the URL is misspelled, or that the site no longer exists, chances are that one or more of your WINS server, DNS server, or default gateway server settings are incorrect. Another probability is that the site requires a reverse DNS verification, and your ISP's or network's DNS entries are incorrectly set. The site may also be on an extremely slow server and you are timing out waiting for it to respond. Contact the ISP to report the problem. If you are the ISP, you will need to isolate which server is in error and correct those under your control and contact the appropriate agencies for the others.

- ✔ **An IP address results in an error page in the browser.** New IP addresses can confuse network routers if the routers are unaware of the destination network or host. First of all, try again, perhaps even a few times. If the IP address entered is valid, it may be that you need to wait until the routers on the network learn of the site.

- ✔ **A commonly used URL is timing out.** One of the routers in the path between you and the URL's Web site may be down or not responding. Try again later. If the problem persists, notify the ISP or NSP (network service provider) upstream from you.

Problems in the hardware

You should know right away if you have problems with the basic hardware of your computer. The monitor is dark, nothing you type displays on the monitor, no lights show on the front of the computer, or if everything else is fine, you cannot log on to the network. These problems really have nothing to do with the Internet itself, but can severely impact your ability to connect.

Most of the problems with what I will call Internet hardware, for the sake of discussion, are usually man-made. I don't mean the man who made the hardware, I mean the man or woman who built the hardware's configuration. Errors in routing tables, bridging tables, or firewall permit or deny tables can directly impact your computer's ability to interact with the Internet. The same holds true for errors in the configuration of your computer as well. If your TCP/IP settings are incorrect, or the wrong protocols are enabled or missing, your connection to the Internet may be less than successful.

Prep Test

1 To verify that an IP address or FQDN is valid, you use _____.

- A ○ IPCONFIG
- B ○ NETSTAT
- C ○ PING
- D ○ TRACERT

2 To display a computer's TCP/IP configuration status, you use_____.

- A ○ IPCONFIG
- B ○ NETSTAT
- C ○ PING
- D ○ TRACERT

3 To display a Windows computer's network interconnections, you use_____.

- A ○ WINLPCFG
- B ○ NBTSTAT
- C ○ ARP
- D ○ DHCP

4 To display the path to reach a remote IP destination and the timings of each hop, you use_____.

- A ○ IPCONFIG
- B ○ NETSTAT
- C ○ PING
- D ○ TRACERT

5 To list statistics about the active network, you use_____.

- A ○ NBTSTAT
- B ○ NETSTAT
- C ○ PING
- D ○ TRACERT

6 The protocol that maintains and displays an address resolution cache is_____.

A ○ PING
B ○ ROUTE
C ○ WINS
D ○ ARP

7 The Windows NT utility used to display the computer names cache is_____.

A ○ NBTSTAT
B ○ NETSTAT
C ○ PING
D ○ TRACERT

8 A hardware device that can be used to isolate network problems, such as bottlenecks or addressing problems, by examining each network packet is a_____.

A ○ Packet engine
B ○ Network analyzer
C ○ Fox and hound analyzer
D ○ Cable certifier

9 Which of the following are considered to be troubleshooting utilities? (Choose two.)

A ❑ PING
B ❑ ARP
C ❑ TRACERT
D ❑ NETSTAT

10 What is a likely cause of a modem that disconnects for no apparent reason after being connected?

A ○ TCP/IP settings
B ○ Call waiting
C ○ ISP circuits are busy
D ○ Modem configuration

Answers

1 *C.* The Packet Internet Groper, while sounding like a tropical fish, is used to determine if a destination address can be reached. *See "Hello. Are you there?"*

2 *A.* The IP Configuration utility has many options that can be used to display different aspects of a computer's TCP/IP configuration. *Review "Displaying the IPCONFIGuration."*

3 *A.* The Windows IP Configuration utility displays all the key information on the computer's network interconnections. *Take a look at "The Windows IP configuration tool."*

4 *D.* The Trace Route command displays the results and timings for each router in the path used to reach a remote computer. *Check out "Tracing the route."*

5 *B.* This one is particularly easy to remember. For statistics on the current network, use the NETSTAT command. *Look over "Checking network statistics."*

6 *D.* This may seem like asking, "Who's buried in Grant's tomb?" However, there are other name caches maintained by other TCP/IP protocols and utilities. The ARP cache is used for address resolution. *See "ARP: Not the beer or the seniors' club."*

7 *A.* As I mention in the answer to question 6, there are several name caches among these utilities. NBTSTAT is used to display the name cache maintained by NetBIOS on Windows computers. *Review "NBT statistics."*

8 *B.* Also called a protocol analyzer, these devices open and analyze network traffic to try to find network throughput and bandwidth problems. *Take a look at "Other troubleshooting tools."*

9 *C and D.* The other tools are verification or diagnostic tools. *Check out "TCP/IP troubleshooting tools."*

10 *B.* The call-waiting signal can be interpreted as a disconnect signal. This option should be turned off before dialing up a remote location with a modem. *Look over "Failing to make your connection."*

Chapter 15

Securing the Internet

• •

Exam Objectives

▶ Listing common suspicious activities on the Internet

▶ Defining Internet security controls

▶ Explaining how a VPN secures data

▶ Using antivirus software

• •

Security on any network is a serious matter, but security on networks attached to the Internet is absolutely essential. The issue isn't whether your system will be hacked, infected with a virus, or otherwise violated, but how soon in the near future it will happen. Like a flashing neon sign, a network with weak defenses against intruders and other nasties is broadcasting to the dark forces of the Ether, "Just do me!"

If you are one of those people that has managed to remain untainted while ignoring all warnings of impending doom and danger and leaving your network or workstation completely unprotected, you need to visit your local gambling hall, bingo parlor, lottery window, and race track as soon as possible, before your luck runs out. You are one extremely lucky person!

However, you may be more like me and have suffered nearly every virus infection released in the past three years, have been hacked more than once, and suspect that your credit card information is intercepted by Realibad terrors for Technostan each time you use it.

Or you could be somewhere in the middle of these two extremes and have heard the rumors and maybe even experienced a virus or two. Your luck is the result of the careful use of the security features of your network operating system, the network hardware, and cautious planning.

The i-Net+ exam considers network security a serious matter and devotes 15 percent of its questions to this one area. Internet security issues are arguably among the most important facing Internet professionals and users alike. Take the time to understand the importance of the topics included in this chapter. If you know how and when the good is used to prevent the bad from happening, you will be ready for the test.

Quick Assessment

Listing common suspicious activities on the Internet

1 A utility like the _____ constantly monitors a system's data stream to detect logon and logoff messages.

2 When a server cannot respond to every request it receives, it will reject some requests with a(n) _____.

3 A(n) _____ storm bombards a site server in an attempt to overload it to the point of shutting it down.

Defining Internet security controls

4 The table or file used to store user access rights on a certain network resource or object is a(n) _____.

5 A(n) _____ is a security mechanism that protects a network and keeps its resources private.

6 Any network that is connected to the _____ is a good candidate for a proxy server.

7 _____ are attached to documents and messages to verify the identity of the sender.

Explaining how a VPN secures data

8 There are two types of encryption keys in use: _____ and _____.

9 A VPN uses a(n) _____ protocol to transmit data over the Internet.

Using antivirus software

10 Antivirus software is also known as _____ and _____.

Answers

1 *Multiple Login Detection Daemon (MLDD).* See "Watching out for multiple logons."

2 *Denial of Service (DoS).* Review "The system is in denial."

3 *SYN or PING.* Take a look at "The great PING flood of '00."

4 *Access Control List (ACL).* Check out "Keeping the list."

5 *Firewall.* Look over "Closing, locking, and bolting the door."

6 *Internet.* See "Proxy servers: Internet traffic cops."

7 *Digital signatures.* Review "Just put your digital scribble right here."

8 *Public, private.* Look over "Public and private keys."

9 *Tunneling.* Check out "Connecting with a Virtual Private Network."

10 *Scanners, inoculators.* Take a look at "Protecting Your System From Infection."

There Is Something Mighty Suspicious Going on Here

The i-Net+ exam objectives prescribe that you know about "various types of suspicious activities" on the Internet. The phrase *suspicious activities* refers to the actions that Internet abusers may use to disrupt, destroy, or otherwise wreck havoc on an Internet site. Not that you or I would ever do something like this, but there are mean and nasty people out there who would — and do.

The maliciousness wielded by the anti-social Internet abusers includes such nastiness as multiple logons, denial of service (DoS) attacks, unsolicited bulk e-mail (UBE) — the polite society name for *spam*, meaning spoofed or forged e-mail — PING floods, and unauthorized access, commonly called hacking. Oh, there are more, but these are the ones that the i-Net+ exam wants you to know about. However, if there is one Internet area of concern to pursue, after the exam of course, the whole topic of Internet security and privacy could be a career in itself.

Are you cloned, or just logged on more than once?

One of the ways a site can be disrupted is through multiple user logons. However, as is often the case, users can innocently log on more than once or they can purposely do so in order to jam up a server.

Watching out for multiple logons

There are detection utilities, such as the multiple login detection daemon (MLDD), that constantly monitor the data stream coming from a connected user looking for logon and logoff messages. When a logon request comes in, the daemon looks to see if the account is already logged on. If it is, the oldest session is terminated, and the new session established.

There is a difference between forgetful and malicious

Evidence of another type of suspicious logon activity is a series of repeated logon failures in a short period of time. It isn't all that unusual for some users, including me, to occasionally forget their account name or password temporarily and require two or three tries to get it right. However, if the logon activity for one or more logon accounts shows repeated multiple logon attempts over and over again, it may be a hacker trying to discover an account and password combination. And it may just be time to change the passwords again!

The system is in denial

The i-Net+ exam questions on suspicious actions and attacks focuses on your ability to determine if an attack is underway and which type of attack it may be. I haven't provided you with much information on prevention or recovery because it is not on the exam. Some guidelines for addressing the the various types of attacks are included in the "An Internet Security Primer" section later in this chapter.

Be careful what you wish for on the Internet; you may just get it. The Web site you launched with the hopes that would become a wildly popular site could be lost under the volume of users accessing it. If a site is saturated by users, and the Web server cannot respond to every request, some requests will be rejected with a denial of service (DoS), an attempt at self-preservation. However, should the site be targeted for a DoS attack, the site and its server may be forced to shut down under the sheer volume of access requests hitting them.

I explain some of the more common types of DoS attacks in the following sections.

My buffer runneth over

Probably the most common type of DoS attack is the buffer overflow attack, which exploits a very common weakness of Web sites. When a Web site is designed, often not much thought is given to how much traffic a site will generate. If a site is programmed without adequate data buffers, it may not be able to handle all the incoming traffic. This weakness, if discovered, can be exploited.

Attackers with inside knowledge can bombard the site purposely, or simply randomly attack sites on the chance a weak site will be discovered. Some of the favorite bombs employed by buffer attackers include e-mail attachments with 256-character filenames, over-sized ICMP (Internet Control Message Protocol) packets, and from addresses longer than 256-characters.

Teardrops of pain

Some of the nastiest tricks that are used to cause DoS attacks simply take advantage of the built-in features and functions of protocols. The teardrop attack makes use of how the Internet Protocol (IP) divides up packets too large for the next router in the path to handle. Each of the fragment packets contains information that enables the packet to be reassembled at its destination. The teardrop attack sends out a stream of packets with confusing information in the second and later packets. If the receiving system cannot handle this situation, it may crash.

Are you spoofing me?

The term *spoofing* refers to the act of sending a message or even a packet to a destination site that contains the address of a third-party. In other words, one party represents itself to a second party as being a third party. Joe tells Sally that he is really Sam.

Sending out packets that cause an innocent by-standing host system to be spoofed is called a *smurf attack*. I'm not sure exactly why; I must not be up on the latest cartoon character lore. Anyway, here is what happens:

1. The attacker sends out an ICMP echo request packet — the same type used in the PING utility — that requests the receiving site to send out a broadcast packet to its local network.

2. The sending site IP address in the request packet is a poor and unsuspecting spoofed host that will receive any denial of service responses.

3. The result is a storm of PING replies that flood the spoofed host, usually overwhelming it.

The attack of the smurfs

Unlike the cute little, snuggly blue cartoon characters, smurf attacks are not nice, cute, or snuggly. A smurf attack is a non-stop bombardment of ICMP echo reply requests that tie up one or more servers to the point that normal activities are disrupted. Another type of smurf attack is a *fraggle attack* (remember the residents of Fraggle Rock?), which uses UDP echo packets in the same way that ICMP packets are used in a smurf attack.

Here are a few Web sites where you can find more information on DoS attacks:

Internet.Com's Webopedia (webopedia.internet.com)

CERT Coordination Center at Carnegie Mellon University (www.cert.org)

Rent-a-Hacker's Evil List (www.rent-a-hacker.com/evil.htm)

Directed attacks: The really mean stuff

While nearly all attacks over the Internet can be classified as a denial of service attack, some types of attacks stand on their own. These attacks are usually the foundation strategies used in other types of attacks. The i-Net+ exam includes questions on four different attack types: PING floods, SYN storms, physical attacks, and computer virus attacks.

The great PING flood of '00

The best nontechnical example of a PING storm, also known as a PING flood, I can think of is the "I Love Lucy" episode in which Lucy and Ethel get jobs in the candy factory and eventually cannot keep up with the amount of candy coming to them on the conveyor belt. So it is with a PING storm.

An attacker employs the PING utility (see Chapter 14 for more information) to bombard a site's server with ICMP reply request packets in an attempt to overload the system to the point of shutting down. Oh, what fun!

Before you try (simply for the sake of research, right?), your Windows PING program can't be used to create a storm, or even a squall for that matter; it is simply a one-time deal. However, some UNIX-based PING programs include options to bounce PING packets back as fast as they are returned or send out a PING packet of a specific size. I tell you this not to encourage such behavior, but rather because you need to know it for the test.

This flood is a SYN

Transmission Control Program (TCP), of the TCP/IP family, must establish a connection between two computers to do its stuff. As a part of setting up a connection, a rapid exchange of messages takes place between the two hosts. As a packet is sent out, it is stored in a buffer so that the sending system can remember which packet is being replied to by the other end. After a reply is received, the packet is removed from the buffer. Inside each packet is a SYN (which stands for synchronize) field. This field contains the sequence number of the packet in the series being exchanged.

The innocence and trust inherent in this connection process is too tempting for some, and ergo, the *SYN flood*. Mean and nasty attackers send out bunches of connection requests to a targeted server and then do not respond to the connection packets sent in reply. This results in the first packet of each exchange remaining in the targeted system's buffers, making it difficult for real connections to be made.

Expect to see questions on the test about SYN and PING floods. So be sure you understand how they happen and their differences.

Catching a bug

A computer virus can also cause DoS attacks as it spreads itself across a network. Virus attacks don't usually target a specific site, but move across the network haphazardly, infecting sites unlucky enough to receive the virus. The DoS attack resulting from a computer virus can be barely noticed — or it can be totally disastrous.

Physical assaults

Somebody may physically attack your system by unplugging the router, disconnecting the cable from the NIC, or performing some other such bit of maliciousness. Although these physical assaults don't directly create a DoS storm, they can create a hardship on another system should traffic on a high-volume server be suddenly rerouted.

An Internet Security Primer

For the i-Net+ exam, you need to know many of the techniques, technologies, and applications used to provide site, message, and transaction security and privacy and how and when they are brought into play. Security and privacy (right after connecting and gaining access) are among the top issues worrying users. As an Internet professional, you should be able to help users, especially business users, apply the right types of security in just the right situations.

The Internet security concepts you should know for the test include access control, authentication, certificates, encryption, and auditing, as well as the technologies and techniques used to implement them.

Letting the good in and keeping the bad out

The topic of access control could fill a book all by itself, but I don't think you'll find *Access Control For Dummies* anytime soon. Unfortunately, it is way too much of a moving target for somebody to lock down all in one place, especially when it concerns the Internet. However, here are some generic concepts you should review as you prepare for the i-Net+ exam.

Keeping the list

At the core of the security systems in nearly all operating systems, including network operating systems, is an access control list (ACL — not to be confused with the injury common to sports). An ACL is a table or file that details the access rights each account has for the system's or network's resources, such as directories (folders), files, and even hardware devices. The ACL associated with each resource or object lists the exact actions a user can take with the item. For example, the ACL for a disk file lists which users have read, write, or execute privileges for the file. The use of an ACL is supported by Windows NT, Netware, and most UNIX operating systems, although it is implemented differently by each.

Filtering the packets

A packet filter, which is more like a packet peeker, looks at the source and destination addresses of an IP packet to decide if the parties involved have the proper authorization to complete the action. If the sender (from either the internal or external network) is authorized to send messages or requests to the destination, then the packet filter takes no action. Otherwise, the transmission is blocked.

A packet filter does not provide enough security to protect your system, because you will undoubtedly need to make exceptions. For example, you probably want e-mail to reach your system and you can't possibly know all the potential source addresses. So, you allow all e-mail to come through, which opens a small doorway into your network.

Closing, locking, and bolting the door

A firewall is a security mechanism, either hardware or software, that protects a network and keeps its resources private. Taking its security a step farther than a packet filter (see "Filtering the packets"), a firewall enables you to define filtering rules that specify by address, port, type, or activity the packets that are allowed in or out of a network. However, a firewall does work very much like a packet filter, in that it filters all packets and, based on its rule set, determines whether a packet should be forwarded on to its destination (either inside or outside the local network). The packets a firewall sees are either from the internal network going out, or from the external network coming in.

Typically, a firewall is located before, in the case of hardware, or on, in the case of software, the network's gateway server. Networks that include a Web server, FTP server, or an intranet, most definitely should have a firewall implemented.

Proxy servers: Internet traffic cops

Proxy servers are used on networks that connect to the Internet. Not all networks have a proxy server, but most definitely should. A proxy server, hardware or software, sits between network workstations and the Internet, where it can provide security, administrative, and caching services.

A proxy server may include some of the same filtering capabilities as a firewall, and may also manage one or more dialup lines, making the connection to the ISP transparent to the user. However, nearly all proxy servers provide caching services that work to make bandwidth usage more efficient.

To most network users, the proxy server is transparent. When they send out a URL seeking to download a page, they usually don't know if it's live or if it's proxy. If a network user sends out a URL request, the proxy server, after clearing the request through its filtering rules, first checks its cache of previously downloaded Web documents. If the requested page is there, it is sent back to the requesting workstation; otherwise, the request is forwarded to the Internet. When the requested page is returned, it is matched up to the request and sent on to the requesting user, as well as being cached for future reference.

Some good sites to find out more about firewalls and proxy servers are

- ✔ National Institute of Standards and Technology (`csrc.ncsl.nist.gov/nistpubs/800-10`)
- ✔ SOS Corporation (`www.soscorp.com/products/BS_FireIntro.html`)
- ✔ Microsoft Corporation (`www.microsoft.com/proxy`)
- ✔ 4Firewalls.Com (`www.4firewalls.com`)

Can you prove you are who you say you are?

One of the basic functions of access control is to permit only authorized users to have access to resources or complete certain types of transactions. Like all else on the Internet, there are a variety of ways to control who has access to resources or to prove that they are who they say. Here are the ways access control is accomplished, or at least the ones you may find on the i-Net+ exam.

May I see some ID, please?

When you log on to your network or on your ISP's system, you evoke the most common of all Internet security systems: authentication. Authentication is the process that verifies that someone is who they claim to be. This is the process that confirms that just because you know your account name and password, you are you. If there is any shortcoming to authentication, it is that anyone who knows your password and account name can also be you. Like Arthur said in the movie *Arthur*, "Don't you wish you were me? I know I do!"

Because of the built-in insecurities of passwords, some Internet entities, especially Internet businesses, require something more. A *digital certificate* — a form of electronic credit card issued by a certification authority — includes your name, a certificate serial number, its expiration date, a copy of your public key (see the "Coding and decoding messages" section later in this chapter), and the digital signature of the authority that issued the certificate.

Don't confuse a digital signature (see the next section) with a digital certificate. The digital certificate is your letter of credit, letter of introduction, and authority to complete a financial transaction, all in one.

Just put your digital scribble right here

A digital signature is your electronic signature. Digital signatures are attached to documents, messages, and even electronic checks, and can be used by anyone needing to verify the identity of a message or document's sender, or that a document has not been altered from its original form. A digital certificate contains the certificate authority's (CA) digital signature, which allows anyone needing to verify its credibility to do so. The CA is the company that issues the certificate, and providing the assurances that everyone is who they say and that the transaction is valid.

You can't say you didn't do it

One of the more confusing of the access control techniques used on the Internet is non-repudiation. *Non-repudiation,* which means that I may want some form of proof that you entered into a transaction with me so you cannot later deny that you did, is becoming a common access control and security element of e-commerce.

In effect, even though I may have your logon and password, and perhaps even a digital certificate, to prove that you entered a secured site to open a transaction, I may need more. What non-repudiation does is prevent you from ever denying that you were on the site, opened a transaction, or promised to pay me. To gain this type of proof, I would use a non-repudiation service to obtain a certificate of non-repudiation of origin, non-repudiation of submission, or non-repudiation of delivery in the form of a digital signature. (If you think that was hard to read, remember that I had to type it!)

Coding and decoding messages

Encryption is the technology behind digital certificates and signatures, as well as other security schemes, such as SSL (secure socket layers) and S/MIME (Secure Multi-Purpose Internet Mail Extensions).

Encryption and decryption

I'm sure you have daydreamed at some point about being a secret agent, coding and decoding secret messages that you had to eat after learning their contents. The use of secret codes in espionage and other dark and nefarious activities is very much like what happens with encrypted data over the Internet.

Encryption is converting data into a cipher — a form that is not easily interpreted by anyone not knowing the special key that unlocks the code. *Decryption,* the opposite of encryption, is converting the encoded data back to its original, understandable form. It is important that you understand that the encryption process on a computer involves a mathematical algorithm to convert the digital form of the original message into its encrypted form. Why? Because, it is even more important that you understand that there is a kind of undo algorithm, called a *key,* that converts the data back to its original form.

Public and private keys

There are two types of *keys,* or decoding algorithms, used on the Internet:

- **Public keys,** issued by certificate authorities (CA), are distributed algorithms that are used to encrypt or decrypt a message or digital signature. A message encoded with a public key by its sender can only be decoded using the private key of the receiver.

- **Private keys,** which are issued by a CA and closely held by their owners, are not distributed with a message. A message encoded with a private key by its originator can only be decoded using a public key by its receiver.

Public keys are also referred to as asymmetric keys and private keys are referred to as symmetric keys. Some of the CAs issuing public and private keys are

- Check Point Software Technologies, Ltd. (www.checkpoint.com)
- RSA Security, Inc. (www.rsasecurity.com)
- Verisign, Inc. (www.verisign.com)

Pretty darn good privacy

In addition to digital certificates, an encryption scheme called Pretty Good Privacy (PGP) encrypts an e-mail message that can be decrypted by anyone to whom you provide your public key. PGP, which is available either as freeware or in a commercial version, has become the standard for e-mail encryption. Here's the URL where you can get more information on the freeware PGP: http://web.mit.edu/network/pgp.html.

How secure are your sockets?

Netscape developed the SSL (Secure Sockets Layer) that manages message (primarily financial transactions) security over a network, such as the Internet. SSL is referred to as a layer because it operates between the Session and Transport layers of the OSI model, where it intercepts and manages security matters. SSL, which is a built-in part of Netscape's Navigator browser and Web server software, uses both public and private keys, as well as digital certificates.

By the way, a *socket,* as in Secure Sockets Layer, is the combination of an IP address and the TCP port used to establish a transaction session.

Sending secure e-mail

The S/MIME (Secure Multi-Purpose Internet Mail Extensions) protocol is based on the MIME (Multi-Purpose Internet Mail Extensions) protocol used to send e-mail and attachments over the Internet. (See Chapter 7 for more

information about MIME.) S/MIME applies RSA public-key encryption to
e-mail messages, is widely supported by virtually all browsers, and has been
proposed, along with PGP/MIME, as an Internet standard.

Sending secure electronic transactions

SET (Secure Electronic Transaction) is a system for securely handling financial transactions over the Internet, and was developed by some of the great
financial companies of our time (Visa, MasterCard, Microsoft, and others).
SET incorporates a number of other secure protocols, including SSL and digital certificates. Under SET, a series of digital signatures and certificates
(called *electronic wallets*) are passed between the parties of a transaction,
buyer, seller, and banker, to complete the transaction securely.

Local versus global encryption schemes

There is much debate and choosing up sides around the world concerning
private keys. Some countries — the United States, Great Britain, and France
among them — have taken the position that a system of licensed private key
banks be created, to which law enforcement agencies would have access. The
opposing point-of-view — from free-thinking Canada, Australia, Denmark, and
others — is that private means private.

There are a wide range of encryption algorithms and standards in use around
the world. One of the more popular is the Data Encryption Standard (DES).
DES is so hard to crack that the U.S. government has restricted it to use only
inside of the U.S. When you consider that DES has over 72 quadrillion possible keys that can be used to encrypt a message and that the keys are issued
at random from the whole range of possible keys, you can see why the government might be worried that secrets are being sent out of the country.

Checking the past to secure the future

There are a few utilities and features on nearly all servers, usually built into
the operating system, that can help you to check out what has been happening on a system over a certain period of time. These features, which combine
to make up the audit system on your computer, include log files, auditing
logs, intrusion detection utilities, and often some analysis software.

Log files and audit logs

While my favorite type of log is pecan, most operating systems create and
manage logs of several different events that routinely occur on a system.
Generally, there are three types of system log files:

✔ **Application log files:** This log contains entries on events, messages, and
  errors created or detected by applications and services running on the
  network.

- ✔ **Security log files:** This log contains entries relating to security events and alerts. An *alert* is a benchmark or threshold, pre-set by the system administrator, at which point a log entry is created.

- ✔ **System log files:** This log contains messages, events, and errors posted by the operating system's internal services and drivers.

Who goes there?

If someone is trying to hack into your system, you may want to know about it. In addition to security log entries that track unsuccessful logon attempts, you may want to invoke an intruder detection system, which is a kind of silent software alarm system that records suspicious attempts to enter the system. The Novell NetWare NOS has a fully developed intruder detection alerting system, and some freeware utilities are also floating around, such as the ARPWatch for UNIX systems. These systems detect when an IP and MAC address combination that is not in the local-hosts files is attempting to access system resources.

Analyzing events of the past

Windows NT includes a utility called the Event Viewer that enables you to analyze and report the contents of its audit system logs. Nearly all other major operating systems have a similar feature that can be used to display all or only certain types of events in a given period of time.

Do you have permission to be here?

If you plan to let remote users access your network or even just the file server, there is one other mechanism, file-level permissions, that can be applied to a system to protect it. Nearly all operating systems use some form of file-level permissions to restrict or permit remote users access to programs and data files on the system.

For purposes of the i-Net+ exam, the individual permissions that can be generalized to all systems are:

- ✔ **Read:** Allows a user or group of users to open, but not change, a file or to access and list the contents of a directory or folder.

- ✔ **Write:** Allows a user or group of users to open, change, and rewrite a file. Can also, depending on the system, allow the user to remove the file, which is not always the best permission to grant someone, even those you trust.

- ✔ **No access:** Restricts the user from opening a file or listing the contents of a directory or folder. A sort of "No Trespassing" sign for data and program files.

Connecting with a Virtual Private Network

First, an actual private network is a LAN, which is only completely secure if it consists of only a single workstation that is never turned on. However, a LAN must eventually be connected to the outside world, even if it is only to connect to another part of the same enterprise. Adding a connection to the outside world, especially over the Internet, exposes the innocence of the LAN to the dangers that lurk along the wire. So what's a security-conscious administrator to do? One solution, rather than turning off the network, is a virtual private network (VPN).

A *VPN* is a private network that uses a tunneling protocol to transmit data over the Internet privately and securely. A packet that is to be sent over the VPN is encrypted and then placed inside a container packet that carries its data as well as its source and destination addresses over the network. At the receiving end, the packet is removed from the tunneling protocol container, decrypted, and sent on to its destination.

A VPN extends a company's intranet to become an extranet when it connects two remote sites. The VPN is also an excellent way for traveling employees to securely access their company's network resources or to simply peruse their e-mail. The remote site or employee connects locally through an ISP and then connects to the company server via the Internet. So, if the Sales Manager in Honolulu wants to connect to the company server in Walla Walla, WA, he or she connects to Internet Hawaii and then uses the Internet to connect to the Walla Walla server. This is all conducted on a free local call!

Tunneling through the Internet

The most commonly used tunneling protocol is PPTP (Point-to-Point Tunneling Protocol), which is the de facto standard for point-to-point VPN transmissions. Another popular VPN solution involves the use of a VPN gateway server (usually proprietary) and VPN remote-user client software (definitely proprietary). Nearly all major Internet connectivity device manufacturers, including Cisco, Cabletron, Shiva, and Nortel, have a VPN gateway device in development or already available on the market.

Working on the second layer

Another protocol used for VPNs is L2TP (Layer 2 Tunneling Protocol). It gets its name from its creation as a combination of Cisco System's Layer 2 Forwarding (L2F) protocol and the emerging Internet Protocol Security

(IPSec) guidelines developed by the IETF (Internet Engineering Task Force). IPSec was specifically designed to be used with the IP protocol and as a result has wide support. It is expected to become the security standard for all VPNs on the Internet.

The tunneling protocol that supports IPSec is L2TP.

Remember this definition for the test: a VPN is encrypted communications using a tunneling protocol over the Internet. However, there are a couple of more things you need to know about VPNs.

A VPN can be used to securely connect remote employees to a company's network. This would include telecommuters, traveling employees, and those people so dedicated to their work that they check their e-mail while on vacation. Can you imagine that?

A VPN can also be used to interconnect two companies using an extranet. The relationship of the two companies may include such activities as EDI (Electronic Date Interchange) for order placement, inventory-checking, order status, and others.

Protecting Your System from Infection

By now you have either heard or have first-hand experience with what can happen when bad people do not have enough to do — computer viruses. A *virus* is a computer program that can be a simple innocuous joke or a full-fledged attack on the integrity of your system.

New viruses seem to germinate almost daily; they can infect a computer or network in many ways and show up in just as many, including reboots, lock-ups, blue screens, weird pictures displayed on the monitor, corrupted or missing data, disappearing disk partitions, or boot disks that don't. Usually, if these symptoms are showing up, your system is sick and it may already be too late to save it. However, you can do more than just make it comfortable. If you act fast, you may be able to affect a miracle by inoculating it and ridding it of its potentially life-threatening bug. The best cure as well as defense against virus infection is antivirus software, also called *scanners* or *inoculators*. (Gosh, I love all this medical-sounding jargon!)

For the i-Net+ exam, you need to know what computer viruses are, but more importantly, you need to know about antivirus software and when and why it is used.

Liberally applying the antivirus solution

The major antivirus solutions include utilities to protect all parts of a network, including its servers and workstation clients. Products such as Computer Associates' Innoculan (www.cheyenne.com), Network Associates' Total Virus Defense (www.nai.com), and Trend Micro's InterScan (www.antivirus.com) all include antivirus scanners and inoculators for not only the network resources, but also for incoming and outgoing e-mail, downloaded Web documents, and in- or outbound FTP files. These solutions obviously run on the server and, if properly updated with new virus databases on a regular basis, serve to protect the server and its resources from attack and infection.

Debugging the client

Viruses reach network server and client computers in a variety of different ways, but the most common causes of infection are e-mail message attachments such as documents, worksheets, graphics, or downloaded demo programs that are in reality a Trojan horse hiding a virus, and compressed binary files downloaded using FTP. While some server-side antivirus systems can detect viruses in these forms, some can't, and not all servers are protected against infection. It is not an uncommon practice that antivirus protection is left to the clients.

A network client, especially one with access outside the local network, should definitely have antivirus software installed. This software should be used regularly to scan the entire disk of the system and its memory. How frequent "regularly" is depends on how exposed the client may be. In addition, the virus database that the scanner or inoculator uses to identify the germs must be kept up to date. Updated antivirus software is your only defense (outside of never turning the computer on).

Prep Test

1 Common Denial of Service attacks include which of the following? (Choose all that apply.)

A ❏ Buffer attack overflow

B ❏ Teardrop attack

C ❏ Smurf attack

D ❏ SYN flood

2 The file that details the access rights users have on a particular shared network resource or object is the _____.

A ○ Security access manager

B ○ Access control list

C ○ Security access list

D ○ Shared access list

3 The security device that examines the source and destination addresses of packets to determine if the sender has the authority to complete the transaction is a _____.

A ○ Firewall

B ○ Gateway

C ○ Packet filter

D ○ Proxy server

4 The security device that sits between a network's workstations and the Internet, providing security, administrative, and caching services, is the _____.

A ○ Firewall

B ○ Gateway

C ○ Packet filter

D ○ Proxy server

5 The security device — either software or hardware — that protects a network from unauthorized access is a _____.

A ○ Firewall

B ○ Gateway

C ○ Packet filter

D ○ Proxy server

6 The _____ process verifies an account's logon name and password.

A ○ Logon verification
B ○ Password verification
C ○ Entry-level security
D ○ Authentication

7 The encryption key that is distributed with an encrypted message to be used to decode the message's content is a(n) _____.

A ○ Public key
B ○ Private key
C ○ Global key
D ○ Universal key

8 Which of the following are protocols or technologies used to secure financial transactions over the Internet? (Choose two.)

A ❏ S/MIME
B ❏ SET
C ❏ SSL
D ❏ PGP

9 The most commonly used tunneling protocol is _____.

A ○ PPP
B ○ SLIP
C ○ PPTP
D ○ TCP

10 Computer viruses can be transmitted by which of the following? (Choose all that apply.)

A ❏ E-mail attachments
B ❏ A Trojan horse file
C ❏ A compressed file
D ❏ A text file

Answers

1 *A, B, C, and D.* This is not meant to be a trick question. There are both attacks and floods, and in most cases, the attacks are floods *and vice versa.* Any packet that triggers a rapid sequence of other packets, each invoking a DoS on its targeted server, is both a flood (of packets) and a DoS attack. *See "The system is in denial."*

2 *B.* While the other choices may sound more likely, the ACL keeps track of which users have which rights and privileges with a file or object. *Review "Keeping the list."*

3 *C.* A packet filter filters packets. I can't explain it much simpler than that. A packet filter looks into each packet, seeking to filter out those packets that do not have the authorization to send to the destination address in the packet. *Look over "Filtering the packets."*

4 *D.* Not to be confused with the real server, the proxy server acts on behalf of the system at the point it connects to the Internet. *Check out "Proxy servers: Internet traffic cops."*

5 *A.* Taking its name from the barriers built into buildings that prevent a fire from spreading, a firewall is intended to provide a formidable barrier to unauthorized users. *Take a look at "Closing, locking, and bolting the door."*

6 *D.* Authentication deals with the verification of an account name and password combination. The assumption is that if someone knows both an account name and its related password, they are either who they claim to be, or have been authorized by the owner to use them. *See "May I see some ID, please?"*

7 *A.* As its name implies, a public key is provided publicly so that an encrypted message can be decoded by its recipient. A private key, on the other hand, is never sent out and is retained by its owner to encode messages. *Review "Public and private keys."*

8 *B and C.* S/MIME and PGP are used to encode e-mail and attachments, not that an e-mail message couldn't be a financial transaction, but it may not be either. SSL and SET are specifically used to encode and decode financial transactions. *Look over "How secure are your sockets?" and "Sending secure electronic transactions."*

9 *C.* PPTP (Point-to-Point Tunneling Protocol) is included in the TCP/IP protocol suite on most operating systems. There are several proprietary tunneling protocols used between the VPN gateways of a vendor, but PPTP is the most commonly used tunneling protocol. *Check out "Connecting with a Virtual Private Network."*

10 *A,B,C,and D.* All of these, and a whole lot more, are ways to transmit a computer virus. Just like with human diseases, you must know where the media you place in your computer have been, keep your computer innoculated with up-to-date antivirus software, and always practice safe computing. *Take a look at "Debugging the client."*

Part V
Doing Business on the Internet

The 5th Wave   By Rich Tennant

"Just how accurately should my Web site reflect my place of business?"

In this part . . .

Somewhere along the way, somebody discovered that
the Internet could be used very effectively for conducting all sorts of business. However, it is not just a
simple matter of offering something for sale. While it is
getting closer everyday to being that simple, for now and
for the i-Net+ exam, you need to know about many of the
issues, limitations, and restrictions surrounding what is
commonly called e-commerce.

What you must know for the test includes the issues
related to working in a global environment, the Web and
Internet mechanisms used for attracting and retaining an
audience, and the issues involved in copyrighting, trademarking, and licensing.

You should also be aware of the difference between an
intranet and an extranet, as well as how they both differ
from the Internet, including how they are relate to each
other.

Chapter 16

Internet Business Planning

• •

Exam Objectives

▶ Identifying the issues of a multinational Web business

▶ Contrasting push and pull technologies

▶ Differentiating intranet, extranet, and the Internet from a business standpoint

▶ Explaining the use of copyrights, trademarks, and licenses

• •

*R*ecently I had the occasion to speak to an e-commerce merchant who was struggling with the enormity of the things he had not considered before launching his Web business. The thought that anyone outside the United States would see his Web site had never occurred to him, much less that they would actually buy anything from him. You'll never guess the origin of the first order: The buyer was from Africa.

Opening a Web store may be much easier than opening a storefront on Main Street or in a shopping mall. However, operating the Web store is no less complex, and in many ways, which I discuss in this chapter and the next, it can be even harder. There are those that see the action of publishing a Web page to be akin to issuing an open-ended contract to the entire world. You are asking, "Please buy my stuff!" or "Please use my services," and the whole world will judge you and your business instantaneously based on the look of your front (page) door.

As a certified Internet professional, you must concern yourself with the legalities of what you do on behalf of your customer. Your customers depend on you to know how the Internet operates, as well as how to avoid its pitfalls and take advantage of its benefits. Regardless of the type of network your work will use, it must adhere to the laws and rules governing its content.

This is why the i-Net+ exam includes questions on the objectives that I cover in this chapter. To protect yourself and your customers, you must know the legal and moral guidelines governing the Web and its content as much as you need to know the different ways content can be launched and shared over a network. "Is it legal?" is just as important as, "Is it for private, local, or global use?"

Quick Assessment

Identifying the issues of a multinational Web business

1 The major issues to be considered when operating a multinational Web business are _____, _____, _____, and _____.

2 One of the ways around the multinational currency issues of a Web-based business is accepting _____.

3 The de facto language of the Internet is _____.

Contrasting push and pull technologies

4 When you download information from a remote source to your desktop, you are using the _____ model.

5 _____ technology delivers new or updated information to your desktop as it becomes available.

Differentiating intranet, extranet, and the Internet from a business standpoint

6 A(n) _____ is a private network that provides information to only users of that network.

7 A(n) _____ is a network that provides information to the internal users of a company's network as well as trusted external users.

8 The _____ is a dynamic, global network of unlimited size.

9 The laws of _____ and _____ exist to protect intellectual property.

Explaining the use of copyrights, trademarks, and licenses

10 _____ is anything of value that is unique, original, or inventive, and produced by human intellect.

Answers

1 *Currency, language, shipping, legal.* See "It Takes a World to Make a Web."

2 *Credit cards.* Review "Money makes the Web world go 'round."

3 *English.* Look over "Can you speak my language?"

4 *Pull technology.* Check out "Pulling and Pushing Over the Web."

5 *Push.* Take a look at "Pulling and Pushing Over the Web."

6 *Intranet.* See "Working on the inside."

7 *Extranet.* Review "Sharing with the outside world."

8 *Internet.* Check out "Inside, Outside, and All Around: Intra-, Extra-, and Internets."

9 *Copyrights, trademarks.* Take a look at "The Tangled Web of Copyrights and Trademarks."

10 *Intellectual property.* See "The Tangled Web of Copyrights and Trademarks."

It Takes a World to Make a Web

That the Internet and the World Wide Web are global networks is simultaneously their best and worst feature; and this paradox faces anyone wanting to conduct business over the Web. The Internet and the Web are boundary- and territory-less marketplaces that at times can defy or at least challenge the "normal" business and marketing rules. The good news is that you won't have to rent a storefront, equip a showroom, and hire lots of smiley, pushy salespeople. The bad news is that you will immediately have around a million or more competitors all vying to get the attention, and business, of every Web user.

So, you register your domain (not the one you really wanted, but what the heck), get your Web site created and hosted, and arrange for all the other electronic commerce tools and services you need. (See Chapter 17 for more on e-commerce.) You might think that now you'd be all set to go, but not so fast there, future millionaire! There are a few major issues you may want to consider first:

- ✔ **Currency issues:** Not everyone in the world uses the same money.

- ✔ **Language issues:** Did you hope to sell to people outside of your country that may not speak your language?

- ✔ **Shipping issues:** If you do take international orders, how are you going to get them to the buyer and at what price?

- ✔ **Legal issues:** Are you sure you understand the legal ramifications of selling products to residents of foreign lands? Do you understand the issues of selling products to residents of your land?

For the i-Net+ exam, you should understand that these are the major issues facing anyone wanting to do multinational business over the Internet. You won't need to know how to solve them in every possible situation, but you should have some ideas on how to deal with each in general. The following sections provide some ideas for you to consider.

Money makes the Web world go 'round

If you plan to offer goods to the whole Web community, or at least to the segment that speaks the same language as you, you may need to deal with the exchange of foreign currency. Even within the groups of countries that speak English, Spanish, or French, there are several different currencies. Consumers spend dollars in the United States, Canada, and Australia, but they are different dollars in each country that are worth different amounts of each other. You must be ready to deal with this issue in order to best serve your new customers. Remember, it doesn't take much to lose a Web customer, and confusion over money and how much an item costs may be enough for a potential customer to just click away in frustration.

One of the better ways around this problem is to accept credit cards. Credit card companies compute the current foreign exchange and charge the customer the correct amount for the product or service. Chapter 17 includes a discussion on credit cards and merchant accounts.

Another way to handle the financial side of your transactions is to use one of the electronic money systems. Various companies, banks, and even credit card issuers on the Internet can help you set up your cyber-cash register. These techniques — all of which are uniquely proprietary — all employ encryption technologies and electronic funds transfer processing to allow Web shoppers to pay for their goods. Some of the e-money companies available on the Internet are:

- ✔ CyberCash (www.cybercash.com)
- ✔ Mondex (www.mondex.com)
- ✔ eCash, formally DigiCash (www.ecashtechnologies.com)
- ✔ NetChecque (www.isi.edu/gost/info/NetCheque)

Pricing an item for foreign currency is another problem altogether. So far, U.S. dollars seems to be the common currency of the Internet, but you must decide whether or not this will affect your sales or not. A customer that is not able to make the currency conversion, may forsake your site for one that provides better information. You could list your prices in more than one currency, but the drawback to this is that exchange rates change quite frequently (at least daily).

If you expect to sell items into different countries with different currencies, perhaps you should provide a link to a currency calculator for your customers, such as Xenon (www.xe.net) or MSN's Expedia site (www.expedia.msn.com).

Can you speak my language?

This fact probably comes as a surprise to most of my fellow Americans: Not everyone in the world speaks English. In fact, more people speak Spanish, Chinese, and very likely, Swahili than English, the standard language of the Internet. That doesn't mean everyone to whom you are trying to sell a product or service can read it. If you truly want to be successful with users in or from countries where English is not spoken, then you may need to translate your Web site into the languages of the areas you want to target.

If you cannot translate your Web pages, at least use simple language, lots of pictures, easy to read numbers, and obvious navigation. Come to think of it, that's not bad advice for pages in any langugage.

If the venture is large enough, meaning if you have enough money, you may want to consider translated Web sites located at mirror sites in other countries or available from hyperlinks on the primary language home page.

Shipping overnight to Timbuktu

Okay, so you have taken an order charged to the buyer's credit card. Now you have to get the goods to your customer. Several shipping companies provide service worldwide, including Airborne Express, UPS, DHL Worldwide Express, and Federal Express. Visit these companies' Web sites to get an idea of the services and rates to various countries around the world:

- ✔ www.airborne.com
- ✔ www.ups.com
- ✔ www.dhl.com/
- ✔ www.fedex.com/

Don't forget the good old postal service; they also ship via express and priority mail (2-5 days) to other countries at fairly reasonable rates (www.usps.gov).

One of the headaches associated with shipping internationally is the paperwork involved. For a shipper in the U.S. sending goods to foreign countries, you must deal with filling out international air bills, and for many countries, you must be able to work out the volumetric weight of the package. Most of the international shippers have customer service people to help you.

A few more international business issues you should be aware of

Some international business issues to which you should pay special attention (for your business and the exam) are:

- ✔ Import duties and tariffs may be an issue when shipping certain items into a country. Your shipping company should be able to help you with this.
- ✔ When doing business in Europe, you may need to price goods and conduct business in in the new Euro currency.

✔ Avoid using local slang, references, or colloquialisms on your site. Remember that just because you know where Mt. Skyhi or Lake Outendaboonies are and what a geoduck is, you can't be sure that customers outside your local area do. In fact, you should assume they don't. Use general and well-known references and terminology that are commonly associated with an area, if you must use them at all.

✔ Some products just may not be appropriate for international shipping, such as fragile goods, fresh vegetables, and the like. At best, the special handling they may require can be very expensive. So, consider what you sell and where very carefully.

✔ Some countries do not allow certain products to be shipped into the country. Such things as meats, agricultural products, firearms, and more are prohibited. Your shipping company should be able to help you with a list of what cannot be shipped to whom. If you are focusing on one or more specific countries, you may also want to contact their consulate or trade delegation (maybe even the country's Web page). Other legal considerations are discussed in the next section.

The law of the lands

Ignorance of the law won't protect you should you violate an international law. Don't worry, you won't have to reenact the *Midnight Express* for violating an international commercial law, but you should try to be fully aware of the laws that govern commerce around the world. So far, Internet business has grown largely without too much legal and political pressure, and just about everything, within reason and the law, goes.

An excellent Web site for information on doing business of any kind, and especially internationally, is the Global Internet Project at `www.gip.org`. This site has excellent information on Internet-based business operations at home or abroad.

Shipping companies can help you with what you can ship into certain countries. In addition, you can contact the consulate of the country in question for specific information.

Pulling and Pushing Over the Web

When you download a Web page and view it with a browser, you are using what's called *pull technology,* which gets its name from the fact you're pulling the page from its source to your computer. The content was identified, downloaded, and displayed using a search-oriented action. If the site is regularly updated, you would only know about the updated information should you happen to download it. If you don't revisit the site, you remain ignorant of any updated information. You can waste a lot of time accessing and downloading documents to see if anything has changed. This is the downside of pull technology.

Push technology attempts to make the retrieval of updated information more efficient. Push technology delivers new or updated information directly to users from content providers and Web publishers. In much the same way that you subscribe to a magazine or newsletter, you can select the specific information sources you want to have delivered to you. Push technology is also called *webcasting,* and the information sources are also called *channels.*

Several different push technology clients are competing to establish the Internet standard. Some of the more popular clients available are

- ✔ **AvantGo** (www.avantgo.com)**:** This client displays HTML information and applications, including forms, tables, and graphics, on handheld computers.

- ✔ **BackWeb** (www.backweb.com)**:** This innovative software package periodically delivers free multimedia clips on subjects of interest to you. These messages can include animations, audio messages, wallpapers, or screen savers.

- ✔ **Downtown** (www.incommon.com)**:** This client enables you to create preferred site channels on a toolbar and then continually searches your channels and sites for new content, which it automatically downloads.

- ✔ **Microsoft Internet Explorer** (www.microsoft.com)**:** This browser integrates a webcasting model in the form of its Active Channels, which bring personalized content to your Windows desktop. Internet Explorer is also available for the Apple Macintosh, but features like Active Channels are not.

- ✔ **Castanet** (www.marimba.com)**:** The Castanet system is comprised of a Castanet Transmitter which automatically maintains software versions and data across the Internet by pushing information to the Castanet Tuner on host computers, ensuring programs and files are the latest, up-to-date versions.

- ✔ **PointCast** (www.pointcast.com)**:** This is one of the pioneering products of push technology. PointCast is like having your own personal, fully-customizable Internet news network.

Basically, all you need to get in on all of this immediately available and up-to-the-minute information is a push client. Push clients are all free, so far, and readily available from the publisher's site. A great site to visit for more information on push technology is www.pushcentral.com.

Inside, Outside, and All Around: Intra-, Extra-, and Internets

Intranets, extranets, and the Internet can be grouped together as the answer to the question, "Name three words that end with 'net.'" Each is a type of network that uses TCP/IP protocols to deliver information and other content to users, but they differ in terms of the scope of the network over which they operate.

You definitely need to know how the Internet, an intranet, and an extranet are different. Since there are no essay questions on the i-Net+ exam, you will only need to know whether an intranet or extranet is best in a given situation. So, focus on their basic functions and applications.

Of course, you know my friend, the Internet

I sincerely hope that you know what the Internet is and can identify it when contrasted to the intranets and extranets on the i-Net+ exam. Just in case, here is my quick and easy definition of the Internet:

> The Internet is a dynamic network of computer networks with unlimited size and global scale, based on a common communications protocol called TCP/IP.

The keys to the definition of the Internet are global, dynamic, public, and TCP/IP.

Be sure you don't confuse the Internet with the World Wide Web, which is a network of documents interrelated through hypertext links and stored across the Internet. The World Wide Web is a layer of documents and activities that operates on the foundation of the Internet. The Web is, in effect, a subset of the Internet.

Working on the inside with an intranet

An *intranet* is a private network that provides information only to users of that network. An intranet is built completely inside of a company or enterprise, and although many local area networks (LANs) are referred to as intranets, it can also include WAN technology as well. Access to an intranet is normally limited only to company employees, and a firewall is used to ensure the security of the network. Intranets use TCP/IP protocols and generally resemble the Internet in form and function.

Sharing with the outside world through an extranet

An extranet is an intranet taken to the next level. In addition to the employees within a company, there are often outsiders, such as suppliers, vendors, partners, customers, or other businesses, with whom the company may want to gather data or share information and processing. In other words, an extranet is a subset of an enterprise's intranet to which access has been granted to outsiders.

To provide the security and privacy required for the extranet to work, certain networking tools, such as a firewall, digital certificates, message and data encryption, and even a virtual private network (VPN) are applied. These networking security tools help ensure the internal network's integrity throughout the extranet. See Chapter 15 for more information on the security features listed.

Extranets can be used:

- ✔ Implement electronic data interchange (EDI), which can be used to create purchase orders, update shipping data, and handle other transaction-oriented data entry.
- ✔ Share product information, inventory status, pricing, and other private or exclusive information among companies.
- ✔ Facilitate collaboration on joint projects by several companies.
- ✔ Conduct online banking and financial management with one or more banks.

The Tangled Web of Copyrights and Trademarks

All Web site developers need to know at least the fundamentals of the laws governing copyrights and trademarks, regardless of whether they are developing business sites or personal sites. A Web site is created by combining text, graphic images, and possibly sounds, animation, or software. The laws of copyrights and trademarks exist to make sure that creators of content are protected against unauthorized use of their intellectual property.

Okay, so what is intellectual property? The term may sound like vaporware, or the clear blue sky, but *intellectual property* is anything unique, original, and inventive produced by a human intellect that also has enough commercial value to be worth protecting. Intellectual property covers a vast array of things, including: ideas, inventions, books, speeches, industrial processes, chemical compounds, computer programs, slide shows, lectures, lists of intellectual properties, and the like.

I wasn't stealing; I was only borrowing

The laws of copyrights and trademarks exist to protect intellectual property. On the Internet and the Web, just about everything you see is protected under copyright law in one way or another, by the copyright laws of one country or another. And don't think that just because something is copyrighted in a foreign country that it is fair game. All but a couple of the countries in the civilized world either are a party to or have adopted the agreements of the Berne Copyright Convention (a kind of Copyright League of Nations).

One thing that the agreements of the Berne Convention do is give each of the participating countries a very long arm that is able to reach across country boundaries to prosecute violator's of their copyright laws. In fact, the Internet is probably the hardest medium on which to pull off a copyright violation. There is no hiding on the Internet, everything you do is globally accessible, and you can, and will be prosecuted by foreign governments for copyright violations. So be sure you have permission before you use something that you did not create.

The creator of the intellectual property is its owner. Only the owner can use it as he or she wants. If you want to use the copyrighted intellectual property created by another person, you must at least ask and receive permission, usually in written form, to use it. The worst case scenario is that you may have to pay for the right to use it.

Copyright protections extend to:

- ✔ **Literary works:** This includes fiction, non-fiction, newspaper, software, catalogs, lists, articles, and ads — including want ads. Anything produced in written word is a literary work and is protected. There are many sites on the Web and internet that publish copyrighted works on the Internet, such as iUniverse.com (www.iuniverse.com) and Elsevier Science (www.elsevier.com). The documents and books on these sites are considered published documents, even though they have not been physically printed, and are protected under the copyright laws.

- ✔ **Graphic images:** This includes drawings, cartoon strips, photographs, maps, and scanned images of copyrighted works. Even cartoon characters, taken out of the context of a cartoon strip or movie, are protected.

- ✔ **Animation:** Moving images in the form of movies, videos, animated GIF files, interactive multimedia, captured television, and so on, are protected by copyright.

> ✔ **Sound:** All types of sound recordings, including music, vocals and instrumentals, spoken words — even recorded noises from nature and the world around us — are protected once they have been encapsulated as an object that can be played back.

There are intellectual property works that are in the public domain. This means that ownership or claim to these works has been abandoned or was never claimed. Public domain works are free of property rights and belong to the community at large. They do not have copyright protection and can be used freely by anyone. The problem with public domain works is knowing if they truly are in the public domain. There are sites on the Web that research and catalog public domain or royalty-free art, music, and images. Some sites for public domain works are:

> ✔ Public Domain Images (`www.pdimages.com`) for public domain art and images
>
> ✔ SoftDisk's "The Naked Word" (`www.softdisk.com/comp/naked/`) for public domain e-text and e-books
>
> ✔ Haven Sound's "PD Info" (`www.pdinfo.com/`) for public domain music

If it isn't obvious by now, here's a hint: If you didn't create it, you don't have the right to use it without permission.

Hey, that's mine!

When you create a work of art, an enthralling piece of music, or a master-piece of literature (such as this book for instance) and fix it into a tangible format, it is automatically protected under copyright laws. You aren't required to register your copyright with a national copyright office (such as the U.S. Copyright Office, for example). However, should you ever need to protect your rights under the copyright laws and go after somebody that infringes on your copyright, remember that it is much easier to prove your ownership and rights with a registered copyright.

Anything you create and publish on the Web or the Internet is automatically covered by the copyright laws. This means you can use the copyright symbol (©) immediately.

If you wish to copyright material, a good Web site to visit for assitance and information is "The Copyright Website" produced by Benedict O'Malley (`www.benedict.com`). Don't confuse a copyright with a trademark, though (see "Dealing with trademarks" later in this section). Remember that the merit of an intellectual property is not material to the law, only its originality. In other words, no matter how good the art is, how pleasing the sound is, or how much — or how little — sense the words make (thank goodness for this one), they are still protected by copyright laws.

The law prohibits you from the following actions:

- ✔ **Copying:** You cannot reproduce, copy, duplicate, or largely imitate copyrighted works.

- ✔ **Modifying:** You cannot modify a copyrighted work in order to create a seemingly new work.

- ✔ **Distributing:** You cannot sell, rent, lease, loan, or permit the unauthorized use of a copyrighted work.

- ✔ **Performing:** You cannot enact, show, recite, play, or transmit a copyrighted work without the express written consent of the originator.

- ✔ **Displaying:** You cannot display or playback to a public audience a copyrighted work without written permission.

The forgiveness of fair use

If you wish to use copyrighted materials for a quote, as a reference, or make or illustrate a point, you may be able to do so under the provisions of what is called the Fair Use Doctrine, which is a provision in most copyright laws. Copyrighted material can be used in certain situations under the fair use provisions, such as for a critical review, in a classroom or as part of a course, a news report, or a research document. To use a copyrighted work, with its creator credited or not, four factors of use must be considered under the fair use provisions:

- ✔ **The purpose of the use.** Is it a commercial use or for a non-profit or educational purpose?

- ✔ **The form of the original work.** Some works need more copyright protection than others, for example recorded sound and works of art.

- ✔ **The percentage of the original work used.** Is the original work exerpted or essentially copied on the whole?

- ✔ **The value of the original work.** Does the use of copyrighted material impact the market value of the original copyrighted work?

By and large, you can use parts of copyrighted works for purposes of education, research, or parody. However, it is always better to ask permission of the creator first.

Dealing with trademarks

A trademark is a word, phrase, name, or symbol used to distinguish the goods or services of an individual or company from other goods or services.

You are probably very familiar with dozens of trademarks, all of which are distinguished by either of the ® or ™ symbol, or both. On the front cover of this book, *For Dummies*® is a registered trademark.

You can create a trademark and establish it by using it. However, should you ever want to defend your rights or restrict its unauthorized use, you must register the trademark with the trademark authority in your country. In the United States, it is The U.S. Patent and Trademark Office. You can use the trademark symbol (™) right away, but you shouldn't use the registered trademark symbol (®) unless you have actually registered the trademark.

Before you begin using a trademark, you should have a patent and trademarks attorney perform a trademark search. This search should identify not only the trademarks that are identical to the one you want to use, but also any that may be similar enough to be confusing to prospective customers.

If the trademark you want to use is not in use and does not create identity confusion, you can then proceed to register it. Once again, use a trademarks attorney for the best results.

As a Web developer, you should know that it is illegal to use a trademark without the permission of its owner. Companies do not often grant permission for their trademarks to be used by another party. However, if you feel you must use the trademark, be sure you ask permission. If the answer is no, find something else to use.

The word *Internet* cannot be used to describe the service associated with a trademark. Instead, a more generic phrase such as "a computer network on a global scale" or the like must be used.

Show me your license

Licensing of intellectual property is quite common in the computer world. I'm sure you have meticulously read the EULA (end-user license agreement) on the media envelope of every software package you have ever purchased. You have also committed to memory the contents of the license agreement screen when you installed the software. If so, then you know exactly what licensing is all about.

When you buy a software package, you do not take ownership of it; you are merely granted a license for its use. The same type of arrangement is available for graphics, music, and other objects that you can embed in a Web document. Acquiring a license for the use of software, art, and sound before you use it publicly protects the originators and honors their rights as the owners of the object's copyright.

An excellent Web site to visit for an example of the language used in copyright, trademark, and licensing agreements is www.graphiccorp.com.

Prep Test

1 What are some of the issues facing the Web entrepreneur wanting to do business internationally? (Choose three.)

A ❑ Product quality

B ❑ Language

C ❑ Currency exchange

D ❑ Shipping

2 Which of the following is one way to avoid currency exchange issues when accepting orders from foreign countries?

A ○ Accept only your nation's currency

B ○ Accept major international credit cards

C ○ Accept only postal money orders

D ○ Accept only cash

3 What are two of the many issues you must deal with when shipping internationally? (Choose two.)

A ❑ The size of the package

B ❑ Completing international air bills

C ❑ Computing volumetric weights

D ❑ Finding an international carrier

4 Which of the following terms refers to the Internet technology model used to search out and download a page on demand?

A ○ Push technology

B ○ Pull technology

C ○ CUSeeMe

D ○ Surfing

5 Which of the following terms refers to the Internet technology model that automatically seeks out updated information and delivers it directly to your computer?

A ○ Push technology

B ○ Pull technology

C ○ PushMePullYou

D ○ Active Desktop

6 Which definition best describes the Internet?

A ○ A private network providing information to only users of that network

B ○ A private network providing information to users of the network plus trusted outside users

C ○ A dynamic, global public network based on the TCP/IP protocol

D ○ A public global network that provides information to its subscribers

7 Which definition best describes an intranet?

A ○ A private network providing information to only users of that network

B ○ A private network providing information to users of the network plus trusted outside users

C ○ A dynamic, global public network based on the TCP/IP protocol

D ○ A public global network that provides information to its subscribers

8 Which definition best describes an extranet?

A ○ A private network providing information to only users of that network

B ○ A private network providing information to users of the network plus trusted outside users

C ○ A dynamic, global public network based on the TCP/IP protocol

D ○ A public global network that provides information to its subscribers

9 Which of the following choices defines the phrase *intellectual property*?

A ○ Public property

B ○ Vaporware

C ○ Virtual property

D ○ Unique, original, and inventive works produced by human intellect

10 Copyright protections extend to which of the following? (Choose all that apply.)

A ❑ Literary works

B ❑ Graphic images

C ❑ Animations and multimedia

D ❑ Sound

E ❑ Web page content

F ❑ Reproductions of copyrighted works

Answers

1 *B, C, and D.* Not that the quality of your products is unimportant, but it is not necessarily an issue for a multinational business specifically. *See "It Takes a World to Make a Web."*

2 *B.* Major international credit card companies take care of currency conversion issues for you at the current exchange rate. This eliminates the need for constant updating and maintenance of your Web site. *Review "Money makes the Web world go 'round."*

3 *B and C.* International air bills include customs declarations and other data requests that must be completed carefully and accurately. Most international carriers have instructions on their Web sites. *Take a look at "Shipping overnight to Timbuktu."*

4 *B.* Pull technology is the fancy name for what you and I do every day: Search out a site, download it, and browse it. *Check out "Pulling and Pushing Over the Web."*

5 *A.* Push technology, per your instructions, seeks out updated content on specified pages and delivers it to your computer for your review. *Look over "Pulling and Pushing Over the Web."*

6 *C.* The keys to the definition of the Internet are global, dynamic, public, and TCP/IP. *See "Inside, Outside, and All Around: Intra-, Extra-, and Internets."*

7 *A.* Intranets are inside a company and therefore are used only by users inside the company. *Review "Working on the inside."*

8 *B.* The *extra* is the key to the definition of this type of network. The addition of outsiders is extra to the intranet. *Look over "Sharing with the outside world."*

9 *D.* Intellectual property should also have some value attached to it, or else it would not be an issue. *Check out "The Tangled Web of Copyrights and Trademarks."*

10 *A,B,C,D,and E.* Reproductions of copyrighted works are just reproductions, hopefully made with the permission of the copyright holder. *Take a look at "I wasn't stealing; I was only borrowing."*

Chapter 17

The Business of E-Commerce

● ●

Exam Objectives

▶ Defining Internet-commerce practices

▶ Describing business-to-business operations

▶ Using electronic-money systems

▶ Explaining common Internet marketing tools

▶ Creating customer-oriented business sites

● ●

*1*f you don't think that business has discovered the Internet and its capacity for reaching customers, then you have not been using the Web lately. If anything owns the Internet and the Web, it is the global business community. It is a rare Web site that does not 1) belong to a business, 2) include at least one banner ad, or 3) contain a plea to visit the page's sponsors. It has gotten to the point that the business of the Internet is business, with apologies to Calvin Coolidge.

Add just a pinch of anarchy to the openness and ubiquity of the Internet, and you have an environment made for anyone — and I do mean anyone — who has ever wanted to own and operate his own business. Opening an e-commerce business is as easy as putting up a Web page that offers goods or services for sale or trade. Staying in business and succeeding — well now, those are other matters. I have no facts to support it, but I'd venture that e-businesses have soared past restaurants and sporting good stores to claim the title of the most common type of business failure. E-businesses come and go, seemingly in the same day.

For the i-Net+ exam, you need to be familiar with several key e-commerce terms and concepts. This chapter does not give too much detail on any one of the concepts or terms, but some background is needed on a few so that you can relate them to their usage.

I would recommend that as you read this chapter you try to visualize a business of your own in which you use the concepts, technologies, and processes discussed. This will help you see how the various electronic business and commerce tools are applied, and the fantasy of becoming the next Amazon.com or eBay is a nice break from your studies.

Quick Assessment

Defining
Internet
commerce
practices

1 An online business that buys and sells goods with electronic money is engaging in _____.

2 A Web site offering an online catalog, a shopping cart, and credit card payment processing is a(n) _____.

Describing
business-to-
business
operations

3 The online tool that enables businesses to share business information electronically is called _____.

4 Three encryption technologies that can be used for securing Web e-commerce transactions are _____, _____, and _____.

Using
electronic
money
systems

5 A(n) _____ acts as a go-between, accepting an invoice from the merchant and paying the invoice from the buyer's wallet.

6 A microtransaction involves money amounts usually paid with _____.

7 A(n) _____ account enables you to accept credit cards for online purchases.

Explaining
common
Internet
marketing
tools

8 A(n) _____ clusters links to complementary Web businesses together in one Web location.

9 The mainstay of Web marketing is the _____ ad.

10 The acronym FAQ refers to _____.

Creating
customer-
oriented
business
sites

Answers

1 *E-commerce.* See "E-Business versus E-Commerce."

2 *Virtual storefront.* Review "The Land of E's."

3 *EDI.* Take a look at "Sharing data electronically."

4 *SET, SSL, RSA.* Check out "Locking the safe."

5 *E-cash service.* Look over "E-Cash, E-Check, or E-Charge?"

6 *Coins.* See "Can you change an e-twenty?"

7 *Merchant.* Review "Merchant accounts."

8 *Online mall.* Check out "Hanging out on the mall."

9 *Banner.* See "Waving your banner."

10 *Frequently asked questions.* Review "Keeping the Customer Happy."

E-Business versus E-Commerce

Absolutely the most important term and concept of business on the Internet is *e-commerce,* also referred to as merely *EC,* and occasionally called *e-business.* Actually, e-commerce and e-business are technically different things, but in general they can be used interchangeably.

Officially, *electronic commerce* — e-commerce — is conducting a business online. This includes the buying and selling of goods and services using electronic money transactions involving credit cards or digital cash. On the other hand, *electronic business* — e-business — is actually conducting a business on the Internet, which goes beyond buying and selling over the Web to include customer services, marketing, and perhaps e-meeting an e-partner via e-mail.

The Land of E's

The world of Internet commerce is also the land of e's. Just about every term or concept involved starts with an *e* — for example, e-commerce, e-business, e-mail, e-checks, e-cash, e pluribus unum, and so on. When Amazon.com sells a book, Dell sells a computer, or Land's End sells a pair of pants, all over the Web, it is an e-tailing e-commerce transaction, perhaps from their extranet, confirmed by e-mail, paid with e-cash, and it's easy. E-commerce and all of its elements combine on the Web to provide both the buyer and the seller with a value-added service.

E-commerce includes several elements:

- **Virtual stores:** These Web sites offer online catalogs and electronic shopping carts and checkout services. This is business-to-customer activity, which is the most visible part of an e-commerce enterprise.

- **Business-to-business commerce:** This may also involve an online catalog, possibly protected by a password or registered names issued only to established customers. Business-to-business activities may also include online ordering, order tracking, bill paying, and other business-related activities.

- **Electronic Data Interchange (EDI):** This is a key element in e-commerce and e-business software packages now emerging. Although EDI has been around since the dialup and bulletin board days, it is becoming extremely popular due to the ease with which an HTML form can be created and the emergence of such tools as XML (Extensible Markup Language) and other extranet tools.

✔ **E-mail and other electronic correspondence:** E-mail and fax messages sent over the Internet are used more and more commonly to send quotes, orders, general business correspondence, and contracts, as well as notices, ads, and announcements to customers, vendors, and business-to-business partners.

✔ **Demographics:** Many business Web sites are used to collect demographic and contact data from visitors. Under the guise of a survey, a contest entry, a request for information, and many other inducements, visitors provide their name, street address, phone, age, income, e-mail address, Web site, and other personal information. This type of data is invaluable to a business because the customers have prequalified themselves as interested in the company's products, if not only its Web site.

✔ **Security:** Privacy concerns of customers and the business alike have driven the development of security methods and procedures that protect the data contained in an e-commerce transaction from interception and illicit use. Security is now built into the major browser software. Users and businesses can also use digital certificates to further secure their transactions using encryption.

Opening the virtual store

The Internet store is open 24-hours a day, 7-days a week, 52-weeks a year. Its doors are always open, rain or shine, day or night, sickness or health, richer or poorer — I'm sure you get the idea. A virtual storefront on the Internet instantly has franchises in every networked home and office around the world. This global electronic marketplace has projected sales well into the billions of dollars, and sales are not limited to high-tech goods. Books, clothing, music, office supplies, gardening, and even groceries are finding lucrative markets on the Web.

The Web also serves as perhaps the world's largest yard sale. Not every e-commerce site is a sophisticated, multi-level shopper's bonanza. Many are simple Web pages offering a single product or service. The minimum requirement for a virtual storefront is a Web page that shares your business name, its e-mail address, and some description of the product you are offering.

Doing business with business

The Internet and the Web provide the efficient business tool kit that companies have been after for some time. The continuing fantasy of the paperless office has a glimmer of becoming a partial reality on the Web. Intercompany activities, such as placing an order, tracking shipments, and paying bills, can be done quickly, easily, and securely on a Web page.

Sharing data electronically

One of the primary tools of business-to-business functions on the Internet is EDI. This tool, a dialup tool that was around before the Web, enables me to access your Web page, place an order for your widgets, and receive an order acknowledgement, all in one session. This interchange eliminates the need for a paper purchase order to flow between us, saving the time filling it out and the cost of the form and the postage to mail it. Typically, EDI is an extranet tool (see Chapter 16 for more information) and is protected behind passwords and other types of security to prevent unauthorized use (see Chapter 15 for more information on Internet security).

Talking the e-talk

The use of e-mail and FAX over the Internet is now a mainstay for e-business. Although some people see the barrage of unsolicited e-mail as just another form of junk mail, the prudent use of e-mail and electronic FAX is an easy way to send information and announcements of business activities. Of course, you run the risk that the mail will be discarded unopened, just like the paper mail. However, the savings from using e-mail can far outweigh its downsides.

As long as you identify the source openly and provide the recipients a way to remove themselves from your mailing list, e-mail is perfectly legal and a lot more convenient for both parties. Subscription-based e-mail newsletters are a friendlier and more effective way to go for some businesses.

With the improvements being made in voice over the IP (VoIP), the Internet is also becoming a tool for voice communications. Companies are springing up almost daily to provide nearly free long-distance services over the Internet.

Who's out there?

A full range of tools is available to help a business track how its e-commerce site is used. These tools range from simple to sophisticated. A *hit counter,* an example of a simple application, counts the number of times a page is downloaded, including each time you look at it yourself. Sophisticated demographic and statistics packages use *cookies* and other data capture techniques to track which pages of a site a visitor opens and even which elements the user's mouse moved over.

An effective way to use the Web as a sales lead generator is to include a request for more information on your Web site. Other ways of collecting customer information include e-mail newsletter signups, contests, surveys, and opinion polls.

Armed with the information collected by the site-tracking tools and that supplied by the customer directly, your salespeople can contact potential customers with the knowledge of exactly which of your products or services they viewed during their visit to your site.

Locking the safe

The rapid development of security tools available for Internet and Web transactions has made e-commerce possible. I don't know about you, but I've always been just a little uncomfortable about entering my credit card number into a Web page. However, if the business assures me that my transaction is secured, I relax enough to actually complete the transaction and not just bail out.

There are different types of security used on the Web for business transactions. Here are the most common ways to secure a business transaction:

- ✔ **Verifying the user:** In much the same way that intranet users must use account names and passwords to access the network, one of the more common ways used to secure a transaction is to assign authorized users account names and passwords.

- ✔ **Access control:** In addition to an account name and a password, you can also assign levels of access to Web site resources through directory and file permissions assigned to individual users or groups of users. For example, your Gold Account users may have the run of the Web site, although the lowly Bronze Account users can only order from the open catalog.

- ✔ **Encryption:** You can encrypt e-mail transactions using digital certificates and programs like PGP (Pretty Good Privacy). Web transactions can also be secured using SET (Secure Electronic Transaction), SSL (Secure Sockets Layer), and RSA (Rivest, Shamir, and Adleman — the developers). Electronic-money transactions also use encryption technologies. See Chapter 15 for more information on certificates and encryption tools.

E-Cash, E-Check, or E-Charge?

To have e-commerce, you must have money. In order to buy or sell something, you must have a medium of value to exchange, and in most cases money is that medium. This doesn't mean that the barter system isn't a good way to exchange goods and services, but money has become the most accepted way to purchase something.

When you buy something on the Web, there is the problem of paying for it. Until such time as your diskette drive becomes a money transport device, some other means must be used to get your money to the vendor without resorting to snail-mailing cash. Enter electronic money, or e-money.

Can you change an e-twenty?

There are actually many different forms of *electronic money,* but the generic types are

- ✔ **E-cash:** Typically, electronic cash systems provide anonymity for the payer. The e-cash service acts as a go-between, accepting the merchant's electronic invoice and paying it from the buyer's wallet. There are a number of electronic cash systems on the Internet, including DigiCash, CyberCash, First Virtual, and NetCash.

- ✔ **Microtransaction:** This type of electronic money system allows for purchases that result in amounts normally paid in coins. In the U.S., a microtransaction would include amounts less than one dollar and even fractions of cents. One microtransaction service is Millicent.

- ✔ **E-check:** The FSTC (Financial Services Technology Consortium) is defining the standards for issuing and accepting electronic checks over the Internet. When you issue an electronic check, typically from an Internet bank, you sign it digitally using a digital certificate (see Chapter 15). The service that issued the digital certificate vouches for you to the merchant and your bank, and the bank issues an electronic funds transfer to the payee. CheckFree and NetCheque are among the growing number of services processing e-checks.

To see a good site with links to various forms of electronic money, visit Michael Pierce's Network Payment and Digital Cash site (Ireland) at `ganges.cs.tcd.ie/mepeirce/Project/oninternet.html`.

Merchant accounts

Merchant accounts are adapted from the normal business world, meaning the non-Internet business world. A *merchant account* is a specialized account that enables a company to accept credit card purchases. On the Internet, not accepting credit cards for payments can severely limit your sales potential. However, some merchant account banks are now also processing phone sales for merchants that charge the purchase price of the goods to their telephone bills.

Some merchant accounts are online and can be directly linked to your Web site. Others require that you accept the order via e-mail or over the phone and then process it much like a mail-order transaction using Web-based or dialup authorization and settlement processing.

Visit the Cybank Web site (www.cybank.net) for a look at the features of a merchant account.

Marketing on the Internet

It is a common mistake to confuse marketing with selling. *Selling* — even over the Internet — involves exchanging goods for money and the occasional coaxing involved to make the exchange happen. On the other hand, *marketing* involves creating awareness of your company, products, services, and the value you add to a sale. Marketing also tries to create a desire to visit your place of business and buy your products. On the Internet, these goals do not change. In fact, the only thing different about marketing on the Internet is where your place of business is located.

Location, location, location

One of the fundamental principles of marketing is business and product location. On the Internet, there are no main street corners or on-the-square locations. You must use whatever means available to get your business in front of potential buyers and then create a Web site environment that invites them to return.

Depending on the scope and size of your Internet business, you may want to consider the use of an Internet marketing firm. By *size*, I mean the amount of sales you are seeking. Internet marketing firms can assist you with your company image, Web site design, registration with search engines, banner design and placement, and perhaps joining an online mall.

Visit the /MouseTracks/ Web site (nsns.com/MouseTracks/) for a list of tips and resources that you can use to improve your e-business' marketing.

Hanging out on the mall

Online malls increase your exposure on the Web by clustering many complementary e-businesses together in a form of online strip mall or shopping center. Online malls can be specialized and oriented around a common theme, such as Pet.Com (www.pet.com), the FashionMall (www.fashionmall.com), or The House of Ireland (www.hoi.ie). Online malls can be generalized malls, such as CyberShop (www.cybershop.com), Shopping.Com (www.shopping.com), or NetPlaza (www.netplaza.com). An online mall also can be a regional mall, such as the Australian CyberMalls (aumall.com.au), The Mall of Texas (www.malloftexas.com), or the TahoeMall (www.tahoemall.com).

The benefit of an online mall is that you can gain exposure to customers seeking a shopping site ready to buy a product. The downside may be the cost and the potential for joining a mall of limited exposure. Some online malls are free to join, but most are fee-based with fees ranging from a flat monthly fee to a percentage of your sales coming directly from the mall.

Waving your banner

The mainstay of Web marketing and advertising is the *banner ad,* a small rectangular-shaped advertisement about 50 by 500 pixels. A banner ad is usually also a hypermedia link to the business advertised on the face of the banner or to the marketing service that placed the banner. Banner ads are everywhere on the Web and often their placement is more calculated than you might think. There are several ways to have your banner placed on the Web:

- ✔ By arrangement
- ✔ Through a banner exchange
- ✔ Through a banner placement service

I'll show yours if you show mine

If you have a good working relationship with another company with whom you do not directly compete, you may be able to place your banner ad on its Web site by mutual arrangement. You and the other Web site owner can agree to place each other's banners and links on your Web sites. This is normally done as a courtesy and without a fee. Be careful with whom you affiliate your banner; your banner will be judged by the company it keeps.

Joining the faithful

You can register your banner and Web site with most of the better banner exchanges for free. If you abide by their rules, your banner is placed into the rotation of banners, often thousands of banners, and shown on the Web sites of other registered banner owners. To have your banner included, you must agree to prominently display the banners of others along with advertising for the banner service on your Web site.

If you want to improve the number of times your banner is shown, or request a special placement, there is a fee involved. The granddaddy of the banner exchange services is the LinkExchange service. Visit its Web site at www.linkexchange.com for information on this type of service.

Carefully calculated placements

A banner placement service can help you place your banner ad exactly where, when, and to whom you want to display it. This type of service, also called an *Internet* or *Web marketing service,* works with the owners of search engines, indexes, directories, and highly visited Web sites to place your ad on specific pages or exactly where the audience with just the right demographic is likely to be looking.

Have you ever noticed that when you use a search engine to search for subjects relating to buggy whips, the banner ad at the top and bottom of the search results page is for a buggy whip company? If you believe that this is a mere coincidence, then you and I need to talk about ocean view property in Idaho. Banner ads can be displayed based on certain key words entered into the search criteria. The logic is that chances are if you are searching for information on buggy whips, then you will be interested in clicking through a banner ad to reach a company selling that very thing.

What am I bid?

Another method to acquaint users with your products and services is putting sample products on one or more of the online auctions. Services such as eBay, Amazon.com, Auction Universe, First Auction, and even Yahoo! Auctions provide you with a ready market looking for a bargain. You are allowed to link your auction item descriptions to your Web site, which is an excellent — and free — way to bring potential buyers to your site.

E-catalogs: The postman's best friend

Publishing an online catalog requires about the same amount of layout and setup as a print catalog. The differences are in cost and flexibility. If you print thousands or millions of print catalogs for mailing to potential customers, you cannot easily change your product lines for the time that the catalog is valid. The print catalog, although still preferred by some customers and businesses alike, is expensive to print and mail and is quickly outdated.

On the other hand, the online catalog may be expensive, or at least time-consuming, to produce — but it does not need to be mailed and can be changed immediately. You could send an e-mail to customers telling them that the new catalog is online. Once again, the mailing expense is eliminated.

Online catalogs can be catalogs of other catalogs, such as Catalog City (www.catalogcity.com), or reproduction of print catalogs, such as J. Crew (www.jcrew.com), or solely produced as an online catalog, like that of Diedrich Coffee (www.diedrich.com).

Keeping the Customer Happy

Any business operating over the Internet must carefully consider its customer relations policies and procedures. More future sales are lost after the first sale than before it. Attracting customers to your Web site is quite a challenge, no doubt about it, but keeping the customer after the sale is the real challenge.

How you handle customer inquiries, problems, complaints, and suggestions has more to do with your business' success than almost any other part of your operations. This is true for both on- and off-line businesses.

Here are some things you can do to manage your online customer relations:

- ✔ **Online self-service shopping:** Including an electronic shopping cart on your Web site is one way to help the customer buy more than a single item at a time. How easy the shopping cart system and its check out are to understand determines if this is an audience-enhancing feature or a customer repellent.

- ✔ **Promoting self-service:** Allow the customers to help themselves if at all possible. This can be done with Web pages dedicated to frequently asked questions (FAQs), troubleshooting guides, tips, tricks, and steps the customer can use to solve common problems or dispel misunderstanding.

- ✔ **Web chat support:** Allow customers to seek help via the Web. Using a Web chat forum for quick help from any of your customer-oriented Web pages keeps the customer engaged and less likely to bail out of the transaction. A recent study showed that over 60 percent of all online sales transactions are never completed.

- ✔ **Dialup support:** If appropriate to your products or services, you should bear in mind that when you choose to do business on the Internet, you are now a 24-by-7 operation. People viewing your page 12 time zones away may have a question or need help outside of your "normal" business hours. Shoppers on the Web expect you to be there.

- ✔ **Follow through:** If you offer the product with certain shipping, then deliver. Never assume that word of mouth is less likely to affect your business on the Web because the customers are far-flung. Newsgroups can be brutal to an uncaring and non-customer-oriented business.

Prep Test

1 "An online business that accepts electronic money transactions as payment for goods and services" best describes which one of the following?

- A ○ An e-business
- B ○ A virtual store
- C ○ E-commerce
- D ○ E-tailing

2 The electronic tool that enables companies to share data electronically is _____.

- A ○ EDI
- B ○ E-mail
- C ○ FTP
- D ○ PPTP

3 Which of the following technologies are well-suited for e-business communications? (Choose three.)

- A ❑ E-mail
- B ❑ PGP
- C ❑ Fax
- D ❑ VoIP

4 Which of the following is not a type of security used for e-commerce transactions?

- A ○ Encryption
- B ○ Account names and passwords
- C ○ Credit-card numbers
- D ○ Access levels and permissions

5 Which of the following offers one alternative to sending unsolicited e-mail?

- A ○ Invite users to send you an e-mail when they want to see information on your company.
- B ○ Invite users to sign up for a newsletter or listserv that is e-mailed periodically.
- C ○ Post all news on your Web site only.
- D ○ Use cookie data to direct mail to all visitors.

6 E-mail can be encrypted using which of the following? (Choose two.)

A ❑ PGP

B ❑ PPTP

C ❑ A digital certificate

D ❑ FTP

7 If an online purchase results in the amount due being $0.52, which type of financial transaction should be used?

A ❑ E-cash

B ❑ E-check

C ❑ Microtransaction

D ❑ Macrotransaction

8 Merchant accounts offer a wide range of features, but what is the foundation feature of all merchant accounts?

A ○ E-checks

B ○ Credit-card processing

C ○ Phone cash

D ○ Microtransaction processing

9 What are the types of online malls? (Choose three.)

A ❑ Online

B ❑ Generalized

C ❑ Regional

D ❑ Specialized

10 The rectangular-shaped advertising and marketing graphic commonly used on the Web that is approximately 50 by 500 pixels is called a _____.

A ○ Placement ad

B ○ Web ad

C ○ Border ad

D ○ Banner ad

Answers

1   *C.* E-commerce involves buying and selling for money online. E-business includes e-commerce, but also includes many of the other normal business functions that are also conducted online. *See "E-Business versus E-Commerce."*

2   *A.* EDI (Electronic Data Interchange) is a standardized process used by businesses to share business information, such as purchasing, orders, and shipping. *Review "Sharing data electronically."*

3   *A, C, and D.* There are other means also used to communicate between companies over the Internet, such as FTP, a VPN, and more. *Look over "Talking the e-talk."*

4   *C.* As nervous as some folks are about using their credit card number anywhere on the Web, I doubt that using this number for an ID number would be a good idea. *Check out "Locking the safe."*

5   *B.* Giving customers the option of receiving your information avoids the possibility of alienating them with unsolicited e-mail or faxes. *Take a look at "Talking the e-talk."*

6   *A and C.* PPTP (Point-to-point tunneling protocol) is used to create virtual private networks (VPN). Although e-mail can be sent over the VPN in encrypted form, PGP and digital certificates can be used to directly encrypt e-mail. *See "Locking the safe."*

7   *C.* Microtransaction systems, such as Millicent, process transactions normally paid in coins (for example, less than one dollar in the U.S.). *Check out "Can you change an e-twenty?"*

8   *B.* Any other features that work for your business add to the value of a particular merchant account, but it is credit-card processing that you are really after. *Take a look at "Merchant accounts."*

9   *B, C, and D.* All online malls are, well, online. You can find virtually any kind or style of mall you want on the Web, but they should all fall into these three general categories. *Review "Hanging out on the mall."*

10   *D.* Banner ads are literally everywhere on the Web. In fact, I was going to put one on this page for one of my other books, but the editors stopped me. *Look over "Waving your banner."*

Part VI
The Part of Tens

The 5th Wave   By Rich Tennant

JERRY CRAMS FOR THE EMOTICON SECTION OF THE i-NET+ CERTIFICATION EXAM.

Oo-I know this one! It's...uh...

C'mon Jerry. Over 800 more to go.

In this part . . .

*O*nce you have scheduled yourself to take the test, you can begin preparing for the test in earnest. This part includes some great places to get study guides, test demonstrations, and other information to help you prepare. I don't believe that you can see too many different styles of test preparatory materials, but I would use caution on which ones you buy. Some are definitely better than others. Visit the Web sites, try out the demonstrations, and use the tools that best work for you.

When your test day finally arrives, I have included a list of things you should think about or do before, during, and after the test. The i-Net+ test is administered on a personal computer, and you cannot use study materials, notes, or anything besides good old brainpower to take the test. The test is not tricky; it is an honest measurement of your knowledge and understanding. So, remain calm. If you have carefully prepared yourself, you'll do just fine.

Chapter 18

Ten Really Great Web Sites for Study Aids

• •

In This Chapter

▶ i-Net+ exam study materials on the Web

▶ Other resources you can use to prepare for the i-Net+ exams

• •

*V*ariety is one of the keys to preparing for the i-Net+ exams. By using a number of different study tools and aids, you can see many ways of asking the same question. This helps prepare you for whatever wording and approach the i-Net+ test uses.

There are a number of sites on the Web that simulate the test content and format fairly accurately. Some are free; some aren't. The free ones are certainly worth their cost; the others — *caveat emptor*. You will need to balance how much you wish to spend on study aids to prepare yourself for a $125 to $175 test. Of course, if you don't pass, the cost of the test begins to multiply. Be cautious when buying study aids, and look for the bargains that are out there.

The Web sites, and other resources, listed in this chapter are resources I believe you will find helpful without having to spend a fortune. Please understand that all of these sites actually did exist at the time I wrote this book. If any of these resources have disappeared, you should search for others. Keep in mind that searching for "i-Net+" will get you nowhere because both the dash (-) and the plus (+) are search characters used to indicate "without" and "especially" respectively. You should search for "inetplus" or "Internet certification" (you'll have to weed through the A+, CNE, and MCSE stuff). Another way to find study materials is to visit CompTIA's site (www.comptia.org) and use the banners and ads included on the i-Net+ pages.

By the way, www.inetplus.com is *not* an i-Net+ materials site, but you can get some nifty freeware there.

CompTIA.org

www.comptia.org/certification/inetplus/inetplus.asp

This should be your first stop when preparing for the i-Net+ exams. This site is the proverbial "horse's mouth" for the i-Net+ tests. CompTIA recently redesigned this site, so that it is much faster and better organized than in the past, and it has the answers to just about any question you would have about taking the test.

If you are looking for preparation courses, materials, or practice tests, the CompTIA site also displays a series of commercial training company banner ads.

Super Software, Inc.

www.rotw.com

The Super Software crew have once again produced an excellent no-frills and to-the-point study aid that is reasonably priced and well-worth it. This is a company I personally recommend to you.

CramSession.com

www.cramsession.com

As of the day this was written, the CramSession folks had not listed an i-Net+ product. However, I am positive that by the time this is published, they will have one. If not, I am sorry to have wasted your time looking. If they do, you can count on it being perfect for that last-minute cram before the test.

As you get closer to the exam day, use this site to finely hone your memory banks for the test. CramSession.com can also be used as you first get started to outline the areas you need to study.

ProSoftTraining.Com

www.prosofttraining.com

Prosoft offers hands-on i-Net+ courses at training sites around the United States and throughout the world. Visit their Web site for specific locations and costs. The classes are offered directly from Prosoft, its strategic partners and affliates, as well as through Prosoft Certified Training Centers around the world.

GTSPartners.com

www.gtspartner.com

If you are interested in finding an instructor-lead class, this may be the site for you. They also have a training partner that offers online classes.

Visit their site to get a very concise list of the skills and knowledge included on the i-Net+ exam.

Wave Technologies, Inc.

www.wavetech.com/trainingsolutions

Wave Technologies is another training company that produces high quality training materials. They have a new product called a self-study career pack for the i-Net+ test that includes a manual, study guide, CD-ROM, practice tests, and support. This is one of the pricier packages, but you can count on the quality being good.

Use the "What's New" menu option on their Web site to find the i-Net+ information.

Connected: The Internet Encyclopedia

www.freesoft.org/

This site, which is provided through the efforts of Brent Baccala, provides a very complete library of Internet information. It may well be one of largest sites on the Internet with 5000 plus pages and over 100 megabytes of content. This is an excellent site to peruse for general knowledge and to use to lookup specific terms that you are having trouble understanding.

The TechWeb Encyclopedia

```
www.techweb.com/encyclopedia
```

Operated by the CMP Media, Inc., this is another great site on which you can enter a specific term or concept and get both a well-worded definition as well as a few reference links that can be used to study further.

Whatis.com

```
www.whatis.com
```

Perhaps the best all around reference on the Internet for computing, networking, and Internet terms and concepts, Whatis.com allows you to select the term you wish to find directly using a directory of terms conveniently located at the top of the frameset. Use this site when all other sources for a definition have failed you.

Amazon.com, Barnesandnoble.com, Borders.com, and Fatbrain.com

```
www.amazon.com
www.barnesandnoble.com
www.borders.com
www.fatbrain.com
```

"What," you ask, "are book sellers doing in the list of i-Net+ sites?" Although this book is by far the most complete and informative reference you will find to prepare you for the i-Net+ exam, you may want to hedge your bet and find other ... *For Dummies* and IDG made Books to help you prepare for the exam (see the "Other Resources You Should Consider" section later in this chapter).

Well, whether you use Amazon.com, Barnes and Noble, Borders, Fatbrain, or another online bookstore, these sites can provide you with a list of other i-Net+ exam guides, cram books, and question banks available in print. The test simulators are good, especially if you buy some of the complete test banks, but a study guide in print form is a good way to study away from the PC, whether you're on an airplane, in the bath, or out on a date (this is important stuff).

Visit the above sites and search for "i-Net+."

Other Resources You Should Consider

Perhaps the best resources are some of my favorite books from my favorite publisher, not to mention some of my favorite authors:

E-mail For Dummies, 2nd Edition, by John R. Levine, Carol Baroudi, Margaret Levine Young, and Arnold Reinhold

HTML 4 For Dummies, 2nd Edition, by Ed Tittel and Natanya Pitts

Internet Searching For Dummies by Brad Hill

Setting Up An Internet Site For Dummies by Jason Coombs, Ted Coombs, David Crowder, and Rhonda Crowder

Small Business Internet For Dummies by Greg Holden

TCP/IP For Dummies, 3rd Edition, by Candace Leiden and Marshall Wilensky

The Internet For Dummies, 6th Edition, by John R. Levine, Carol Baroudi, and Margaret Levine Young

Web Graphics For Dummies by Linda Richards

In spite of the fact that this list is a shameless plug for *For Dummies* books, these books are an entertaining and informative way to brush up on your networking knowledge. You need to have some fun while studying, and at least this way you'll have an excuse for that smile on your face.

Chapter 19

Ten Test-Day Tips

Get Me to the Test on Time

When you schedule your exam, you will be asked first of all where you would like to take the test. If you are uncertain, the friendly, helpful Sylvan Prometric counselor (see Chapter 1 for more information on the friendly Sylan counselors), can help you choose the one closest to your home or find the most exotic location you would like to visit (After all, who wouldn't want to go all the way to Hawaii just to take a grueling I-Net+ exam?). The only reason I mention the location at this time is that the operating days and hours of your test location are the only limits on when you can choose to take the test. Taking the i-Net+ test, or any Sylvan Prometric exam, is not like the SAT, GMAT, or GRE tests where you are given a time and date to show up . . . or else. You are free to pick the time and date that works best for you.

When I took the i-Net+ exam, it was at a community college about an hour away that was only open Monday through Thursday, 8:00 AM to 2:30 PM. My other nearby choice was a site about 3 hours away that was open all day and into the evening, as well as Saturdays. So, if the first choice testing center doesn't meet your time needs, look for another that does.

Before you leave home

Be sure you have the following items in your possession before you leave your home or workplace to take the test:

✔ **Two pieces of identification:** One must have both your picture and your signature and the other must bear your name.

✔ **Your study materials:** Be sure you have your cram notes and the Cheat Sheet from the front of this book, plus any other study materials you wish to use for your last minute cram.

You may want to also be sure that you have enough gas to get your to the test site, or the right change for the bus or public transportation or parking. You won't need pens, pencils, paper, staplers, paper clips, protractors, blue books, or any other of that type of stuff for the test. The test is online and you are provided note materials, which you must turn in.

Arrive early

Make sure that you get to the testing center at least one-half hour before your test time, or perhaps earlier if you want to do some last minute cramming. The last thing you want or need is to be rushing to make the test time (that you set yourself, remember) and be agitated and rushed when you begin the test. Get there early, find a quiet place, have a cup of coffee, tea, Postum, or whatever helps you relax, and go over the *i-Net+ Certification For Dummies* Cheat Sheet included in the front of this book and your notes.

Arrive early enough to allow time for such unscheduled and unexpected things as checking into the testing center or having to find a parking permit. You may even want to get the location's phone number from Sylvan Prometric and contact them directly before you leave from home or the office and ask what you may need to do about parking and checking in.

Review Your Notes One Last Time

In the time right before you check in for the test, review the things guaranteed to be on the test: TCP/IP protocols, networking concepts, Internet security concepts, connectivity devices, and all of the Instant Answer icons throughout this book. In most cases, these items all have a list or sequence of items. Right before the test you should review any reminders you have developed. You may not benefit by cramming conceptual topics, but a last-minute cram with lists and sequences can help you focus on the test.

Check In on Time

A few minutes before your scheduled test time, check in with the test administrator. Be sure that you have the two pieces of identification you are required to show. Only one piece of identification needs to be a picture ID, so your driver's license, passport, or work badge (as long as it also has your signature on it) should work. The second piece of ID only need to have your full name on it. A credit card, library card, or the like should do fine.

Since this is a closed book test, you can't carry your notes or books with you into the testing area, so surrender them without whimpering. Don't play tug of war with your notes; keep yourself relaxed and focused on the test. Remember that this test is something you volunteered for and that it is a good thing to have behind you.

One thing you should keep in mind is that even if you fail, you have at least then seen the test and will definitely know what to study for next time. In addition, the i-Net+ exam report tells exactly how you did in each area and what each area covers. So, regardless of the result, the test should be a positive experience. I know, this is easy for me to say, it isn't my money.

Do a Brain Dump, but Do It on the Plastic

You're not allowed to bring any paper into the testing area at all. In most test centers, you will be given sheets of plastic and a grease pen, a dry-erase board and a dry-erase pen, or sometimes one or two sheets of paper and a pencil (perhaps surprisingly, none of the centers use Etch-A-Sketch). These items are for you to use for notes during the test. You must turn them in after the test. Ask for or take as many notes as you think you need to.

After you're situated at your assigned station and have been given your basic instructions, unload your memorized lists by writing them down on the board, plastic, or paper. Write down as many lists and sequences, and special relationships such as client-side and server-side programming languages, as you can remember. You can then refer to your notes during the exam without getting flustered about whether you're remembering something correctly.

Do the Tutorial!

At the beginning of the test session, you will be offered a tutorial on the different types of questions, illustrations, response types, and the Sylvan Prometrics testing system. Do yourself a favor and go through the tutorial. No matter how many times you've taken the test machine, or even if you are a Sylvan Prometrics veteran, this testing experience is likely very different, and much better, than any you have experienced prior. Don't think that if you've seen one online test, you've seen them all. Take the time to casually move through the tutorial. Your time doesn't begin until you finish the tutorial and actually start the test. Even if you've seen it before, you can use the tutorial as a way to relax, adjust your chair, keyboard, and mouse, and get in the mindset for the exam.

Ready, Steady, Go

When you're ready to begin, take a deep breath, clear your head (or at least try to), and start the exam. You have 90 minutes to answer the 65 questions on the exam. The distribution of questions on the test should be very close to that shown in Table 19-1.

Table 19-1	i-Net+ Question Distribution by Domain
Domain	*Number of Questions*
Internet Basics	7
Internet Clients	14
Development	14
Networking	18
Internet Security	10
Business Concepts	7

Take your time, but check the time remaining (it displays in the upper-right corner of the display) occasionally. Even if you're not a particularly fast test-taker, you should have plenty of time as long as you stay on task.

Mark Questions You Want to Think About

The Sylvan Prometric test software allows you to mark a question with a check box in the upper-left corner of the screen, so you can review it again later. You should also make a note on your plastic as to why you have marked this question, such as the following:

33. Is it A or D? First impression is D.

41. B or D?

61. Isn't this asked a different way earlier in the test?

Avoid the temptation to mark every question. You really don't need to mark a question to review it later, but the software will let you step through only the marked questions, if you choose.

Answer Every Question

Some people recommend that you read through an entire test before you begin answering its questions. Don't waste your time reading the entire exam before starting. Instead, answer all the questions you're sure of and mark the one's you're not. If you're in the least bit hesitant on a question, choose your best choice, and then mark it.

If you forget to answer any questions, the testing software will indicate that these are incomplete. At this point you have the opportunity to go back and answer them.

No Hootin' and Hollerin' Please

The good, and sometimes bad, part of taking a Sylvan Prometric interactive online test is that you get your results immediately. As soon as you finish the test, you know not only whether you passed or failed, but are even given a printed report that tells you how well you did in each section. Of course, if you pass, you may not much care about which areas you could improve on until later. However, if you fail, this information is the positive part of an otherwise disappointing time, and can be helpful for your next attempt.

Note: When you do receive your passing test score, it is considered bad manners to celebrate boisterously at your terminal. However, when that happens, take along my congratulations and those of the entire *i-Net+ Certification For Dummies* team for a job well done!

Part VII
Appendixes

The 5th Wave   By Rich Tennant

STUART FAILED TO SUFFICIENTLY PREPARE FOR THE BALLOON FOLDING PORTION OF THE i-Nett EXAM.

I'm sorry, Stuart, but this just doesn't look like anything.

In this part . . .

This part contains sample questions for each section of the i-Net+ exam to help you prepare for the test. I have tried to give you about the same number and type of questions as you will find on the actual exam. For many reasons (memory being foremost), I am prevented from just giving you the exact questions you will find on the test. The questions you will see on your test are very likely different from those that I saw when I took the test, although they cover the same material.

Please remember that my questions are intended to help you find your weaknesses. They are not a list of the questions you'll find on the actual exam. If you can answer my questions fairly easily, I suggest that you also can explain why each wrong answer is wrong. Then, I think you'll be ready.

Included with this book is a companion CD-ROM that contains many tools to help you prepare for the test, including a test engine that will generate practice tests for you in a variety of combinations.

Appendix A
Sample i-Net+ Exam

*H*ere are sample questions representing all of the objective areas of the i-Net+ examination. The i-Net+ test has 70 questions spread over the 6 test domains. You must get 70 percent correct to pass the exam and receive your i-Net+ certification. In this appendix I have provided you with the same number and ratio of questions you can expect to find on the actual test.

These questions are not the exact questions you will find on the i-Net+ exam, but are instead examples of the topics and question formats you should expect to see on the test. Practice with these questions, and if you do well, you are probably just about ready to take the i-Net+ exam.

There is one type of question I am unable to reproduce for you here in the book. On at least one question, you will be asked to look at a diagram and then answer a question or two about it. For example, you may be asked to identify a particular network device from a group of devices. So, study all of the Internet and network layout diagrams you can find and be sure you can identify all of the features and devices included.

As you go through these questions, it is a good idea to also be sure that you know why an answer choice is wrong. Good luck!

The following questions are samples of what you may find on the i-Net+ examination in each of the exam domains.

i-Net Basics

1 The rules that govern how data and control signals are sent between two communicating computers or network devices is a

A ○ Network operating system
B ○ Protocol
C ○ Daemon
D ○ Client

2 The device that responds to requests from network clients is a

A ○ Client server
B ○ Cache server
C ○ Server
D ○ Application server

3 How many major NAPs form the Internet backbone in the United States?

A ○ 4
B ○ 6
C ○ 10
D ○ 12

4 Which of the following is an effective way to speed up Web page download time for end-users?

A ○ Proxy/cache server
B ○ Additional RAM on the Web server
C ○ Additional hard disk space on the Web server
D ○ VPN

5 Which of the following is likely to have the greatest impact on the Web page download time for end-users?

A ○ Modem speed
B ○ Many large high-resolution graphic files embedded in a Web page
C ○ Large text documents
D ○ Bandwidth from ISP to backbone

6 What feature can the user change to speed up page download and display time?

A ○ Caching on the server
B ○ Browser display properties
C ○ Caching on the client
D ○ Adding RAM to the client

7 Which of the following would retrieve the most specific information on chocolate cookies with no chocolate chips?

A ○ Cookies
B ○ "Cookies+chocolate-chips"
C ○ Cookies and chocolate no chips
D ○ Chocolate cookies with no chocolate chips

i-Net Clients

8 The most commonly used protocol for connecting two computers over a dialup connection is

A ○ SLIP
B ○ TCP
C ○ IP
D ○ PPP

9 FTP clients and servers control the transfer of documents over the Internet using which two commands?

A ○ Put
B ○ Send
C ○ Download
D ○ Get
E ○ A and D
F ○ B and D

10 In which of the following scenarios would Telnet most likely be used?

A ○ Transferring a document via FTP
B ○ Logging onto a remote computer
C ○ Downloading a Web page
D ○ Using a dialup connection to connect to a remote computer

11 Which of the following is most likely the subnet mask for 204.200.106.1?

A ○ 255.0.0.0
B ○ 255.255.0.0
C ○ 255.255.255.1
D ○ 255.255.255.255

12 The Internet service that is used to translate FQDNs into IP addresses is

A ○ WINS

B ○ ARP

C ○ DNS

D ○ RARP

13 The command used to add an alias name to a computer in a HOSTS or DNS file is

A ○ ANAME

B ○ CNAME

C ○ LINK

D ○ LMHOST

14 To configure your Web browser to use the services of a caching server, you would enable which feature?

A ○ Use of client-side caching

B ○ Use of server-side caching

C ○ Use of proxy server

D ○ Use of DHCP

15 The protocol that governs the format of attachments to e-mail is

A ○ POP3

B ○ IMAP

C ○ SMTP

D ○ MIME

16 To minimize problems when installing new or updated application software on a client computer, you should first do what?

A ○ Disable the NIC

B ○ Disable the anti-virus software

C ○ Update the anti-virus software

D ○ Disconnect the network connection

17 A cookie stored on your client computer by your browser does not include an expiration date. When will this cookie expire?

A ○ 300 days

B ○ 500 days

C ○ Never

D ○ At the end of the current browser session

18 The length of a cookie is

A ○ Variable from 50 to 150 bytes
B ○ Fixed at 1,500 bytes
C ○ Fixed at 50 bytes
D ○ Fixed at 300 bytes

19 The purpose of a cookie is to

A ○ Record everything a user does at a site
B ○ Capture site security information for later use
C ○ Provide a link to the hard disk of a user's computer
D ○ Scan a user's computer for private information

20 The best protection against computer viruses is to

A ○ Never use e-mail to download MIME documents
B ○ Never use disks from other parties
C ○ Install and update anti-virus software
D ○ Enable the filtering features on your Web browser

21 The logical address of a client computer is also called a(n)

A ○ MAC address
B ○ IP address
C ○ Physical address
D ○ Default gateway

22 When the Internet client is assigned its logical address as it logs onto the network, which protocol is in use?

A ○ TCP
B ○ IP
C ○ PPP
D ○ DHCP

Development

23 A set of pre-programmed functions that can be used by a computer programmer to perform a group of related tasks is a(n)

A ○ API
B ○ CGI
C ○ DLL
D ○ SQL

24 Server-side programming, which is commonly written in the Perl language, generally follows which program standard?

A ○ API
B ○ CGI
C ○ DLL
D ○ SQL

25 The language used to interface with a relational database is

A ○ API
B ○ CGI
C ○ DLL
D ○ SQL

26 Which of the following can be dynamically linked into a computer program?

A ○ API
B ○ CGI
C ○ DLL
D ○ SQL

27 Which of the following is not a server-side programming language?

A ○ Java
B ○ JavaScript
C ○ Perl
D ○ C++

28 The markup language usually associated with an extranet is

A ○ HTML
B ○ SGML
C ○ XML
D ○ VRML

29 The language used to create three-dimensional virtual worlds is

A ○ HTML
B ○ SGML
C ○ XML
D ○ VRML

30 Which of the following is not a client-side programming language?

A ○ Visual Basic

B ○ ASP

C ○ JavaScript

D ○ Perl

31 Which server-side programming language can be compiled into portable objects?

A ○ Java

B ○ JavaScript

C ○ VBScript

D ○ Perl

32 In which of the following situations would a link between the Web page and a database be appropriate?

A ○ A chronological listing of recent academic journals

B ○ An online ordering system that shows real-time inventory levels for ordered items

C ○ An e-tail shopping cart that includes merchant account credit card processing

D ○ All of the above

E ○ None of the above

33 HTML commands are referred to as

A ○ Attributes

B ○ Hyperlinks

C ○ Anchors

D ○ Tags

34 In HTML, such feature values as size, color, and style are declared with a(n)

A ○ Anchor

B ○ Tag

C ○ Attribute

D ○ Meta

35 Look over the following HTML code sample. What syntax error(s) do you detect?

```
<HTML>
<HEAD>
<TITLE>i-Net+ Sample Question #35</TITLE>
</HEAD>
Sample Question #35 is looking for HTML errors.
</BODY>
</HTML>
```

A ○ <META> is missing

B ○ <BODY> is missing

C ○ </TITLE> is not required and can be deleted

D ○ </BODY> is optional and can be deleted

36 Which of the following tags set is used to create an alphabetical list in HTML?

A ○ <UL> ... </UL>

B ○ <DIR> ... </DIR>

C ○ <LI> ... </LI>

D ○ <OL> ... </OL>

37 To create a space in an HTML form that you wish users to use to enter their name, you would insert which of the following?

A ○ OPTION

B ○ TEXTAREA

C ○ INPUT

D ○ SELECT

38 Which of the following graphic file formats are not supported by most browsers without an add-in viewer?

A ○ GIF

B ○ JPEG

C ○ PNG

D ○ TIFF

39 Which of the following Web graphic file formats supports transparent back-grounds?

A ○ JPEG

B ○ PCX

C ○ GIF89

D ○ TIFF

40 The multimedia technology that allows a downloading file to begin playing before the entire file has been downloaded is called

A ○ Video-on-demand
B ○ Cascading media
C ○ Streaming media
D ○ Plug-and-play

41 Which of the following is not a multimedia file format?

A ○ QuickTime
B ○ Flash
C ○ Shockwave
D ○ RealPlayer
E ○ None of the above

Networking

42 If you are able to connect to your ISP via a dialup modem and can view the ISP's Web page and others hosted at the ISP, but cannot access Web pages from the Internet, what is the likely source of the problem?

A ○ The network configuration of your client
B ○ The configuration of your browser software
C ○ The ISP's Web server
D ○ The ISP's Internet connection

43 Which of the following is the best cure for improving the performance of a slow Web server?

A ○ Additional hard disk space
B ○ Additional network adapters
C ○ Additional RAM
D ○ Additional outgoing bandwidth

44 At which level of the DNS hierarchy are you less likely to find host information?

A ○ Lowest level
B ○ Top-level
C ○ Regional level
D ○ None of the above (host information is on all levels of the DNS hierarchy)

45 Which of the following is not a valid top-level DNS domain?

A ○ .com
B ○ .edu
C ○ .gr
D ○ .us
E ○ .bus
F ○ .gov

46 Which of the following is not a valid private IP address?

A ○ 192.168.2.101
B ○ 172.25.2.101
C ○ 10.100.2.101
D ○ 127.0.0.1

47 Which of the following protocols supports flow-control?

A ○ SLIP
B ○ FTP
C ○ ICMP
D ○ PPP

48 The tunneling protocol that supports the IPSec standard is

A ○ PPTP
B ○ PPP
C ○ L2TP
D ○ CSLIP
E ○ None of the above

49 The point-to-point protocol that supports encryption is

A ○ PPP
B ○ SLIP
C ○ UDP
D ○ TCP

50 Which of the following is not a description of a network firewall?

A ○ Restricts outside access to the internal network
B ○ Restricts remote user access to internal resources
C ○ Services remote user requests for file transfers
D ○ Restricts internal user access to external resources

51 The TCP/IP utility used to verify if an IP address is a valid location is

A ○ PING
B ○ TRACERT
C ○ NETSTAT
D ○ WINIPCFG

52 The TCP/IP utility used to determine if a problem exists in the route between two Internet sites is

A ○ PING
B ○ TRACERT
C ○ NETSTAT
D ○ WINIPCFG

53 Which of the following is not a protocol used with e-mail systems?

A ○ POP3
B ○ SMTP
C ○ IMAP
D ○ LDAP

54 The TCP/IP protocol that translates physical network addresses into logical network addresses is

A ○ WINS
B ○ ARP
C ○ DNS
D ○ LMHOSTS

55 The data communications technology that uses faster downloads and slower uploads using existing telephone lines that are constantly connected is

A ○ ISDN
B ○ PPP
C ○ Frame relay
D ○ ADSL

56 The router that serves as a network's portal to and from the Internet is known as a

A ○ Gateway
B ○ Bridge
C ○ Firewall
D ○ Hub

i-Net Security

57 The process that verifies the user's account name and password combination is called

A ○ Access control
B ○ Authentication
C ○ Verification
D ○ Auditing

58 The use of public and private keys to encode transmitted data is called

A ○ Decryption
B ○ VPN
C ○ Encryption
D ○ Access control

59 Which of the following is not a VPN function?

A ○ Remote employees checking e-mail
B ○ Telecommuters connecting to the network
C ○ Extranet companies accessing each other's data
D ○ Free access to the company's Web site

60 When an attacker sends out packets that represent the sender as a third-party site, it is called

A ○ Spoofing
B ○ Spamming
C ○ Spooking
D ○ Smoking

61 When a system is bombarded with incoming ICMP reply request packets, the system is under what type of attack?

A ○ SYN attack
B ○ Smurf attack
C ○ PING attack
D ○ Spoofing attack

62 The security mechanism that is used to provide security assurance and decryption instructions to the receiver of an encrypted message is a

A ○ Certificate authority
B ○ Digital certificate
C ○ Certificate of authority
D ○ MIME instructions

63 The file-level access permissions that can be assigned to a remote user are

A ○ Read, write, execute

B ○ Open, change, delete

C ○ Read, write, no access

D ○ Read, modify, execute

64 You are installing a new version of your browser software; which of the following step sequences would you follow?

A ○ Remove the older version, reboot the system, install the new version, test the software

B ○ Deactivate the anti-virus software, install the new version, reboot the system, test the new version

C ○ Install the new version, reboot the system, update the anti-virus software, test the browser

D ○ Install the new version, reboot the system, test the new version

65 Which of the following network structures is an internal network that is not attached to the Internet or behind a firewall?

A ○ Internet

B ○ Extranet

C ○ VPN

D ○ Intranet

Business Concepts

66 When can you legally begin applying the copyright symbol (©) to work you have created?

A ○ Only after you register the copyright with the patents and copyright authority

B ○ Only after you have contacted a copyrights and patents attorney

C ○ At the moment you publish the work

D ○ None of the above (The use of the copyright symbol holds no special meaning.)

67 The data transfer technology that automatically transfers updated information to a Web client is called

A ○ Pull technology

B ○ Push technology

C ○ Active desktop

D ○ Agent technology

68 Which of the following HTML code sets represents the method used for including copyright information in the Meta area of an HTML document?

A ○ `<meta http-equiv="copyright" content="Ron Gilster, 2000">`
B ○ `<meta name="copyright" content="Ron Gilster, 2000">`
C ○ `<metadata="copyright" description="Ron Gilster, 2000">`
D ○ None of the above (Copyright data cannot be included in the meta area of a Web page.)

69 When developing an e-commerce site that will offer products to an international market, which of the following should be avoided?

A ○ The use of credit cards
B ○ The use of local references and colloquialisms
C ○ Shipping information to all markets
D ○ Customs and import/export information

70 The type of account that includes credit card approval and processing is a

A ○ Credit card processing account
B ○ E-commerce account
C ○ Merchant account
D ○ Shopping cart account

Answers

1 *B.* A protocol establishes the rules and guidelines to be followed by two computers, devices, or programs when they communicate for a specific purpose. TCP is a protocol, and TCP/IP is a protocol suite. *See Chapters 2 and 12.*

2 *C.* Okay, perhaps an application server and even a cache server may respond to requests from clients as well. What you need to remember is that clients and servers together form client/server networks, such as the Internet. *See Chapter 2.*

3 *D.* Just remember this number. There are majors and sub-majors, but for purposes of the i-Net+ exam, there are 12. *See Chapters 2 and 12.*

4 *A.* You may think this is a trick question, but if you consider it carefully, you'll understand that RAM and disk space impact only the performance of the server itself and have no affect on the Internet. *See Chapters 3 and 12.*

5 *B.* Even more than modem speed, the size of the graphics in a Web document directly impact its download time. *See Chapter 3.*

6 *C.* If users frequently visit the same sites, and if most of the site content objects rarely change, client-side caching can help speed up a page's display and download times. *See Chapter 4.*

7 *B.* Search-data wild cards can be used to focus the search to specific information within a broader general subject. *See Chapter 3.*

8 *D.* By far, the Point-to-Point Protocol is the most commonly used protocol to connect dialup users to ISPs. *See Chapters 5 and 13.*

9 *E.* FTP clients "get" and FTP servers "put." Documents are transferred from the FTP server to the FTP client through this combination of commands. *See Chapter 7.*

10 *B.* Telnetting to a remote system means logging onto it to run programs or access data. *See Chapter 7.*

11 *D.* 204.200.106.1 is obviously a Class C address, right? That means you would most likely use the default standard subnet mask for Class C addresses. *See Chapter 12.*

12 *C.* The Domain Name System consists of a hierarchy of database tables that can be accessed to convert domain names into IP addresses and vice versa. *See Chapter 12.*

13 *B.* This out-of-left-field question is on the i-Net+ exam, so just remember computer name (CNAME) for the test. CNAME really means canonical or alias name. *See Chapter 12.*

14 *C.* Most Web browsers have a configuration setting that enables the use of a proxy or caching server. *See Chapter 6.*

15 *D.* MIME is the protocol that allows e-mail clients to know the format and type of a file attached to an e-mail message. *See Chapter 7.*

16 *B.* Anti-virus software will often detect updates to a file as a potential virus, which is its job. During installations of application software and upgrades from trusted sources, you should deactivate the anti-virus software to avoid problems. *See Chapter 15.*

17 *D.* Cookies generally have expiration dates, some way into the next millennium. Those that don't have expiration dates go away when you close your browser. *See Chapter 7.*

18 *A.* Cookies are small and won't fill up a hard disk. *See Chapter 7.*

19 *A.* In general, cookies are well-intentioned small files that allow the Web sites you visit to better serve you. *See Chapter 7.*

20 *C.* Installing an anti-virus program doesn't complete the job. The virus files must be kept up-to-date as well. *See Chapter 15.*

21 *B.* A MAC address is the physical address of a network node, and the default gateway is the address of the router or device that connects the network to the Internet. *See Chapters 2 and 6.*

22 *D.* Dynamic Host Configuration Protocol (DHCP) is used to assign IP addresses to network nodes as they log into the network. This is the method used by most ISPs to assign an IP to dialup customers. *See Chapter 6.*

23 *A.* An Application Program Interface (API) is a library of related routines and objects that can be applied by a computer programmer to create programs that accomplish a particular task. An API consists of DLLs. *See Chapter 8.*

24 *B.* CGI is a server-side standard for interaction with and processing of client data. *See Chapter 8.*

25 *D.* SQL is the language commonly used to request data from and post data to relational database systems. *See Chapter 8.*

26 *C.* The name dynamic link library (DLL) should be your first clue to this answer. DLLs contain objects that can be linked into computer programs to perform specific tasks. DLLs are the embodiment of most APIs. *See Chapter 8.*

27 *B.* JavaScript is a client-side programming language. Remember this question and answer, and don't be surprised if you see something like it on the test. *See Chapter 8.*

28 *C.* XML (Extensible Markup Language) is the foundation language for extranets. *See Chapter 2.*

29 *D.* Virtual Reality Modeling Language (VRML) is used to create three-dimensional worlds that can be viewed with a Web browser. *See Chapter 2.*

30 *D.* Okay, so there's some controversy over whether ASP is client-side or not, but not to worry, Perl is definitely not a client-side language. Be ready for questions like this, where more than one answer could be right, but only one is really and completely right. *See Chapter 8.*

31 *A.* There may be a question on the exam regarding compiled objects. If there is, the answer is Java. *See Chapter 8.*

32 *B.* If you really think about the applications listed, only one requires up-to-the-minute information. The others could be linked to a database, but could just as easily be periodically updated manually. *See Chapter 8.*

33 *D.* HTML commands are merged into a document with a series of tags that can be interpreted by a Web browser when the document is downloaded. *See Chapter 9.*

34 *C.* Be sure you know the difference between HTML tags and attributes. *See Chapter 9.*

35 *B.* `<BODY>` is a required tag along with `</BODY>`. Meta tags are optional and if a `<TITLE>` tag is present, it should have a `</TITLE>` closing tag. *See Chapter 9.*

36 *D.* OL stands for ordered list. Ordered means that the list will be in some sequence, whether numbered or lettered. You may also see the DIR tag on the test and remember that it creates directory lists. *See Chapter 9.*

37 *C.* INPUT tags create input boxes. OPTION tags define selections in a SELECT list. A TEXTAREA is used for comments and larger text entry areas. *See Chapter 10.*

38 *D.* GIF and JPEG are the standard graphic file formats, although PNG is beginning to replace the GIF format. However, TIFF files need an add-in viewer to be displayed. *See Chapter 11.*

39 *C.* There are two GIF formats around (well, three if you count GIF89a and GIF89b as two). GIF89 allows the background color of an image to change to the color of the background on which it is placed, becoming seemingly transparent. *See Chapter 11.*

40 *C.* There are several streaming media formats, including MP3, AVI, and RealMedia. *See Chapter 11.*

41 *D.* RealPlayer is a Web browser helper-application that plays back streaming media formats. *See Chapter 11.*

42 *D.* If you are able to connect to the ISP and see the resources stored at that site, then the problem must be upstream from there. *See Chapters 5 and 14.*

43 *C.* RAM is almost always the best cure for slow computers and will speed up a server if the bottleneck is the server itself. *See Chapters 5 and 14.*

44 *B.* As you approach the higher levels of the DNS hierarchy, the emphasis shifts from specific host computers to domains. *See Chapter 12.*

45 *E.* Businesses use the .com domain, and, so far, there are no bus companies with a domain or three-letter country domains on the Internet. *See Chapter 12.*

46 *D.* This address is actually the IP address set-aside for loopback testing of network adapters. *See Chapter 12.*

47 *D.* PPP supports software flow control (XON/XOFF). *See Chapter 13.*

48 *C.* Look for the L2TP protocol on the test. You may even see a question like this one on the test. *See Chapters 13 and 15.*

49 *A.* PPP, the most commonly used dialup point-to-point protocol, supports a number of different encryption algorithms. *See Chapter 15.*

50 C. While a firewall may pass on the request (on port 21) for a file transfer, it does not itself take part in the actual FTP activities. *See Chapters 13 and 15.*

51 A. PING sends out an echo request message to a specific IP address, and if the site exists it should respond. *See Chapter 14.*

52 B. You may or may not see TRACERT on the exam, but just in case, you should know what it does. *See Chapter 14.*

53 D. LDAP is a directory protocol and not an e-mail protocol. Be sure you know what answers are wrong, right along with why the correct answers are correct as a part of your studies. The other protocols listed are all e-mail protocols. *See Chapters 2 and 13.*

54 B. The Address Resolution Protocol (don't you just love the protocol names that say what they do?) builds a table in memory — the ARP cache — that is used to translate MAC addresses to IP addresses. *See Chapter 13.*

55 D. Be sure you know what DSL stands for (Digital Subscriber Line) and what each of the other link types are and when they are used, including ISDN, frame relay, and ATM. *See Chapter 13.*

56 A. Actually, it is the default gateway, but be sure you understand the definition that forms this question. *See Chapter 13.*

57 B. Authentication verifies that a user has access to a system and delineates the services the user may access. *See Chapter 15.*

58 C. Encryption converts a message stream into a cipher before it is transmitted. Decryption converts it back to its original form using public or private keys. *See Chapter 15.*

59 D. A virtual private network (VPN) provides secured access to a network and its resources. *See Chapter 15.*

60 A. Spoofing is the method used by attackers to try to mask the source of the attack — an electronic way of pointing the finger at someone else. *See Chapter 15.*

61 C. A SYN attack is carried out with TCP packets that have a synchronization field. Smurfs are requests for broadcasts and there is no such thing as a spoof attack, except perhaps at the local watering hole. Spoofing is trying to pass yourself off as somebody from some other network. *See Chapter 15.*

62 *B.* A digital certificate vouches for the sender and the encryption of the content. *See Chapter 15.*

63 *C.* In general, file-level permissions are read, write, and no access. On Telnet servers, these permissions are especially important. *See Chapter 15.*

64 *B.* It is always a good idea to deactivate your anti-virus software when installing new applications or upgrades — when they're from trusted sources that is. *See Chapter 15.*

65 *D.* Of course, you know what the Internet is, and an extranet is an intranet with outside extra users from other companies. Remember that intranets do not need to connect to the Internet, though most do. *See Chapter 15.*

66 *C.* You hold the copyright on original works you create immediately, even when they're unpublished. You can mark your work with the copyright symbol immediately when it is published. *See Chapter 16.*

67 *B.* When you download material to your computer, you "pull" it from the source. Automatic agents that "push" data to your computer use push technology. *See Chapter 16.*

68 *A.* Commit this answer to memory. The key here is that copyright is an established HTTP variable and can be set throughout the HTTP-EQUIV attribute. *See Chapter 16.*

69 *B.* Watch those local place references and slang terms. Do as I say and not as I do. *See Chapter 17.*

70 *C.* A merchant account allows credit-card transactions to be processed and then deposited in your bank account. *See Chapter 17.*

Appendix B

What's on the CD

On The CD-ROM:

▶ Sample questions and test engine demos from some of the top names in test preparation materials

▶ Some great links I recommend for i-Net+ test information, study aids, and sample questions

▶ The great QuickLearn game Outpost — to make test preparation fun

▶ The Dummies Certification test engine with lots of sample i-Net+ questions

System Requirements

Make sure that your computer meets the minimum system requirements shown in the following list. If your computer doesn't meet most of these requirements, you may have problems using the contents of the CD.

✔ A PC with a 486 or faster processor.

✔ Microsoft Windows 95 or later.

✔ At least 16MB of total RAM installed on your computer.

✔ At least 40MB of available hard drive space to install all the software on this CD. (You need less space if you don't install every program.)

✔ A CD-ROM drive — double-speed (2x) or faster.

✔ A sound card for PCs.

✔ A monitor capable of displaying at least 256 colors or grayscale.

✔ A modem with a speed of at least 14,400 bps.

If you need more information on the basics of networking, check out some or all of the following books (all published by IDG Books Worldwide, Inc.): *Networking For Dummies* by Doug Lowe; *Upgrading & Fixing Networks For Dummies* by Bill Camarda; *Windows NT Networking For Dummies* by Ed Tittel, Mary Madden, and Earl Follis; *Networking with NetWare For Dummies* by Ed Tittel, James E. Gaskin, and Earl Follis; *Windows NT Server 4 For Dummies* by Ed Tittel; or *Novell's Encyclopedia of Networking* by Kevin Shafer.

Using the CD with Microsoft Windows

Note: To play the QuickLearn game Outpost, you must have a Windows 95 or Windows 98 computer — it will not run on Windows NT. You must also have Microsoft DirectX 5.0 or a later version installed. If you do not have DirectX, you can download it at `www.microsoft.com/directx/resources/dx5end.htm`.

To install the items from the CD to your hard drive, follow these steps:

1. **Insert the i-Net+ CD into your computer's CD-ROM drive.**

2. **Choose Start➪Run.**

3. **In the dialog box that appears, type** `D:/setup.exe` **and then click OK.**

   If your CD-ROM drive uses a different letter, type the appropriate letter in the Run dialog box.

4. **Read through the license agreement, and then click the Accept button if you want to use the CD.**

   After you click Accept, you'll never be bothered by the License Agreement window again.

   The CD interface Welcome screen appears. This interface is a little program that shows you what's on the CD and coordinates installing the programs and running the demos. The interface basically enables you to click a button or two to make things happen.

5. **Click anywhere on the Welcome screen to enter the interface.**

   The next screen lists categories for the software on the CD.

6. **To view the items within a category, just click the category's name.**

   A list of programs in the category appears.

7. **For more information about a program, click the program's name.**

   Be sure to read the information that appears. Sometimes a program has its own system requirements or requires you to do a few tricks on your computer before you can install or run the program, and this screen tells you what you may need to do, if necessary.

8. **If you don't want to install the program, click the Go Back button to return to the previous screen.**

   You can always return to the previous screen by clicking the Go Back button. This feature enables you to browse the different categories and products and decide what you want to install.

9. **To install a program, click the appropriate Install button.**

   The CD interface drops to the background while the CD installs the program you chose.

10. **To install other items, repeat Steps 6 through 9.**

11. **When you finish installing programs, click the Quit button to close the interface.**

    You can eject the CD now. Carefully place it back in the plastic jacket of the book for safekeeping.

In order to run some of the programs on the *i-Net+ Certification For Dummies* CD, you need to leave the CD in the CD-ROM drive.

What You'll Find on the CD

The following is a summary of the software included on this CD.

This CD contains questions related to i-Net+ Certification. The questions are similar to those you can expect to find on the exams. We've also included some questions on i-Net+ topics that may or not be on the current tests or even covered in the book, but they are things that you should know to perform your job.

Dummies test prep tools

QuickLearn Game

The QuickLearn Game is the *For Dummies* way of making studying for the Certification exam fun. Well, okay, if not fun at least less painful. OutPost is a high-resolution, fast-paced DirectX arcade game.

Double-click `Dxinstal.exe` in the Directx folder on the CD, and it will walk you through the installation. As part of the install, you must restart your computer.

Answer questions to defuse dimensional disrupters and save the universe from a rift in the space-time continuum. (The questions come from the same set of questions that the Self-Assessment and Practice Test use, but isn't this way more fun?) Missing a few questions on the real exam almost never results in a rip in the fabric of the universe, so just think how easy it will be when you get there!

Practice Test

The practice test is designed to help you get comfortable with the i-Net+ testing situation and to pinpoint your strengths and weaknesses on the topic. You can accept the default setting of 60 questions in 60 minutes, or you can customize the settings. The practice test also allows you to pick the number of questions, the amount of time, and even decide which objectives you want to focus on.

After you answer the questions, the practice test gives you plenty of feedback. You can find out which questions you got right or wrong and get statistics on how you did, broken down by objective. You can even review the questions — all of them, all the ones you missed, all the ones you marked, or a combination of the ones you marked and the ones you missed.

Self-Assessment Test

The Self-Assessment Test is designed to simulate the actual i-Net+ testing situation. You must answer 60 questions in 60 minutes. After you answer all the questions, you find out your score and whether you pass or fail — but that's all the feedback you get. If you can pass the Self-Assessment test fairly easily, you're probably ready to tackle the real thing.

Links Page

I've also created a Links Page — a handy starting place for accessing the huge amounts of information about the i-Net+ tests on the Internet. You can find the page, `Links.htm`, at the root of the CD.

Commercial demos

i-Net+ Demo, from Specialized Solutions, Inc.

Run the i-Net demo to choose the practice test you want to work on. For more information about Specialized Solutions, visit their Web site at: `www.specializedsolutions.com`

If You've Got Problems (Of the CD Kind)

I tried my best to compile programs that work on most Windows 95 and 98 computers with the minimum system requirements. Alas, your computer may be somewhat different, and some programs may not work properly for some reason.

The two most likely culprits are that you don't have enough memory (RAM) for the programs you want to use, or that you have other programs running that are affecting installation or running of a program. If you get error messages such as Not enough memory or Setup cannot continue, try one or more of the following procedures and then try using the software again:

✔ **Turn off any antivirus software monitor that you may have running on your computer.** Installers sometimes mimic virus activity and may make your computer incorrectly believe that it is being infected by a virus. But don't forget to turn the virus software back on after you're done!

✔ **Close all running programs.** The more programs you're running, the less memory is available to other programs. Installers also typically update files and programs; if you keep other programs running, installation may not work properly.

✔ **In Windows, close the CD interface and run demos or installations directly from Windows Explorer, which can usually be found under the Start➪Programs menu.** The interface itself can tie up system memory or even conflict with certain kinds of interactive demos. Use Windows Explorer to browse the files on the CD and launch installers or demos.

✔ **Add more RAM to your computer.** This is admittedly a drastic and somewhat expensive step. However, if you have a Windows 95 or 98 PC, adding more memory can really help the speed of your computer and enable more programs to run at the same time.

If you still have trouble installing the items from the CD, please call the IDG Books Worldwide Customer Service phone number: 800-762-2974 (outside the U.S.: 317-572-4998).

Index

• C •

• D •

• *X* •

• *Y* •

IDG Books Worldwide, Inc., End-User License Agreement

READ THIS. You should carefully read these terms and conditions before opening the software packet(s) included with this book ("Book"). This is a license agreement ("Agreement") between you and IDG Books Worldwide, Inc. ("IDGB"). By opening the accompanying software packet(s), you acknowledge that you have read and accept the following terms and conditions. If you do not agree and do not want to be bound by such terms and conditions, promptly return the Book and the unopened software packet(s) to the place you obtained them for a full refund.

1. **License Grant.** IDGB grants to you (either an individual or entity) a nonexclusive license to use one copy of the enclosed software program(s) (collectively, the "Software") solely for your own personal or business purposes on a single computer (whether a standard computer or a workstation component of a multiuser network). The Software is in use on a computer when it is loaded into temporary memory (RAM) or installed into permanent memory (hard disk, CD-ROM, or other storage device). IDGB reserves all rights not expressly granted herein.

2. **Ownership.** IDGB is the owner of all right, title, and interest, including copyright, in and to the compilation of the Software recorded on the disk(s) or CD-ROM ("Software Media"). Copyright to the individual programs recorded on the Software Media is owned by the author or other authorized copyright owner of each program. Ownership of the Software and all proprietary rights relating thereto remain with IDGB and its licensers.

3. **Restrictions on Use and Transfer.**

   (a) You may only (i) make one copy of the Software for backup or archival purposes, or (ii) transfer the Software to a single hard disk, provided that you keep the original for backup or archival purposes. You may not (i) rent or lease the Software, (ii) copy or reproduce the Software through a LAN or other network system or through any computer subscriber system or bulletin-board system, or (iii) modify, adapt, or create derivative works based on the Software.

   (b) You may not reverse engineer, decompile, or disassemble the Software. You may transfer the Software and user documentation on a permanent basis, provided that the transferee agrees to accept the terms and conditions of this Agreement and you retain no copies. If the Software is an update or has been updated, any transfer must include the most recent update and all prior versions.

4. **Restrictions on Use of Individual Programs.** You must follow the individual requirements and restrictions detailed for each individual program in the "What's on the CD" appendix of this Book. These limitations are also contained in the individual license agreements recorded on the Software Media. These limitations may include a requirement that after using the program for a specified period of time, the user must pay a registration fee or discontinue use. By opening the Software packet(s), you will be agreeing to abide by the licenses and restrictions for these individual programs that are detailed in What's on the CD" appendix and on the Software Media. None of the material on this Software Media or listed in this Book may ever be redistributed, in original or modified form, for commercial purposes.

Installation Instructions

To install the items from the CD to your hard drive, follow these steps:

1. **Insert the CD into your computer's CD-ROM drive.**

2. **Click Start⇨Run.**

3. **In the dialog box that appears, type** D:/SETUP.EXE.

4. **Click OK.**

   A License Agreement window opens.

5. **Read through the license agreement, and then click the Accept button if you want to use the CD.**

6. **Click anywhere on the Welcome screen that appears to enter the interface.**

   The next screen lists categories for the software on this CD.

7. **To view the items within a category, just click the category's name.**

   A list of programs in the category appears.

8. **For more information about a program, click the program's name.**

9. **If you don't want to install the program, click the Back button to return to the previous screen.**

10. **To install a program, click the appropriate Install button.**

    The CD interface drops to the background while the CD installs the program you chose.

11. **To install other items, repeat Steps 7 through 10.**

12. **When you finish installing programs, click the Quit button to close the interface.**

Discover Dummies Online!

The Dummies Web Site is your fun and friendly online resource for the latest information about ...*For Dummies*® books and your favorite topics. The Web site is the place to communicate with us, exchange ideas with other ...*For Dummies* readers, chat with authors, and have fun!

Ten Fun and Useful Things You Can Do at www.dummies.com

1. Win free ...*For Dummies* books and more!

2. Register your book and be entered in a prize drawing.

3. Meet your favorite authors through the IDG Books Author Chat Series.

4. Exchange helpful information with other ...*For Dummies* readers.

5. Discover other great ...*For Dummies* books you must have!

6. Purchase Dummieswear™ exclusively from our Web site.

7. Buy ...*For Dummies* books online.

8. Talk to us. Make comments, ask questions, get answers!

9. Download free software.

10. Find additional useful resources from authors.

Link directly to these ten fun and useful things at **http://www.dummies.com/10useful**

For other technology titles from IDG Books Worldwide, go to
www.idgbooks.com

Not on the Web yet? It's easy to get started with *Dummies 101*®: *The Internet For Windows*® *98* or *The Internet For Dummies*; 6th Edition, at local retailers everywhere.

Find other ...*For Dummies* books on these topics:
Business • Career • Databases • Food & Beverage • Games • Gardening • Graphics • Hardware
Health & Fitness • Internet and the World Wide Web • Networking • Office Suites
Operating Systems • Personal Finance • Pets • Programming • Recreation • Sports
Spreadsheets • Teacher Resources • Test Prep • Word Processing

IDG BOOKS WORLDWIDE
BOOK REGISTRATION

We want to hear from you!

Visit **http://my2cents.dummies.com** to register this book and tell us how you liked it!

✔ Get entered in our monthly prize giveaway.

✔ Give us feedback about this book — tell us what you like best, what you like least, or maybe what you'd like to ask the author and us to change!

✔ Let us know any other *...For Dummies*® topics that interest you.

Your feedback helps us determine what books to publish, tells us what coverage to add as we revise our books, and lets us know whether we're meeting your needs as a *...For Dummies* reader. You're our most valuable resource, and what you have to say is important to us!

Not on the Web yet? It's easy to get started with *Dummies 101*®: *The Internet For Windows*® *98* or *The Internet For Dummies*® 6th Edition, at local retailers everywhere.

Or let us know what you think by sending us a letter at the following address:

...For Dummies Book Registration
Dummies Press
10475 Crosspoint Blvd.
Indianapolis, IN 46256

BESTSELLING
BOOK SERIES